DATA SCIENCE FROM SCRATCH WITH PYTHON

Concepts and Practices
with NumPy, Pandas, Matplotlib,
Scikit-Learn and Keras

AI PUBLISHING

First Printing, 2019

Edited by AI Publishing
Ebook Converted and Cover by Gazler Studio
Publised by AI Publsihing LLC

ISBN-13: 978-1-7330426-3-5

ISBN-10: 1-7330426-3-6

How to contact us

If you have any feedback, please let us know by sending an email to contact@aispublishing.net.

This feedback is highly valued, and we look forward to hearing from you. It will be very helpful for us to improve the quality of our books.

All the materials needed in this book are available at this link:

https://www.aispublishing.net/dsfswp

About the Publisher

At AI Publishing Company, we have established an international learning platform specifically for Young Students, Beginners, Small Enterprises, Startups and managers, who are new to Data Sciences and Artificial Intelligence.

Through our interactive, coherent and practical books and courses, we help beginners learn skills that are crucial to developing AI and Data science projects.

Our courses and books range from basic intro courses to language programming and data sciences to advanced courses for machine learning, deep learning, computer vision, big data and much more. Using programming languages like Python, R and some data science and AI softwares.

AI Publishing's core focus is to enable our learners to create and try proactive solutions for digital problems by leveraging the power of AI and Data Sciences to the maximum extent possible.

Moreover, we offer specialized assistance in the form of our free online content and ebooks, providing up to date and useful insight into AI practices and Data sciences subjects, along with eliminating the doubts and misconceptions about AI and programming.

Our experts have cautiously developed our online courses, kept them concise, to the point, short, and comprehensive, so that you can understand everything clearly and effectively and start practicing the applications right away.

We also offer consultancy and corporate training in AI and Data Sciences for enterprises so that their staff can navigate through the workflow efficiently, with absolutely no trouble at all,

With AI Publishing, you can always stay closer to the innovative world of AI and Data Sciences.

If you are also eager to learn the AtoZ of AI and Data Sciences and have got no clue where to start, AI Publishing is the place to go.

Please contact us by email at: contact@aispublishing.net.

Book Approach

This book assumes that you know nothing about Data Science. Its goal is to give you the concepts, the intuitions, and the tools you need to actually implement data science programs capable of learning from data.

We will cover many techniques from the simplest and most commonly used to more advance. We will be using actual some python libraries and packages like NumPy, Pandas, Scikit-Learn and Keras.

While you can read this book without picking up your laptop, we highly recommend you experiment with the practical part available online as Jupyter notebooks at:

https://www.aispublishing.net/dsfswp

Table of Contents

Preface

§ Who should read this book?

This book is written for beginners and novices who want to develop fundamental data science skills and learn how to build models that learn useful information from data. This book will prepare the learner for a career or further learning that involves more advanced topics. It contains introduction and very basic concepts used in data science. The learner is not required to have any prior knowledge but some basic knowledge of mathematics is required.

§ Why this book?

This book contains a quick introduction and implementation of data science concepts. The working of each algorithm is traced back to its origin in probability, statistics or linear algebra which helps learner to understand the topics better. The concepts of probability and statistics are defined and explained at rudimentary level to make things simple and easy to comprehend. For intuitive understanding, algorithms have been explained through proper visualizations and various examples.

The practical part of this book contains Jupyter notebooks for each topic. So, one can execute the code and understand the working of the algorithm step by step. You will find it in the following link:

https://www.aispublishing.net/dsfswp

Each chapter begins with an explanation of the chapter's content relevance to data science.

§ What is data science?

Today, we are bombarded with information being generated through machines in all corners of the World. From surveillance cameras, gps trackers, satellites and search engines to our mobile phones and smart appliances in a kitchen, all these entities generate some kind of data. Usually, it contains information about users: their routines, their likes and dislikes, their choices or even work hours.

The most important reason for the growth of machine learning in recent years is the exponential growth of available data and compute power. Surveillance cameras, GPS trackers, satellites, social media and millions of such other entities generate data. Data about users' habits, routiness, likes and dislikes is collected through various apps and during web surfing.

So out of all this data, we need to extract useful and relevant information and this is what data science is all about. Data science is actually "making sense of the data".

Today, the research is more focused to make sense of this data and extract useful information from it. By collecting and analyzing large scale data, not only we can develop useful applications but can also tailor the application for personalized use as per each user's needs. Statistics and probability provide the basis to carry out data analysis in data science. These play a crucial role and most important requirements to learn about.

§ Data science applications

Data science has been applied to a vast range of domains like finance, education, business and healthcare. Data Science is a powerful tool in fighting cancer, diabetes, and various heart diseases. Machine learning algorithms are being employed to recognize specific patterns for symptoms of these conditions. Some machine learning models can even predict the chance of having a heart attack in a specific time frame. Cancer researchers are using deep learning models to detect cancer cells. Research is being conducted at UCLA to identify cancer cells using deep learning.

Deep learning models have been built which accurately detect and recognize faces in real time. Through such models, social media applications like facebook and twitter can quickly recognize the faces in the uploaded images and can automatically tag them. Such applications are also being used for security purposes.

Speech recognition is another success and an active area of research. The machine learns to recognize the voice of a person, can also convert the spoken words to text and can understand the meaning of those words to get the command.

One of the hottest research areas is self-driving cars. Using data from camera and various sensors, it learns to drive as it interacts with the environment. Using deep learning, those cars learn to recognize and understand a stop sign, differentiate between a pedestrian and a lampost and learn how to avoid collision with other vehicles.

§ How to use this book

This book is filled with definitions of methods, tools and algorithms. The book is divided in chapters that cover all the basics concepts and packages used by a Data Analyst using Python. Each chapter will cover a topic in detail, and possibly present exercises and applied projects when applicable.

Frequently, you will encounter three types of box-tags in this book: **Further Readings** and **Hands-on Time**. Examples of these boxes are shown below.

Further Readings

Here you will be pointed to some external reference or source that will serve as an additional content about the specific **Topic** being studied. In general, it consists or packages documentations and cheat sheets.

Hands-on Time

Here you will be pointed to an external file to train and test all the knowledge acquired about a **Tool** that has being studied. Generally, these files are jupyter notebooks (.ipynb), python (.py) files or documents (.pdf).

Further Readings works as a great form of a more detailed and in-depth reference for specific topics. While **Hands-on Time** should work as a break on the flow of the book and prepare the learner to start working directly using the presented tool. All box tags are important, and it is highly recommended to follow their instructions.

1

Introduction

This eBook will give you a fundamental understanding of all data science, machine learning, and deep learning concepts and algorithms. To achieve this, the book has detailed theoretical and analytical explanations of all concepts and also includes dozens of hands-on, real-life projects to help you understand the concepts better.

In the first chapter, you will learn what is meant by data science, why it is currently used everywhere, its areas of applications, and its history and future. Finally, the concluding chapter discusses some notes, tips and tricks to get the utmost benefit from this eBook.

1.1. What is Data Science?

Data science is not a usual field like other traditional fields. Instead, it is a multidisciplinary field, which means it combines different fields such as computer science, mathematics, and statistics. Because data science can be applied and used in various applications and fields, it requires domain expertise in this particular field. For example, if we use data science in medical analysis applications, then we will need an expert in medicine to help to define the system and interpret the results.

So, you might ask, what is the difference between data science, data analytics and big data?

While these terms are used interchangeably, there is a fundamental difference between them.

First, big data means the huge volumes of various types of data: structured data, unstructured data and semi-structured data. We won't get into the details of what is meant by unstructured or semi-structured data because this isn't the scope of this eBook.

However, we can say that the data is semi-structured if it lacks a fixed, rigid schema. So, it has a structure, but this structure is not fixed or rigid. Spreadsheets are good examples of semi-structured data.

On the other hand, unstructured data doesn't have any structure. Text documents and images are good examples of unstructured data.

Data analytics, on the other hand, is more about extracting information from the data by calculating statistical measures and visualizing the relationship between the different variables and how they are used to solve a problem. This, of course, requires data preprocessing to remove any outliers or unwanted features and also requires data post processing to visualize the data and draw conclusions from these visualizations.

Finally, data science came to take the best of the two worlds because it is, as we said, an interdisciplinary field which aims to mine a large amount of all types of data to identify patterns. To identify these patterns, data scientists explore the data, visualize it and calculate important statistics from it. Then depending on these steps and the nature of the problem itself, they develop a machine learning model to identify the patterns.

1.2. Why Data Science?

While the idea of data science was established long ago, it hasn't exploded until the last few years. This can be justified by three main reasons. First, there are currently plenty of data, more than any time in history, and they just keep growing exponentially. Second, we have much better computers and computational power than ever before. A task that can be finished in a few seconds nowadays would have required days with the computers that existed just a few years ago. Finally, we have more advanced algorithms for pattern recognition and machine learning than we did a few years ago.

So, in one sentence, if you want to know why data science is surging now, it is because of the availability of more data, better algorithms, and better hardware.

1.3. Areas of Application

Data science applications are currently countless, so you can do nearly anything. This is because there are data for any task that you may think of, with dozens of algorithms being developed each year to solve these tasks.

However, we will talk about a few famous use cases of machine learning and data science in our daily lives as a lead-in to the next chapters.

1. Healthcare: Machine Learning is currently used in disease diagnosis with accuracies better than professional physicians. It is also undergoing extensive research in drug discovery. Another application is robotic surgery, where

an AI robot helps to perform the surgery with precision higher than the best surgeons.

2. Transport: Tesla cars have auto-pilot which can take control of driving, and thus decrease the number of car crashes dramatically. Machine learning is also used for air traffic control as the whole process is now automated.
3. Finance: Many banks are currently using machine-learning powered software for fraud detection. Also, many people working in the finance sector are currently using machine learning for algorithmic trading. Finally, many corporates have machine-learning software to manage and monitor their employees.
4. Social media: Nearly all social media platforms use machine learning for both filtering spamming and sentiment analysis.
5. E-commerce: Many online shopping websites such as Amazon and eBay use machine learning for customer support, targeted advertising and product recommendation.
6. Virtual assistant: Many start-ups are founded based on the idea of developing a machine-learning powered assistant in one particular field. This assistant can be a chatbot, for example, which can intelligently reply and answer any inquiries in this field.

Finally, as we discussed, these are just a few broad and general applications of data science and machine learning. You can develop your own application in any field that you find interesting and have some experience in. You'll easily be able to achieve this by the end of this eBook.

1.4. History of Data Science

Although the term "data science" has been used in a different context for more than thirty years, it was not really established as a standalone field until recently. Peter Naur used the term data science as a substitute for computer science in 1960, and he later introduced the term "datalogy". He then published a pioneering paper titled "Concise Survey of Computer Method" which used the term data science freely.

However, the godfather of data science is considered to be C.F. Jeff Wu, who gave a fundamental talk called "Statistics = Data Science" back in November 1997. He formalized the data science field as a trilogy of data analysis, data collection, and decision making.

After this talk, data science has been used with an exponential increase in the number of people interested in it.

Further Readings

https://www.dataversity.net/brief-history-data-science/

1.5. Future of Data Science and AI

Following our discussion so far, you can see clearly that the future of data science and AI is very bright. Further evidence for that is the cloud services that have appeared in the last two or three years. Being extremely cheap and fast, they can help develop more advanced machine learning applications in all fields.

So, it will not be surprising to see many tasks, which are currently considered science fiction such as assistant robots and self-driving cars, used in our daily lives.

Further Readings

https://www.dataversity.net/data-scientist-future-will/

1.6. Important Notes, Tips, and Tricks

As we mentioned before, data science is a multidisciplinary subject and includes math, statistics, programming skills and some domain expertise. While we will explore the last two points in this eBook, we highly suggest that you go through your high school, undergraduate or postgraduate studies and revise topics from linear algebra, calculus and statistics classes. We won't go deeply into the math behind algorithms in this course, but we'll cover basic ideas, logic and in some cases formulas to better understand ideas.

Also, to get the utmost benefit from this eBook, finish every single project provided on your own first, and then check the sample solution. Don't read the solution first and convince yourself that you understand everything. You have to write code, develop your logical thinking skills and deal with programming errors and problems. If you start by reading the solution, then you won't acquire any of these three very important skills.

Finally, we encourage you to go through any further reading material that you will frequently find in the upcoming chapters. Although they may contain advanced topics, it will give you an overview of what you can learn next after finishing this eBook.

1.7. About the Author

This book was developed by Ahmed Wael, who is pursuing projects in communication and information engineering, with a concentration on machine learning and big data. He studied AI, ranging from image processing and computer vision, deep learning and neural networks, natural language processing, data visualization and many more. He is currently a mentor tutoring over 100 students from around the world the fundamentals of machine learning and deep learning. In addition, he worked as a data science intern at the world food Program regional office.

2

Preliminary to Understand Data Science

In this chapter, we'll explore in detail the different data science elements in the first section, including statistics and probability, data mining and machine learning (ML), the different types of learning, what is meant by neural networks and deep learning (DL) and finally, what is the link between AI, ML, and DL.

In the second section of the chapter, we will explain fundamental concepts in any machine learning systems: overfitting and underfitting, bias-variance tradeoff and feature extraction and selection.

2.1. Different Data Science Elements

2.1.1. Probability and Statistics

Probability and statistics are essential for any data scientist as they form the basis for data science itself. As experts in probability theory, we can utilize this knowledge to make a prediction, which is the ultimate goal of data science. Also, with the help of statistical analysis, we can explore the data, and based on that, we can decide which algorithm is best suited for our problem.

Another important difference between probability and statistics is that probability is a theoretical mathematics branch, while statistics is more of a practical mathematics branch.

As a data scientist, you should have both the probability theoretical foundations and the statistics analysis understanding.

But before we dive into probability and statistics theories in chapter 4, let's first define some important terms.

Data are collections of facts (measurements, observations, numbers, words, etc.) that have been transformed into a form that computers can process.

Data are stored in columns and rows. The convention is that each row represents one observation, case or example. Also, each column represents one feature or variable.

Because our ultimate goal is to find a function that predicts y values based on x values $Y = f(x)$, it is important to know that x variables need to be independent of each other and called the predictors. On the other hand, y variable is the dependent variable, and it's called the response.

Another two important terms are population and sample.

Again, our ultimate goal is to find a global function to map x into y. Therefore, the whole population as our target for our mapping function will be no different than traditional programming algorithms, which are designed to work on the specified dataset only and are not guaranteed to be generalized to the whole population. The problem is that we cannot have the whole population in our dataset, so we work with a representative sample of the data population. Machine learning algorithms are different from traditional programming algorithms in that their goal is to find parameters that can do the mapping on the entire population based on the given sample.

Outliers are also considered a critical issue that can alter the performance of many machine learning algorithms as we will see in the upcoming chapters. Outliers can be detected by visualizing the data or by calculating special statistical measures that we'll discuss in detail in chapter 4.

Outliers can be dealt with in four major ways: drop them completely, cap them with a threshold, assign new values based on the mean of the dataset for example, or to transform the dataset itself.

Note that the topic of outliers will be revisited multiple times as we go through the datasets, and then we will discuss what is the best way to handle them based on the nature of the dataset itself.

The same issues and solutions will be covered about missing data, which are also frequently found in datasets.

2.1.2. Data Mining and Machine Learning

Let's talk about the difference between data mining and machine learning because both terms are sometimes used interchangeably. This is not completely wrong because they overlap with each other, but they also have subtle differences.

The major objective of machine learning is to induce new knowledge from experiences. The most famous definition of machine learning was coined in 1959 saying, "A computer program is said to learn from experience E with respect to some class of tasks T and performance measure P if its performance at tasks in T as measured by P improves with experience E". By analyzing this definition, we can say that machine learning is more concerned with finding patterns and automatically predicting some output based on that pattern.

Data mining, on the other hand, is carried out by a person on a particular dataset, in a specific situation, with a goal in mind. This person can use machine learning algorithms to find patterns for the sake of finding them or generating some preliminary insights from the dataset.

Also, we can say that machine learning uses data mining techniques, among other techniques to build models that can be used to achieve machine learning tasks.

So, in a nutshell, data mining explains patterns in a specific dataset, while machine learning predicts using models formed from mined data.

2.1.3. Link between Artificial Intelligence, Machine Learning, and Deep Learning

Let us clear the confusion between another three important terms, which are AI, ML, and DL.

Before we explain the difference in words, take a look at this image, which visualizes the difference between them.

By looking at the above image, it is clear that ML is a subset of AI, and DL is a subset of ML.

So, we can say that there is an AI involved in our system if the computer is able to mimic human behavior. AI involves many techniques such as rule-based systems or expert systems. One category of techniques that was showing promising results back in the 80s was machine learning.

Machine learning was promising because it did not use any heuristics or hard-coded algorithms but instead was oriented to mimicking how humans learn instead of mimicking human behavior. So, simply put, machine learning algorithms were developed to find the function that maps the input to the output by feeding the algorithm lots of data and let it decide the best function.

Machine learning performed exceptionally well compared to the traditional AI algorithms because, in some problems, the function that maps the input to the output is too complex for humans to write or derive.

However, machine learning faced the same issues as AI in some tasks, because of the same reason, which is that these algorithms cannot find the complex function that maps the input to the output. An example of this is image classification.

The researchers then tried to come up with an algorithm called neural networks that mimics the human brain.

The neural network consists of a collection of neurons (which are the major elements in the brain) connected in a specific way. By using this algorithm, many complex functions were feasible.

However, the use of the neural network was still limited because of three reasons that we talked about in the first chapter. These reasons are the lack of computational power, the lack of data, and the lack of optimum optimization algorithms for neural networks.

This is because to mimic the brain, we need around 86 billion neurons, and that was not possible by any means.

This is where deep learning, in which more neurons, layers, and interconnectivity came in. How deep learning actually works is the sole topic of chapter 7. But for now, we only need to know the difference between AI, ML, and DL.

2.1.4. Types of Learning

As we saw, learning is the ultimate goal for any machine learning algorithm. Therefore, we must define the different types of learning.

1. **Supervised Learning:**

   In this paradigm, we have our dataset containing the input features and the output features. We try to predict the output from the input by training our machine learning model on the input and by trying to get as many correct predictions as possible.

   Classification is one example of a machine learning algorithm where the goal is to classify objects. Regression is another example where we try to understand the relationships among variables.

2. **Unsupervised Learning:**

   In this paradigm, we only have input features with no corresponding output in our dataset. The target is to discover the structure of the data. Unsupervised learning is used mainly for clustering tasks where we organize the examples into clusters. Another useful application of unsupervised learning is dimensionality reduction where we extract the most relevant information/features. This can help us visualize the data in 2D or 3D and can help to reduce the number of features and thus speed up the calculations.

3. **Reinforcement Learning:**

   In this paradigm, we learn by interacting with the environment. The term reinforcement learning comes from psychology, as psychology purposes that we learn through actions. We have an agent which we want to teach, and this agent learns by doing actions which alter the environment. The environment responds by either rewarding the agent or penalizing it. Based on this, the agent performs either the same action—if it was rewarded—or another action if it was penalized.

   Reinforcement learning is mainly used in skill acquisition tasks such as robot navigation.

2.2. Important Concepts in Data Science and Machine Learning

2.2.1. Overfitting and Underfitting

Before we talk about what is meant by overfitting and underfitting, let us recall what we know so far about the main objective of any machine learning algorithm.

If you remember, the main objective is to recognize the pattern of the data, which can be measured by how well the algorithm performs on unseen data, not just the ones that the model was trained on.

This is called **generalization**, which means performing well on previously unseen input.

The problem in our discussion so far is that when we train our model, we calculate the training error. However, we care more about the testing error (generalization error).

Therefore, we need to split our dataset into two sub-datasets, one for training and one for testing. For traditional machine learning algorithms with small datasets (less than 50,000 instances), we usually split the dataset into 70% for training and 30% for testing. If the dataset is large (more than 50,000 instances), we train on more than 70% and test on less than 30%. For deep learning applications, the datasets are usually too large to the extent that the testing can be done on less than 10%.

Note that your model should not be exposed to the testing set throughout the training process.

You might now ask, are there any guarantees that this splitting operation will give the two datasets the same distribution?

This is hard to answer, but data science pioneers made all their algorithms based on the assumption that the data generation process is I.I.D., which means that the data are independent of each other and identically distributed.

So, what are the factors that determine how well the machine learning algorithm is performing?

We can think of two main factors which result in a small training error and cause a small gap between the training error and testing error.

By defining these two factors, we can now introduce the meaning of **underfitting** and **overfitting**.

We say that the model is underfitting when the training error is large, as the model cannot capture the true complexity of the data.

We say that the model is overfitting when the gap between the training and testing errors is large, as the model is capturing even the noise among the data.

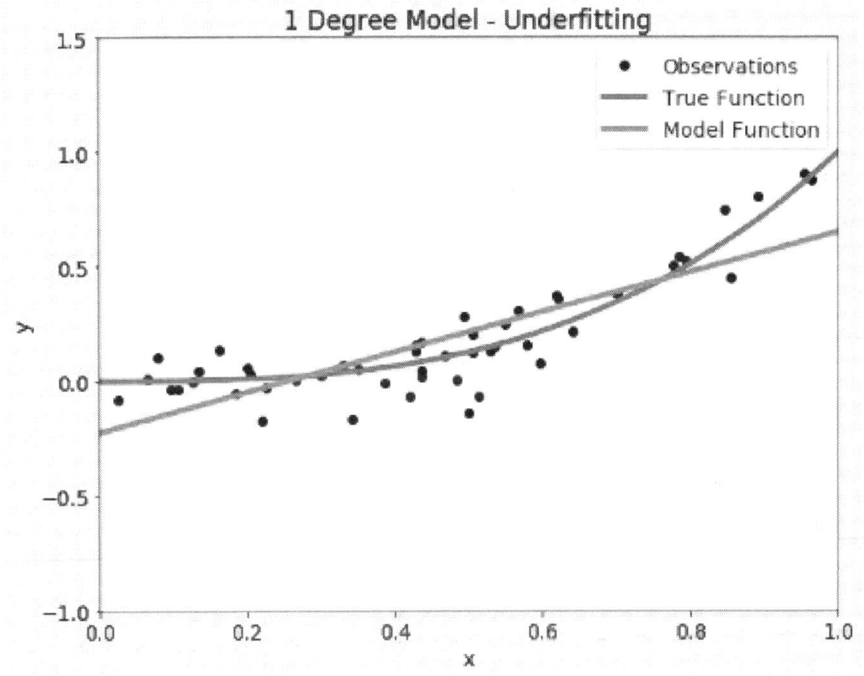

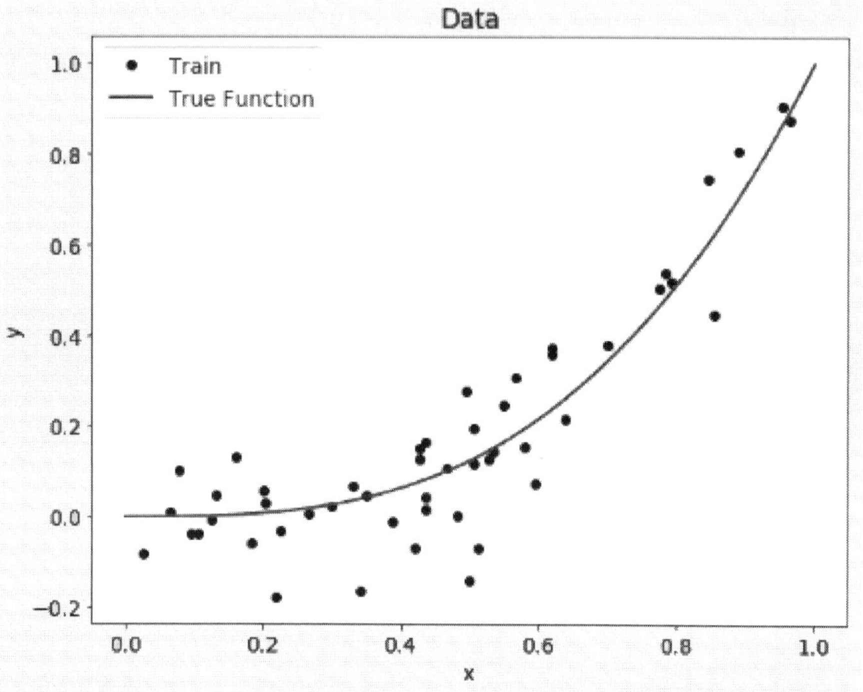
Data
Train
True Function
1.0
0.8
0.6
0.4
0.2
0.0
−0.2
y
0.0
0.2
0.4
0.6
0.8
1.0
x

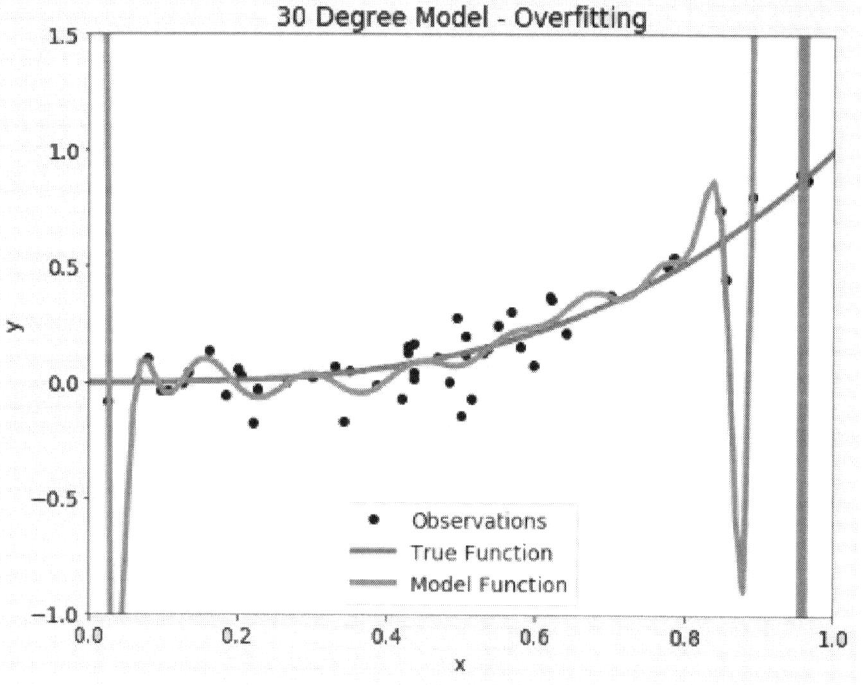
30 Degree Model - Overfitting
1.5
1.0
0.5
0.0
−0.5
−1.0
y
Observations
True Function
Model Function
0.0
0.2
0.4
0.6
0.8
1.0
x

So, you might wonder, can we control this? The answer is yes. It can be controlled by changing the model **capacity**. Capacity is a term that is used in many fields, but in the context of machine learning, it is a measure of how complex a relationship the model can describe. We say that a model that represents quadratic function has more capacity than the model that can represent a linear function.

You can relate capacity to overfitting and underfitting by thinking of a dataset that follows a quadratic pattern. If your model is a linear function, then it will definitely underfit the data no matter what you do. If your model is a cubic function, then it will overfit the data.

Therefore, we can say that the model is performing well, if the capacity is appropriate for the amount of training data it is provided with, and the true complexity of the task it needs to perform. Given that knowledge, we can say with confidence that the model on the left is underfitting because it has low capacity. The model on the right is overfitting because it has a high capacity, and the model in the middle is just right because it has the appropriate capacity.

The solution to underfitting is fairly straight-forward, which is either increasing the size of the dataset, increasing the complexity of the model, or training the model for more time until it fits.

The overfitting solution is a bit trickier because it needs more carefulness. The first solution is to gather more data, of course, but this is not always feasible.

The second solution is to use cross-validation. So, let's stop here and learn what cross-validation means.

So far, we've split our dataset into training and testing, and we said we train our model on the training set for the specified number of iterations, and after the training is finished, we test the model performance by using the test set. But what if we need to test our model after each iteration to discover if it is converging or diverging? This is where a validation set comes to the rescue. The validation dataset is simply another part of the dataset that is used for validating the performance of the model while it is still being trained. So, we split our dataset now into three datasets instead of two.

But the problem is, if the validation set is the same each time, we are back to square one, which prevented us from using the testing set while training our model.

Therefore, to solve this problem, **K-fold cross-validation** was introduced. In this technique, the training dataset is split into k separate parts. The training process is repeated k times. Each time, we randomly choose a subset that is held out for testing the model while the remaining subsets are used for training. The model overall error is the average error of all errors.

Leave-one-out cross-validation is a special type of k-fold cross-validation, where k is the number of instances in the dataset. So, each time we test only on one example and train on the rest. This method, of course, is not used, because we cannot rely on one example. Another reason that it is not used is that it is computationally expensive as we will need to train our model a number of times equal to the size of the dataset to get the overall error.

After understanding what is meant by cross-validation, we can now understand why it is used for preventing overfitting. Now we can monitor our model and stop the training whenever the gap between the training error and validation error is increasing. In fact, this is called early stopping, and we will talk about it in detail in chapter 7.

Another way to limit overfitting is regularization, which means penalizing the model if it is getting too complex for the problem at hand. The mathematics of regularization and how exactly it works will be explained when we get to our first machine learning algorithm in chapter 5.

Other solutions for overfitting exist, but are designed to work on specific algorithms. These solutions will be mentioned and explained when we get to their respective algorithms.

2.2.2. Bias-Variance Trade-off

Given that you understand what is meant by overfitting and underfitting, the concept of bias and variance will be easy to digest.

Before talking about bias and variance, we will classify the various kinds of errors.

First, we have the irreducible error, which comes from the nature of the data itself. For example, when you talk through your mobile phone, your voice signal will always be corrupted by the irreducible error that we cannot fix. While we cannot do anything about this kind of error, it is important to know that it exists so we understand what the maximum limit of accuracy for example, that we can reach when we train our model is.

The second kind of error is, of course, the reducible error. This error can be categorized even more to bias error and variance error.

Bias error is the difference between the average prediction of our model and the correct value which we are trying to predict. We say that the bias error is high if the model is oversimplified. In this case, we have a huge error in both training and testing sets. This is similar to underfitting.

Variance error is the variability of model prediction for the given data or a value that tells us the spread of our data. We say the variance error is high if the model is not generalizing well on the test set. This is similar to overfitting.

By looking at the following figure, the concept of bias-variance tradeoff can be explained thoroughly.

The blue points represent how far we are from the minimum error which is represented by the small red circle. In case of low bias, the blue points—the error—are not very far from the minimum error. In the case of low variance, the blue points are near each other without taking into consideration the minimum error location.

Of course, we want our model outputs to be as close as possible to the minimum error -low bias-, and also the outputs themselves to be consistent and near each other.

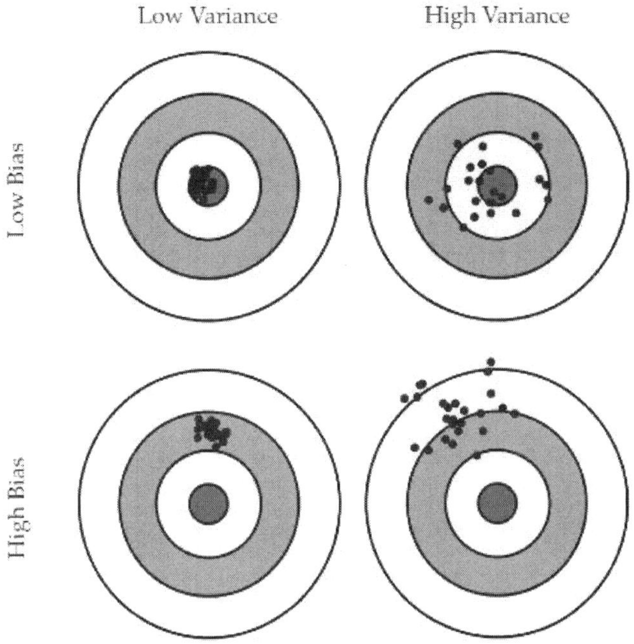

However, there is a tradeoff between bias and variance because as we decrease the model bias, we make it more complex, and thus, we increase its variance. Similarly, when we limit the spread of our data to decrease its variance, there is a higher chance to increase the bias.

By linking that to the model capacity, both increasing the model variance, and decreasing the model bias, will increase the model capacity.

Looking back at the three curves of overfitting, underfitting and fitting we can say that when the model is underfitting, it has low variance and high bias. We can also say that when the model is overfitting, it has high variance and low bias.

To solve the bias error, we try to get a larger set of features.

To solve the variance error, we try to get more training examples and a smaller set of features.

By just looking at the solution, we can see again that solving one of the two problems will negatively affect the other one. Therefore, you should first know which problem, if any, your model is suffering from more, and focus on solving it.

2.2.3. Feature Extraction and Selection

Moving to the final topic of this chapter, feature extraction and selection is an extremely important step in any data science project. Why?

As we agreed, our dataset consists of several examples, each one having a specific number of features, and depending on the task we are performing, we use these features.

The problem with real-world datasets is that many of the recorded features are dependent on each other's, and thus redundant. Even if there are no completely-dependent variables, some features are more important and effective than others, depending on the task at hand. Another issue is that many datasets consist of hundreds or even thousands of features, making the training process impractical and sometimes impossible.

Thus, we need to perform some statistical calculations and visualization in order to know before we start working on the model, which are the most important features in our data.

To do so, we will perform this step as a preprocessing step for all the projects that we will work on together throughout this eBook.

3

Overview of Python and Data Processing

This chapter is divided into three main sections: Python programming language, python data science tools, and real-world data.

In the first section, we will learn the basics of Python programming, its syntax, its data structures, and why not to use R.

In the second section, we will focus more on the tools and libraries that every data scientist should be familiar with including Jupyter notebook, NumPy, Pandas, SciPy, Matplotlib and Scikit-Learn.

In the third and final section, we will begin our journey on how to deal with real-world data using the tools that we mentioned. This will include how to get the dataset, how to import the needed libraries, what the different types of variables are, how to split our dataset, how to preprocess our data, and finally, how to perform k-fold cross-validation.

3.1. Python Programming Language

3.1.1. What is Python?

There is a high chance that you've heard about Python, but perhaps you don't know the complete definition of it. Python is basically an interpreted, high-level, general-purpose programming language that was created back in 1991 by Guido van Rossum.

What do we mean by an interpreted language? It means the instructions that you write—the code—are executed directly without compiling them first into machine-language instructions. On the other hand, a programming language like C++, for example, is called a compiled language as the instructions are first converted into machine language and then executed. Without going into detail, you only need to know that interpreted languages such as Python are much slower than compiled languages. This is basically because the whole code, in the case of compiled languages, is converted into machine language instructions which the hardware of the computers is designed to work on better.

To understand what is meant by a high-level language, the lowest level language that humans can understand and write is the machine language code such as assembly language. The main use of low-level languages is to write programs that will be used on a very specific architecture, which is the case in embedded systems, for example. As we go up to higher language levels, the language becomes more humanly readable and generic for more architecture. However, of course, they will not be optimized for specific hardware.

General-purpose means it can be used for a variety of applications, such as web applications, graphical user interface, games development and of course, data science.

There are many different versions of Python, with two versions, 2.7 and 3.6 being the most commonly used. For beginner or intermediate level programmers, the main difference is in some simple syntax. We will be using 3.6 in this eBook as it has wider libraries support than 2.7.

3.1.2. Installing Python

Before we start working with Python, we have to install it. This can be done in one of three main ways:

1. Official Python Website: This is very easy to follow, but it will install Python only, with no external libraries. Thus, **this method is not recommended**.
2. Miniconda: This will install the conda package manager along with Python. This method has the same disadvantage as the first method as all the external libraries have to be installed manually.
3. Anaconda Distribution: This will install all the packages that you will need in many chapters of this eBook. Also, the installation of any additional packages is very easy and straightforward, and we will mention it when we need it. This is **the recommended method.**

Further Readings

If you want to know more about how to use **Anaconda**, check its documentation here **https://docs.conda.io/projects/conda/en/latest/index.html**

3.1.3. Python Syntax

After installing Python, let's find more about how to use it and work with it.

Every programming language has its own syntax. So, what do we mean by syntax?

The syntax is the rules or the grammar of the programming language, like that of any spoken language such as English or French.

The first thing you will need to know about any programming language is the syntax because this differs very much from one language to another.

The first rule of Python code is the line structure. Any Python program is divided into logical lines, and every one of these lines is ended by a token which is NEWLINE. You do not write this word; it is embedded and hidden in the language. A single logical line can consist of one or more physical lines. If a line contains only comments or is left blank, it is called a blank line, which is ignored by the interpreter.

The second rule is the comments. Comments in Python start with a hash character (#). These comments are also ignored by the interpreter.

The third rule is joining two lines. This is needed when you are writing a long code and need to go to the following line. To do so, we use the backslash character (\).

The fourth rule is writing multiple statements on a single line. This can be done by using a semicolon (;) between the two statements. Then, they will be executed as if they were on two different lines.

The final and most important rule is indentation. While many languages such as Java or C++ use braces ({}) when indicating blocks of code Python uses whitespaces to do this. All the statements within the same block should have the same indentation level.

3.1.4. Python Data Structures

Starting from here, the following sections of this chapter will be divided into two main parts. These are the concepts stated in this eBook, and the code that you will explore and execute that will be provided to you.

To start writing code using any programming language, you need to know that all the data "variables" that you use in your code has to be saved in the memory. You can do an operation like the following for example, and it will be saved in the memory, but where? Can you locate the memory address that contains three? The answer is, of course, no.

```
1 + 2
```

```
3
```

Thus, we need to assign three to a variable that we can refer to after that.

```
x= 1 + 2
print(x)
```

```
3
```

But as we can tell, the data has to be stored in the memory in a structure so we can differentiate between different kinds of variables.

Before we start talking about the different data structures, note that in Python, you don't have to write the type of the variable before it as in other languages. Python is smart enough to interpret the type of the variable from the assignment. To understand more about this, let's discuss the different data structures.

We'll talk first about the basic data types. The most basic data type category is **numbers**. We can show our numbers in three different formats: integer, float and complex. We won't work with complex numbers as they're not really useful in data science. You only need to know that Python, as opposed to other languages, has a dedicated data type for complex numbers. Let us write some basic code and see how Python executes it.

```
x = 1
y = 1.5
z= 1.2j
print(type(x))
print(type(y))
print(type(z))
```

```
<class 'int'>
<class 'float'>
<class 'complex'>
```

As you can see, by using `type` built-in function, we can see which data type Python used for every variable.

Also, if you do any basic operations between an integer and a float, Python will store the result automatically in a float.

```
x = 1
y = 2.5
z= x*y
print(type(z))
```

```
<class 'float'>
```

So, let's now talk about **strings**, which are the second category of the basic data types in Python. Strings are sequences of character data. We can use either single or double quotes to indicate that this variable is a string.

```
s = "Hello World! "
print(s)
print(type(s))
```

```
Hello World!
<class 'str'>
```

String manipulation is best understood by examples. Here are some examples executed in a Jupyter notebook. While you might not know what a "notebook" is in this context, it will be very clear once we reach the second section of this chapter.

As we said, strings are just a bunch of characters. Thus, we can access some of these characters like this.

```
new_s = s[2:5]
print(new_s)
```

```
llo
```

We can also concatenate different strings with each other.

```
newer_s = s + new_s
print(newer_s)
```

```
Hello World! llo
```

We can also multiply a number by a string. This will have the effect of repeating this string a number of times equal to this number.

```
repeated_s = s*4
print(repeated_s)
```

```
Hello World! Hello World! Hello World! Hello
World!
```

We cannot add a number to a string directly like this.

```
add_s_num = s + 4
```

```
---------------------------------------------
------------------------------
TypeError                                 Tra
ceback (most recent call last)
<ipython-input-15-c46ee2a4b7fb> in <module>()
----> 1 add_s_num = s + 4

TypeError: can only concatenate str (not "in
t") to str
```

The error is pretty clear! So, what we do to add a number to a string is this.

```
add_s_num = s + str(4)
print(add_s_num)
```

```
Hello World! 4
```

The same operation can be done with float to number or the other way around.

```
f_to_i = int(3.2)
i_to_f = float(3)
print(f_to_i)
print(type(f_to_i))
print(i_to_f)
print(type(i_to_f))
```

```
3
<class 'int'>
3.0
```

We'll now talk about the **Boolean** data type. This is a data type that was created to be used in conditions and comparisons. This is because the only values that can be stored in Boolean data type are True and False - 0 and 1-.

```
is_true = 1.2 >1
print(is_true)
print(type(is_true))
```

```
True
<class 'bool'>
```

Given that we now understand the basic data types, let us move to more complex data types.

First, we have ***lists***, which are basically a container of variables of any type, stored together. We can write a simple list like this.

```
l = [1,2,5.1,'hi']
print(l)
print(type(l))
```

```
[1, 2, 5.1, 'hi']
<class 'list'>
```

So, to write a list, we use square brackets []. Also, for all indexing, we start from 0 and not from 1. Thus, if we want to do any operation on the second number of this list, then we will write `list [1].` So, what if we need more than one index? Then we can do the following:

```
new_list = l[0:2]
print(new_list)
```

```
[1, 2]
```

If we write the index negative, then it will start from the end of the list.

```
print(l[-1])
```

```
hi
```

We can add two lists together, and we can append or remove one value it/from the list.

```
l_1 = [4,15,7]
l_2 = l_1 + l
print(l_2)
```

```
[4, 15, 7, 1, 4, 5.1, 'hi']
```

```
l_2.append(8)
print(l_2)
```

```
[4, 15, 7, 1, 4, 5.1, 'hi', 8]
```

```
l_2.remove(8)
print(l_2)
```

```
[4, 15, 7, 1, 4, 5.1, 'hi']
```

So, let's now talk about another data structure, which is **Tuple**. The Tuple is a special type of list whose elements cannot be changed.

We say that lists are mutable as we can change their contents at any time, while we cannot do the same with tuples. Therefore, we say that tuples are immutable.

By looking at this simple example, we can see that the only difference in syntax is that we use circle brackets instead of square brackets. We can also see that for indexing, tuples and lists are the same.

```
t = (1,2,5.1,'hi')
print(t)
print(type(t))
```

```
(1, 2, 5.1, 'hi')
<class 'tuple'>
```

To index a value, we use the same syntax as a list.

```
print(t[1])
```

```
2
```

It is immutable.

```
t[1] = 10
```

```
--------------------------------------------
-----------------------------
TypeError                                    Tra
ceback (most recent call last)
<ipython-input-27-5a9388635924> in <module>()
----> 1 t[1] = 10

TypeError: 'tuple' object does not support it
em assignment
```

Moving to the next data structure, we now introduce **dictionary.** The Dictionary is an address-book, where you can find the address of a person by using his name. If we assume that you have his full name, then this name is `unique.` So, we say that every object in the dictionary has two attributes, which are the value and the key. While the key is unique as we said, the value is not. For example, John and Mary -keys- can have the same height -values-, but we cannot do the opposite. This means that we cannot say that John is 170 cm for example, and then say that he is 180 cm. Also, if the height is the key, then we cannot assign the same height to two different persons.

We use curly brackets for indexing, and to connect a key to a value we use a colon (:). Note that while tuples and lists are ordered, dictionaries are not ordered, and can be indexed using the keys.

```
dic = { "john" : 170 , " Mary" : 170}
print(dic)
print(type(dic))
```

```
{'john': 170, ' Mary': 170}
<class 'dict'>
```

Notice that we get the value by using the key instead of the index, as there is order here.

```
dic_2 = {170 : "john", 170 : "Mary"}
print(dic_2)
```

```
{170: 'Mary'}
```

The final data structure is called **set**, which can only have unique values. To create and assign a set, we also use curly brackets but without the colons. It also resembles the dictionary in that it has no order.

```
s = {1,20,4,5,6,1,2,3,4,5,3}
print(s)
print(type(s))
```

```
{1, 2, 3, 4, 5, 6, 20}
<class 'set'>
```

As we can see, the main idea behind sets is we don't have any repeated values. Also, sets do not support indexing.

```
s[1]
```

```
---------------------------------------------
----------------------------
TypeError                                    Tra
ceback (most recent call last)
<ipython-input-41-f8bb2b116405> in <module>()
----> 1 s[1]

TypeError: 'set' object does not support inde
xing
```

So, after talking about the syntax of all the data structures, let's discuss the use cases of each one of them.

First, we use lists when we don't have any special cases that we want to take care of, and we want our list to be ordered for indexing.

We use tuples only when we are sure that the values inside them should not be changed no matter what, so this is the best way to assure that.

Dictionaries are used when we want to have some sort of relation between some unique variables and other non-unique variables. Also, they are very useful in the sense that we do not need to know the index of the variable to get it, as we are only concerned with the key.

Sets are rarely used in data science, but we only use it when we know that any repeated data will be redundant. So, sets can be very efficient in ignoring redundant data to increase the performance of any algorithm.

Now, it's your turn to run the code and experiment with it.

Further Readings

If you want to know more about Python data structures, go to this tutorial here **https://www.tutorialspoint.com/python/python_variable_types.htm**

3.1.5. Why not R?

R is a programming language that was originally developed for the sole purpose of being used for statistical analysis and graphical visualizations. Its syntax is much simpler than Python, and it has more built-in functions that support data manipulation and processing.

However, it's not as widely used as Python because Python has much more support from external libraries than R. Python, and it can be used for other applications, so its use can result in more thorough projects.

Therefore, we choose to work with Python in this eBook because it has a bigger community and can help you explore different areas other than data science.

3.2. Python Data Science Tools

3.2.1. Jupyter Notebook

Jupyter notebook is one of the fundamental tools for any data scientist nowadays. It is an open-source web application that you can use to create and share documents containing code, visualizations, text and equations. Jupyter notebook supports three main languages: Python, R and Julia.

If you followed the installation of Python using Anaconda in the previous section, then you will have Jupyter notebook installed.

Note that all the codes that we will develop throughout this book are embedded in notebooks. Thus, you need to be familiar with the interface.

When you open the application, you will see something like this:

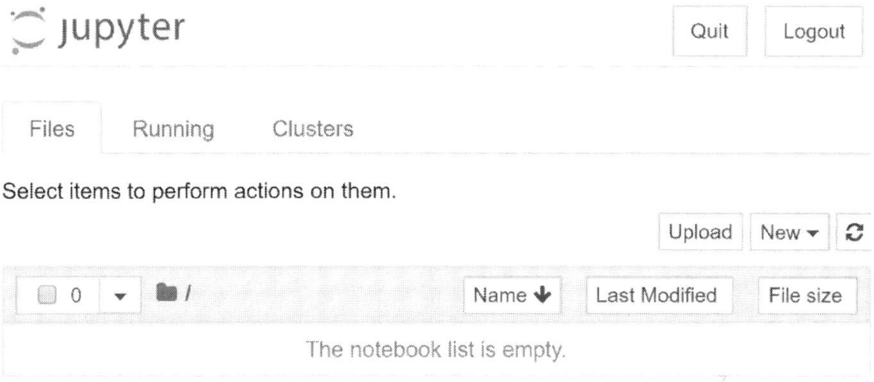

This is the notebook dashboard where you manage your notebooks.

You can create a notebook by clicking New on the right corner. After that, you can create a notebook which looks like this.

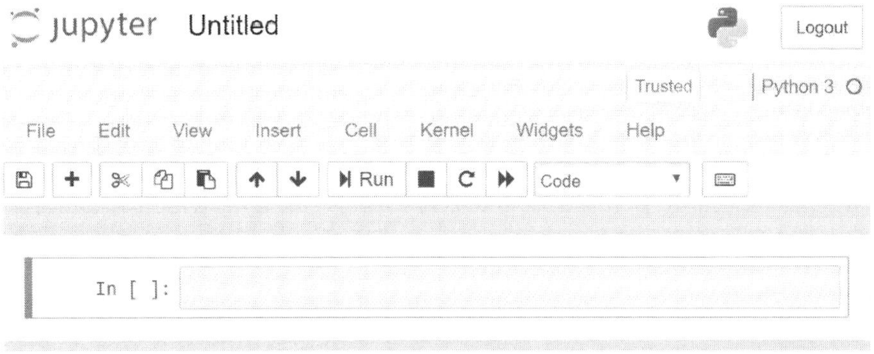

By moving your mouse cursor to any button, you will understand exactly what it does. It is very intuitive.

The main thing you need to know is that what you write is one of two things, either a code cell or a markdown cell. The markdown cell is just for the organization because you write things that will not be executed by Python, such as comments or headlines.

At the end of this section, you will find a hands-on box containing a notebook with even more details.

3.2.2. NumPy

NumPy is short for Numerical Python, which is a library consisting of multidimensional array objects and collection of routines for processing those arrays. Its main use is for mathematical and logical operations on arrays.

NumPy is also installed with Anaconda distribution.

To understand and practice the capabilities of NumPy, let's start writing some code using it.

We can import NumPy using "import", and we usually use a short name for our libraries as we will be mentioning them many times.

```
import numpy as np
```

Create an array using NumPy by doing the following.

```
a=np.array([1,2,3])
print(a)
print(type(a))
```

```
[1 2 3]
<class 'numpy.ndarray'>
```

Now, let us see how to get the shape of any array. This is crucially important in data science, as we are always working with arrays and matrices.

```
a.shape
```

```
(3,)
```

Let us create a multidimensional array.

```
a_2d=np.array([[1,2,3],[4,5,6]])
print(a_2d)
print(type(a_2d))
print(a_2d.shape)
```

```
[[1 2 3]
 [4 5 6]]
<class 'numpy.ndarray'>
(2, 3)
```

Finally, we'll see how to perform the basic operations using NumPy.

```
a1=np.array([1,2,3])
a2=np.array([4,5,6])
print(a1+a2)
print(a1-a2)
print(a1*a2)
print(a1/a2)
print(np.sqrt(a1))
print(np.mean(a1))
print(np.median(a1))
print(np.max(a1))
print(np.min(a1))
```

```
[5 7 9]
[-3 -3 -3]
[ 4 10 18]
[0.25 0.4  0.5 ]
[1.         1.41421356 1.73205081]
2.0
2.0
3
1
```

Further Readings

If you want to know more about NumPy, go to this tutorial here

https://www.numpy.org/devdocs/user/quickstart.html

3.2.3. Pandas

Pandas is another very critical library in data science. It provides high-performance data manipulation and analysis tools with its powerful data structures.

The main unit of Pandas is the DataFrame, which is like an excel sheet with dozens of built-in functions for any data preprocessing or manipulation needed. There is also a data type called Series and another one called Panel. These will be explained when needed.

With Pandas, dealing with missing data or outliers can be very easy. Not only that but also manipulating complete columns or rows of data.

Pandas also supports reading and writing different file types.

Let us look at the fundamentals of Pandas. Again, it is really important that you execute the following code snippets yourself in order to understand better.

We start by importing Pandas.

```
import pandas as pd
```

The following table summarizes the different Pandas data structures.

Data Structure	Dimensions	Description
Series	1	1D labeled homogeneous array, sizeimmutable.
Data Frames	2	General 2D labeled, size-mutable tabular structure with potentially heterogeneously typed columns.
Panel	3	General 3D labeled, size-mutable array.

Series is a one-dimensional array structure with homogeneous data, while the size is immutable. Also, the values of the data are mutable.

```
pd.Series([1,2,3])
```

```
0    1
1    2
2    3
dtype: int64
```

DataFrame is a two-dimensional array with heterogeneous data and mutable size.

```
pd.DataFrame(data= {'col1': [1, 2], 'col2': [3, 4]})
```

	col1	col2
0	1	3
1	2	4

Pandas Panels are not used widely. Thus, we will focus only on Series and Data Frames.

However, you can use Panels when your data are 3D.

Pandas also has many data reading functions such as:

- read_csv()
- read_excel()
- read_json()
- read_html()
- read_sql()

Let us now work with a real-world dataset!

The first step is to change the directory to the one containing the dataset. This can be done using os library.

```
import os
os.chdir('D:')
os.getcwd()
```

```
'D:\\'
```

We will now use the reading function that we have just mentioned.

```
iris_df=pd.read_csv('iris.csv')
iris_df.head()
```

Pandas has a function called "head" that enables us to view the first few elements of a specific DataFrame.

	sepal_length	sepal_width	petal_length	petal_width	species
0	5.1	3.5	1.4	0.2	setosa
1	4.9	3.0	1.4	0.2	setosa
2	4.7	3.2	1.3	0.2	setosa
3	4.6	3.1	1.5	0.2	setosa
4	5.0	3.6	1.4	0.2	setosa

```
cars_df=pd.read_excel('cars.xls')
cars_df.head()
```

	Model	MPG	Cylinders	Displacement	Horsepower	Weight	Acceleration	Year	Origin
0	chevrolet chevelle malibu	18.0	8	307.0	130	3504	12.0	70	US
1	buick skylark 320	15.0	8	350.0	165	3693	11.5	70	US
2	plymouth satellite	18.0	8	318.0	150	3436	11.0	70	US
3	amc rebel sst	16.0	8	304.0	150	3433	12.0	70	US
4	ford torino	17.0	8	302.0	140	3449	10.5	70	US

```
titanic_df=pd.read_json('titanic.json')
titanic_df.head()
```

	datasetid	fields	record_timestamp	recordid
0	titanic-passengers	{'fare': 7.3125, 'name': 'Olsen, Mr. Ole Marti...	2016-09-21T01:34:51+03:00	398286223e6c4c16377d2b81d5335ac6dcc2cafb
1	titanic-passengers	{'fare': 15.75, 'name': 'Watt, Mrs. James (Eli...	2016-09-21T01:34:51+03:00	a6e68dbc16c3cf161e3d250650203e2c06161474
2	titanic-passengers	{'fare': 7.775, 'name': 'Bengtsson, Mr. John V...	2016-09-21T01:34:51+03:00	50cc1cb165b05151593164cdbc3815c1c3cccb55
3	titanic-passengers	{'fare': 10.5, 'name': 'Mellors, Mr. William J...	2016-09-21T01:34:51+03:00	1b3c80a0f49d7a4b050f023381aec7ce40fe4768
4	titanic-passengers	{'fare': 14.4542, 'name': 'Zabour, Miss. Thami...	2016-09-21T01:34:51+03:00	30c3695bc6b529abe6fb6052648f9238371a189b

Now, we'll work with the cars dataset and see how to select a column from it.

```
cars_df['MPG']
```

```
0        18.0
1        15.0
2        18.0
3        16.0
4        17.0
5        15.0
6        14.0
```

We can also choose a specific value in a specific column and row.

```
cars_df.iloc[19,1]
```

```
26.0
```

Moreover, we can choose the values that satisfy a condition.

```
cars_df.loc[cars_df.MPG>20,]
```

	Model	MPG	Cylinders	Displacement	Horsepower	Weight	Acceleration	Year	Origin
14	toyota corona mark ii	24.0	4	113.0	95	2372	15.0	70	Japan
15	plymouth duster	22.0	6	198.0	95	2833	15.5	70	US
17	ford maverick	21.0	6	200.0	85	2587	16.0	70	US
18	datsun pl510	27.0	4	97.0	88	2130	14.5	70	Japan
19	volkswagen 1131 deluxe sedan	26.0	4	97.0	46	1835	20.5	70	Europe
20	peugeot 504	25.0	4	110.0	87	2672	17.5	70	Europe
21	audi 100 ls	24.0	4	107.0	90	2430	14.5	70	Europe
22	saab 99e	25.0	4	104.0	95	2375	17.5	70	Europe
23	bmw 2002	26.0	4	121.0	113	2234	12.5	70	Europe
24	amc gremlin	21.0	6	199.0	90	2648	15.0	70	US
29	datsun pl510	27.0	4	97.0	88	2130	14.5	71	Japan

This can be done even with multiple conditions.

```
cars_df.loc[(cars_df.MPG>35)&(cars_df.Origin=='US'), ]
```

	Model	MPG	Cylinders	Displacement	Horsepower	Weight	Acceleration	Year	Origin
243	ford fiesta	36.1	4	98.0	66	1800	14.4	78	US
293	dodge colt hatchback custom	35.7	4	98.0	80	1915	14.4	79	US
340	plymouth champ	39.0	4	86.0	64	1875	16.4	81	US
372	plymouth horizon miser	38.0	4	105.0	63	2125	14.7	82	US
373	mercury lynx l	36.0	4	98.0	70	2125	17.3	82	US
381	oldsmobile cutlass ciera (diesel)	38.0	6	262.0	85	3015	17.0	82	US
385	dodge charger 2.2	36.0	4	135.0	84	2370	13.0	82	US

Finally, we can create a new column in the DataFrame that the data is saved in.

```
cars_df['MPG_per_cylinder']=cars_df['MPG']/cars_df['Cylinders']
```

Further Readings

If you want to know more about Pandas, go to this tutorial here

https://pandas.pydata.org/pandas-docs/stable/

3.2.4. Scientific Python (SciPy)

SciPy is a very important library for linear algebra operations, and it's also used in Fourier Transformers.

While it is a low-level library compared to other libraries that we will use, it is important to be familiar with it, because you may need to develop your own algorithm from scratch and this library will be of use then.

Note that SciPy library depends on NumPy for all its operations.

We will see how to compute 10^x using SciPy.

```
from scipy.special import exp10
exp = exp10([1,10])
print(exp)
```

```
[1.e+01 1.e+10]
```

SciPy also gives functionality to calculate permutations and combinations.

```
from scipy.special import comb,perm
com = comb(5, 2, exact = False)
print(com)
per=perm(5, 2, exact=False)
print(per)
```

```
10.0
20.0
```

We can also calculate the determinant of a two-dimensional matrix.

```
from scipy import linalg
import numpy as np
two_d_array = np.array([ [4,5], [3,2] ])
linalg.det( two_d_array )
```

```
-7.0
```

Finally, for our discussion, let us calculate the inverse of any matrix using SciPy.

```
scipy.linalg.inv(two_d_array)
```

```
array([[-0.28571429,  0.71428571],
       [ 0.42857143, -0.57142857]])
```

SciPy will not be used that much in our discussions, as we will use more high-level libraries to compute the determinant and other operations. However, it is good to know.

Further Readings

If you want to know more about SciPy, go to this tutorial here

https://docs.scipy.org/doc/

3.2.5. Matplotlib

Matplotlib is the fundamental library in Python for plotting 2D and even some 3D data. You can use it for many different plots such as histograms, bar plots, heatmaps, line plots, scatter plots and many others.

Let's see how to work with it. We'll start by importing it.

```
import matplotlib.pyplot as plt
import numpy as np
```

Then, we generate some random data to plot.

```
x = np.arange(10)
y = 4*x + 5 + np.random.random(size=x.size)
print(x)
print(y)
```

```
[0 1 2 3 4 5 6 7 8 9]
[ 5.55702208  9.05720778 13.01066085 17.02045126 21.69267
435 25.80298672
 29.917964   33.16520441 37.12348891 41.62939263]
```

After that, we plot using the scatter method.

```
plt.scatter(x, y)
```

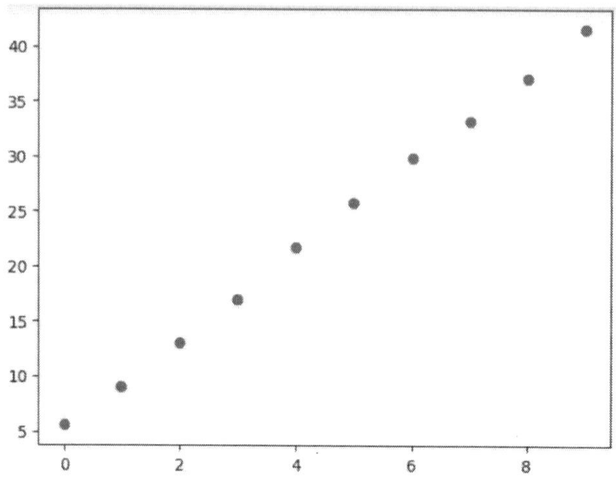

We can make the plot more beautiful.

```
# Use `o` as marker; color set as `r` (red); size proportion to Y values
plt.scatter(x, y, marker='+', c='r', s=y*10)
# How about adding a line to it? Let's use `plt.plot()`
# set line style to dashed; color as `k` (black)
plt.plot(x, y, linestyle='dashed', color='k')
# set x/y axis limits: first two are xlow and xhigh; last two are ylow and yhigh
plt.axis([0, 10, 0, 35])
# set x/y labels
plt.xlabel('My X Axis')
plt.ylabel('My Y Axis')
# set title
plt.title('My First Plot')
```

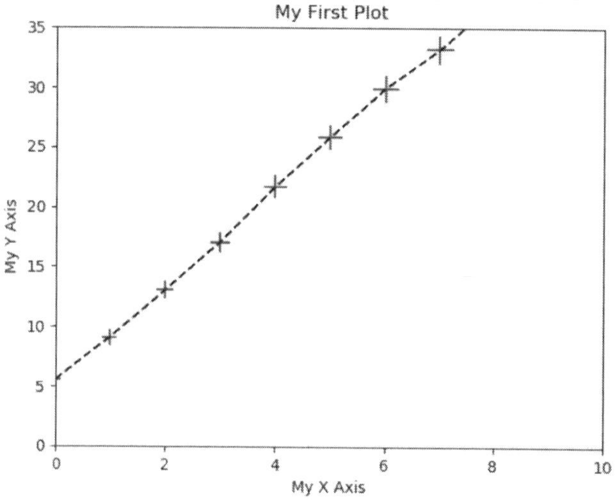

To understand the anatomy of the figure, see the following figure.

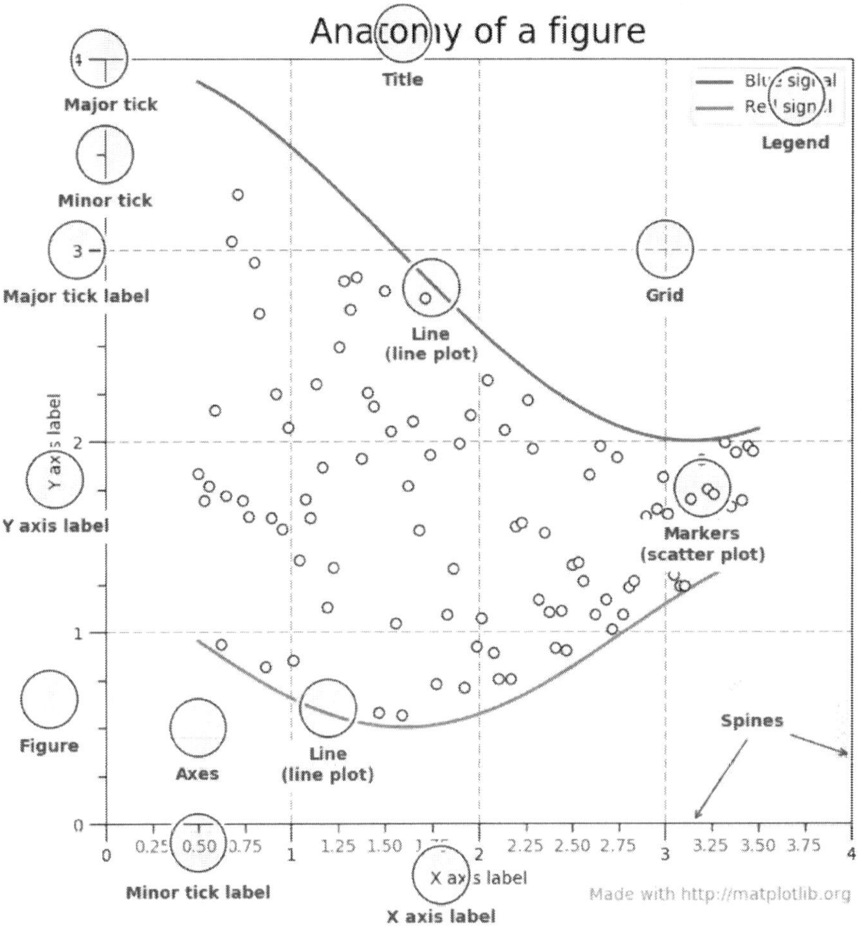

We can also have many sub-plots as follows:

```
# Now the returned `ax` would be array with a shape a 2x2
fig, ax_arr = plt.subplots(nrows=2, ncols=2)

# Now the returned `ax` would be array with a shape a 2x2
for ax_row in ax_arr:
    for ax in ax_row:
        ax.plot(x, y)
```

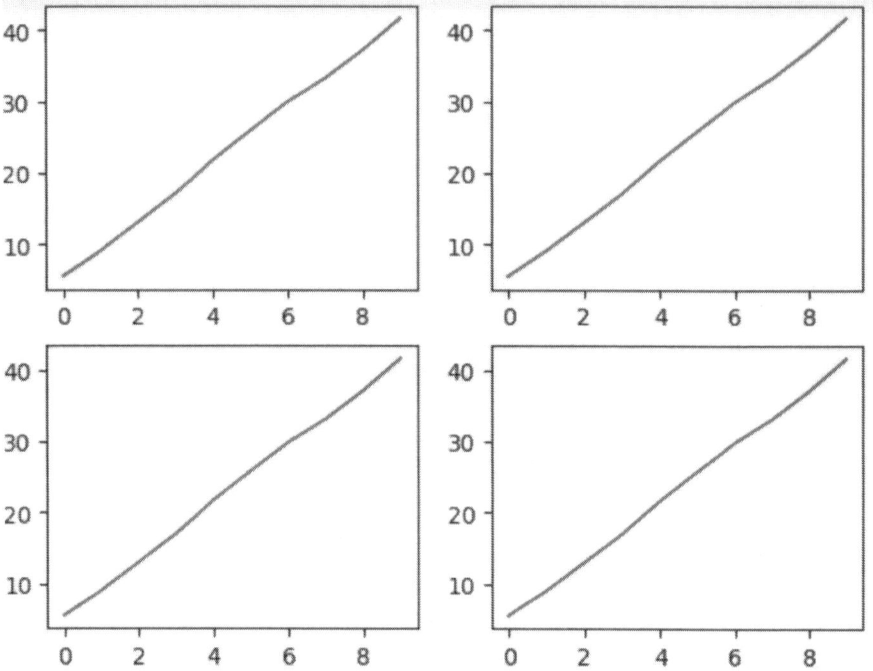

Now, let's use the visualization on a real dataset to enhance our understanding. We will be using the cars dataset once again.

We start by importing the libraries, fixing the path and loading the dataset.

```
import pandas as pd
import os
os.chdir('D:')
os.getcwd()
cars_df=pd.read_excel('cars.xls')
```

Then, we simply call the scatter method and pass our dataset variables.

```
plt.figure(figsize=(15,10))
plt.scatter(cars_df.Horsepower, cars_df.MPG, c=cars_df.Year,
            s=cars_df.Displacement, alpha=0.5)

plt.xlabel(r'Horsepower', fontsize=15)
plt.ylabel(r'MPG', fontsize=15)
plt.title('MPG vs Horsepower by Year and Displacement', fontsize=25)
plt.show()
```

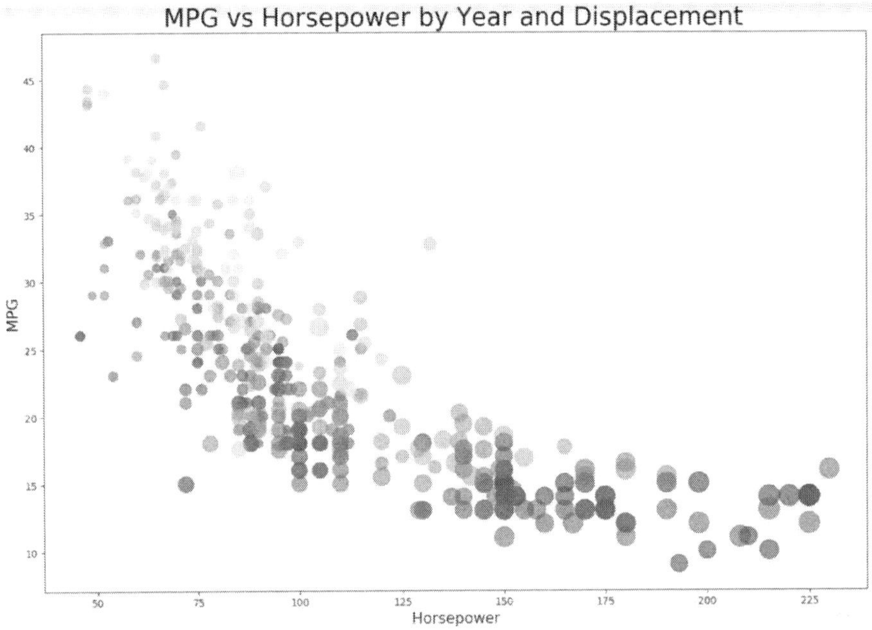

Now, we will experiment and see different kinds of plots: histograms, boxplots, bar plots and line plots. We will start with the histogram.

Let's create some random data with Gaussian distribution.

```
mu, sigma = 15, 1
gaussian_arr = np.random.normal(mu, sigma, size=10000)
np.mean(gaussian_arr), np.std(gaussian_arr, ddof=1)
```

```
(14.990546050758532, 1.0051987624650212)
```

Now, plot this data using a histogram.

```
fig, ax = plt.subplots()
freq_arr, bin_arr, _ = ax.hist(gaussian_arr)
```

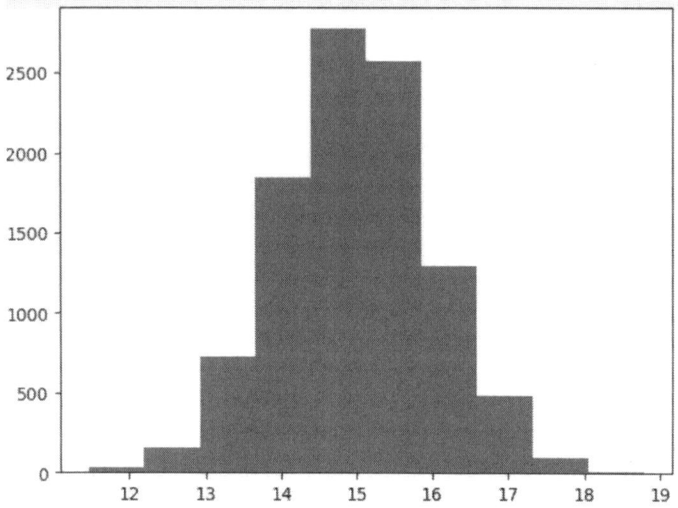

Then, we try to make it look better.

```
fig, ax = plt.subplots()
# Facecolor set to green; transparency (`alpha`) level: 30%
freq_arr, bin_arr, _ = ax.hist(gaussian_arr, facecolor='g', alpha=0.3)
# Add grid
ax.grid()
```

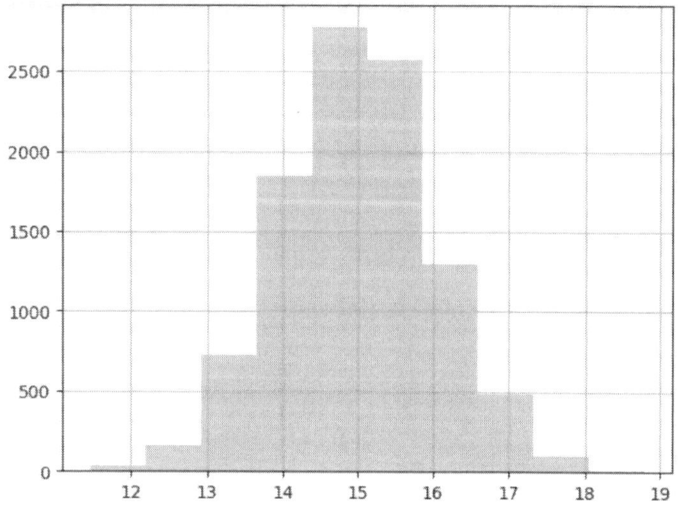

After that, we repeat the same code but on our cars' dataset.

```
cars_df.MPG.hist()
plt.show()
```

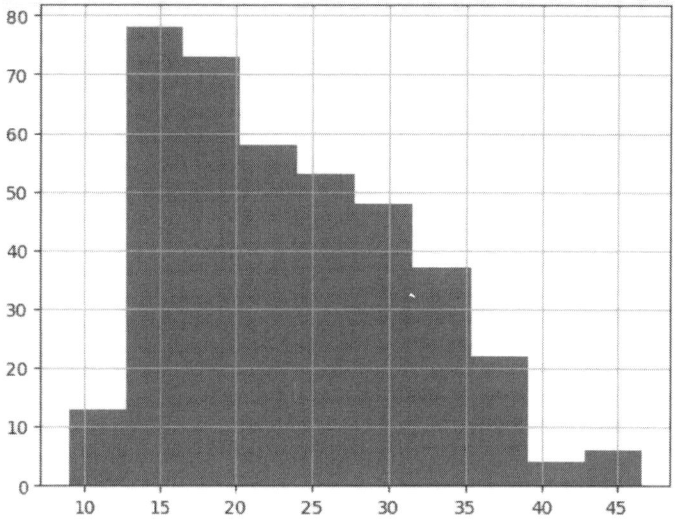

We then use the same data using a boxplot.

```
fig, ax = plt.subplots()
ax.boxplot(gaussian_arr,
           vert=False,  # verticle
           showfliers=False, # do not show outliers
           showmeans=True, # show the mean
           labels=['Gaussian'] # group name (label)
          )
```

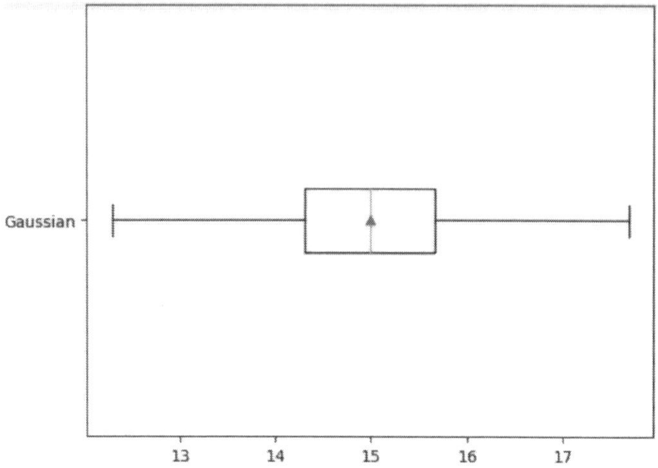

From there, we can experiment with the bar plots and see how they look and used. Here, we combine them with error bars that are frequently used when we have uncertainty about our data.

```
bar_arr = np.array(['Spring', 'Summer', 'Fall', 'Winder'])
freq_arr = np.random.randint(0, 100, 4)
yerr_arr = np.random.randint(5, 10, 4)
```

```
fig, ax = plt.subplots()
ax.bar(bar_arr, freq_arr, # X and Y
       yerr = yerr_arr, # error bars
       color='red',
      )
```

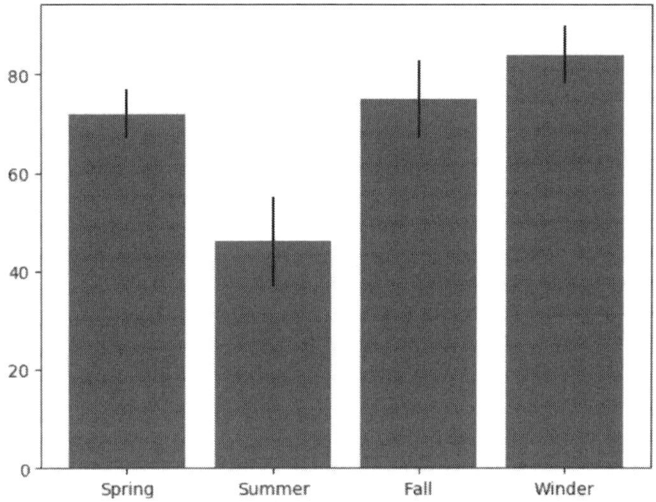

The last type of plot that we'll mention is the line plot. We will artificially generate the data with the following distribution so they can be interpreted easily in the plots.

```
dt = 0.01
t = np.arange(0, 30, dt)
nse1 = np.random.randn(len(t))
nse2 = np.random.randn(len(t))
r = np.exp(-t / 0.05)
cnse1 = np.convolve(nse1, r, mode='same') * dt
cnse2 = np.convolve(nse2, r, mode='same') * dt
s1 = 0.01 * np.sin(2 * np.pi * 10 * t) + cnse1
s2 = 0.01 * np.sin(2 * np.pi * 10 * t) + cnse2
```

Now, we can create two plots in one using the sub-plots function.

```
fig, (ax1, ax2) = plt.subplots(2, 1)
# make a little extra space between the subplots
fig.subplots_adjust(hspace=0.5)
ax1.plot(t, s1, t, s2)
ax1.set_xlim(0, 5)
ax1.set_xlabel('time')
ax1.set_ylabel('s1 and s2')
ax1.grid(True)
cxy, f = ax2.csd(s1, s2, 256, 1. / dt)
ax2.set_ylabel('CSD (db)')
plt.show()
```

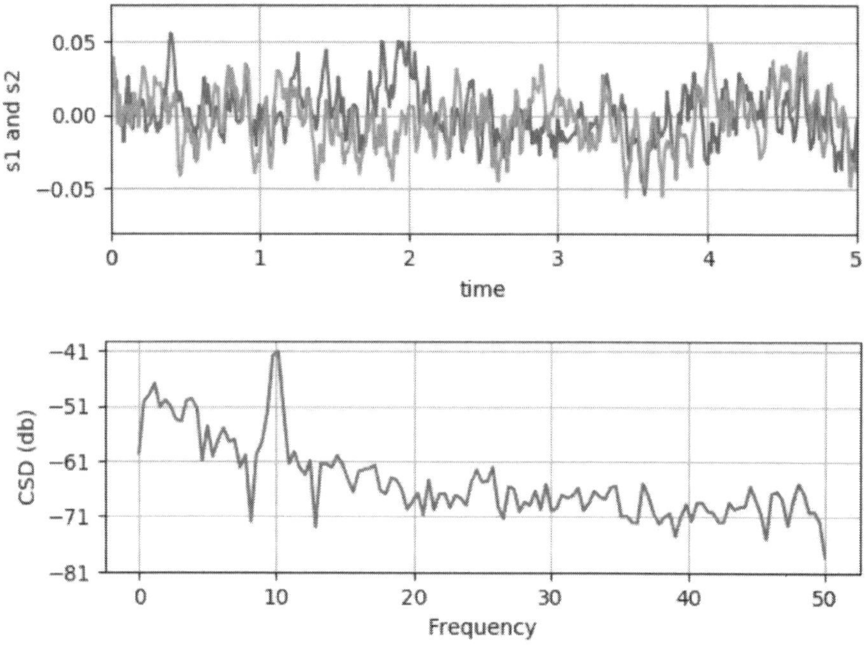

Finally, we can combine the four different types of plots that we discussed in a single plot.

```
fig, ax_arr = plt.subplots(nrows=2, ncols=2,sharex=False, sharey=False)
fig.set_figwidth(12)
fig.set_figheight(8)
# set global title
fig.suptitle("My first subplots")
## first
ax_arr[0, 0].scatter(x, y, marker='+', c='g', s=y*10)
ax_arr[0, 0].plot(x, y, linestyle='dashed', color='k')
ax_arr[0, 0].axis([0, 10, 0, 35])
ax_arr[0, 0].set_title('My First Plot')
## second
ax_arr[0, 1].hist(gaussian_arr, facecolor='g', alpha=0.3)
ax_arr[0, 1].set_title('Histogram')
## third
ax_arr[1, 0].boxplot(gaussian_arr, vert=False, showfliers=False,
showmeans=True, labels=['Gaussian'])
ax_arr[1, 0].set_title('Box plot')
## last one
ax_arr[1,1].bar(bar_arr, freq_arr,
                yerr = yerr_arr, color='gold')
ax_arr[1, 1].set_title('Bar chart')
```

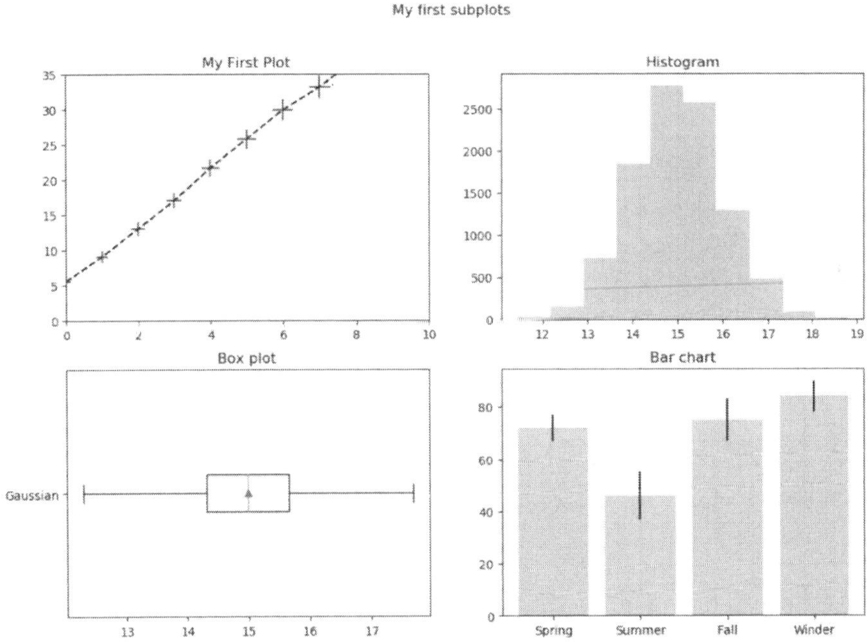

One final thing before we move on. It's worth mentioning that there is another less used library called seaborn, which can help us produce some good-looking graphs.

```
import seaborn as sns
sns.heatmap(cars_df.corr())
plt.show()
```

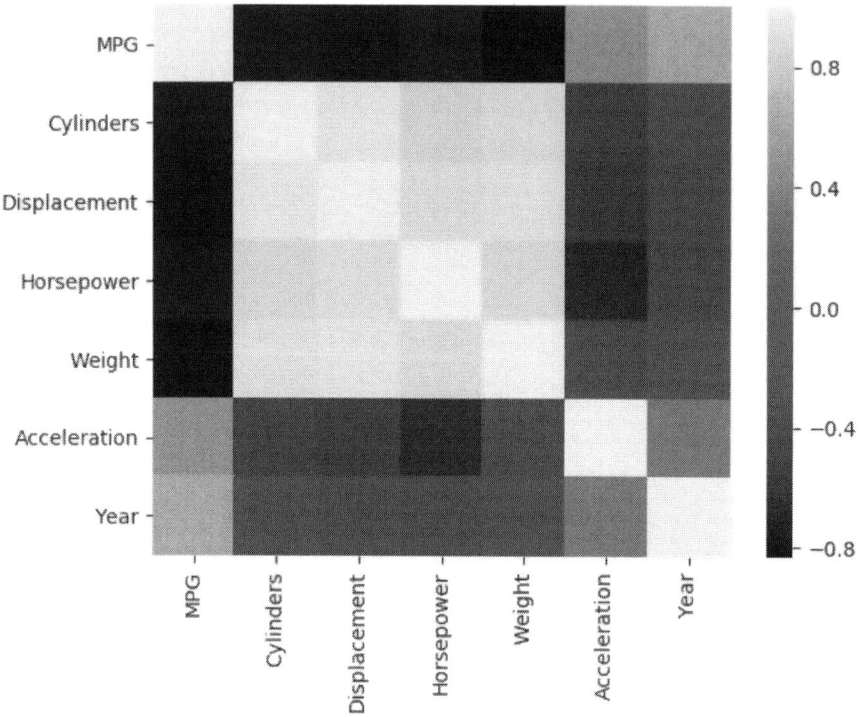

Further Readings

If you want to know more about Matplotlib, go to this tutorial here

https://matplotlib.org/contents.html

3.2.6. Scikit-Learn

Let us now introduce one of the most important libraries for anyone starting machine learning—Sklearn, or Scikit-Learn.

This library includes out-of-the-box ready-to-use machine learning algorithms. It literally has most of the algorithms that we will talk about in the eBook. The beautiful thing about it is that it has very great documentation, but more than that, it is very easy and intuitive to use. We will look at how to use it with a fundamental machine learning algorithm called linear regression, which will be the first algorithm that we will tackle in chapter 5.

The library also provides many utilities for data-preprocessing and data visualization and evaluation.

We start by importing the modules that we will use from sklearn.

```
from sklearn.linear_model import LinearRegression
from sklearn.model_selection import train_test_split
```

We will use linear regression as the algorithm.

```
lm=LinearRegression()
```

After that, we load the cars' dataset to work with.

```
import pandas as pd
import os
os.chdir('D:')
os.getcwd()
cars_df=pd.read_excel('cars.xls')
cars_df.head()
```

	Model	MPG	Cylinders	Displacement	Horsepower	Weight	Acceleration	Year	Origin
0	chevrolet chevelle malibu	18.0	8	307.0	130	3504	12.0	70	US
1	buick skylark 320	15.0	8	350.0	165	3693	11.5	70	US
2	plymouth satellite	18.0	8	318.0	150	3436	11.0	70	US
3	amc rebel sst	16.0	8	304.0	150	3433	12.0	70	US
4	ford torino	17.0	8	302.0	140	3449	10.5	70	US

Following that, we choose x to be all the dataset variables without the origin, the model and the MPG columns. Also, we choose y to be the output variable which is MPG. Moreover, we drop any missing values.

```
x =cars_df.dropna().drop(columns=['MPG','Model','Origin'])
y= cars_df.dropna().MPG
```

Then, we split our dataset into training and testing.

```
X_train,X_test,y_train,y_test=train_test_split(x,y,
                                test_size=0.3,random_state=42)
```

We then fit the model and predict the output. We will understand all the details in chapter 5.

```
lm.fit(X_train,y_train)
```

```
lm.predict(X_test)
```

```
array([26.31050971, 26.24667456, 33.14488022, 27.2244046
2, 29.46550187,
       29.28389189,  7.66404492, 29.42701039, 21.1231744
, 29.36858154,
       12.23470009, 23.80655125, 16.26874891, 28.4271919
4, 21.98956832,
```

Finally, we will plot the data with the predicted outputs.

```
import matplotlib.pyplot as plt
import numpy as np
```

```
# add your actual vs. predicted points
plt.scatter(y_test, lm.predict(X_test))
# add the line of perfect fit
straight_line = np.arange(0, 60)
plt.plot(straight_line, straight_line)
plt.title("Fitted Values")
plt.show()
```

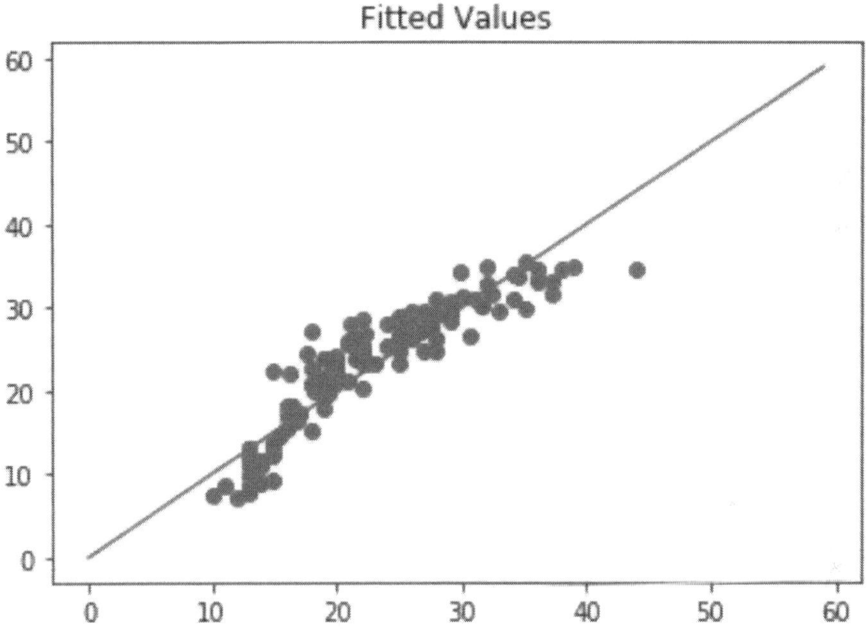

Further Readings

If you want to know more about Sklearn, go to this tutorial here

https://scikit-learn.org/stable/documentation.html

3.3. Dealing with Real-World Data

3.3.1. Importing the Libraries

Importing the libraries can be considered step 0 in any machine learning project. It is recommended to import all your libraries in the first cell of your project.

We will practice how to import the libraries, and most importantly, how to know what libraries you need in your projects throughout the upcoming chapters.

3.3.2. Get the Dataset

The first step in any machine learning project is to upload or load the dataset into your notebook. We have seen this step in-action in the last section where we imported many libraries with different extensions into our code. The dataset can come in different formats such as csv, excel or json. We have used Pandas library to easily load any dataset that we want.

We can also work with an SQL database format or even specific APIs that some websites or servers provide. Moreover, we can work with files coming from other software such as MATLAB. We will see this in practice in the notebooks of this section.

However, we haven't yet mentioned the source of these datasets. Basically, you can collect your own dataset and store them into an excel file, for example. However, this may be an overhead for you when starting your machine learning journey. There are plenty of websites where dedicated data scientists upload their datasets. Some of the most popular websites for this purpose are:

- Kaggle
- WorldBank
- UCI Machine Learning Repository
- Quandl
- Amazon Web Services (AWS) datasets
- Data.Gov

Another very cool service that Google has just launched that it is still in a Beta version is Google Dataset Search engine. This is just the usual Google search engine but dedicated to the search of datasets. You can access it here.

A more advanced approach to create your dataset is via API and web scraping. This will be explored in detail in chapter 9.

3.3.3. Detecting Outliers and Missing Data

So, let's now talk about preprocessing, which is the first actual step in any machine learning project. Data preprocessing is a painful and unenviable task, unfortunately.

The first and the most important step in preprocessing is detecting outliers. We've talked about outliers before. Now it's time to learn how to deal with them.

To detect outliers, you should first look at the general structure of your data and print some statistics of them. Also, you should visualize your data if possible. This is an easy task now that we know how to use Pandas and Matplotlib, specifically.

After detecting the outliers, we can easily write a condition in Pandas DataFrame to filter out the outliers as we saw on a dummy example in the previous section.

Let us practice what we have studied so far.

```
import numpy as np
import pandas as pd
import matplotlib.pyplot as plt
import os
from sqlalchemy import create_engine
```

```
fords=pd.read_csv('fords.csv')
```

```
fords.info()
```

```
<class 'pandas.core.frame.DataFrame'>
RangeIndex: 635 entries, 0 to 634
Data columns (total 7 columns):
Year        635 non-null int64
Mileage     616 non-null float64
Price       629 non-null float64
Color       625 non-null object
Location    635 non-null object
Model       627 non-null object
Age         635 non-null int64
dtypes: float64(2), int64(2), object(3)
memory usage: 34.8+ KB
```

As we can see, the data has 635 examples with seven features. We can also see that there are missing data in some features such as Mileage and Price. Let's visualize the data to see if there are any outliers.

```
fords.Year.hist()
plt.show()
```

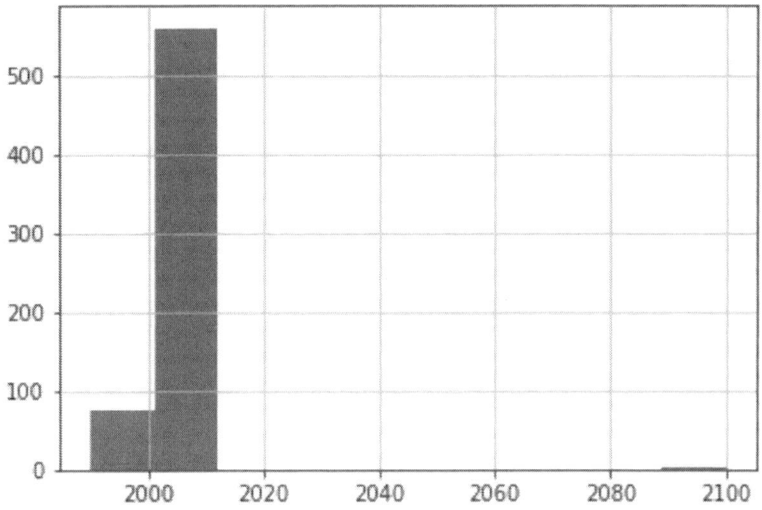

The outliers are clear! They exist at nearly 2090. So, let's filter them out.

```
fords = fords[fords.Year<2090]
```

```
fords.Year.hist()
plt.show()
```

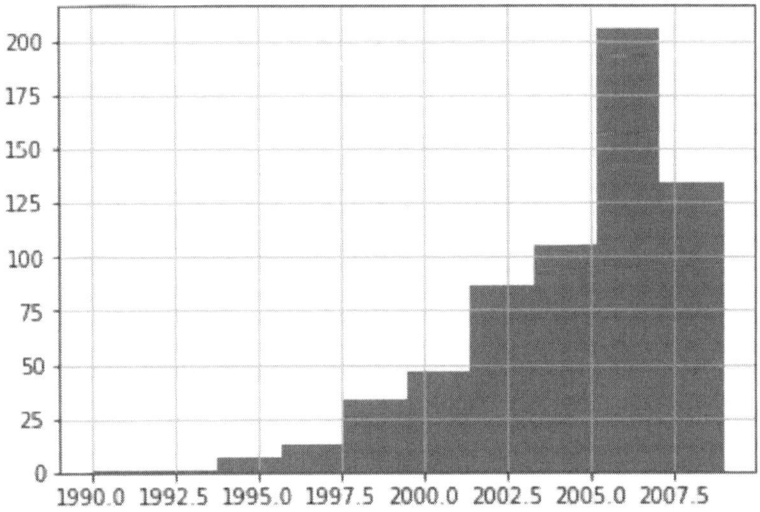

We can delete them using a smarter way as follows:

```
fords=pd.read_csv('fords.csv')
fords=fords.loc[~((fords.Price>8000000)|(fords.Year>2080)),
```

Now, let's drop any missing values.

```
fords.dropna(inplace=True)
```

```
fords.info()
```

```
<class 'pandas.core.frame.DataFrame'>
Int64Index: 598 entries, 1 to 634
Data columns (total 7 columns):
Year        598 non-null int64
Mileage     598 non-null float64
Price       598 non-null float64
Color       598 non-null object
Location    598 non-null object
Model       598 non-null object
Age         598 non-null int64
dtypes: float64(2), int64(2), object(3)
memory usage: 37.4+ KB
```

3.3.4. Dummy Variables

The second preprocessing step in all machine learning projects is to know if we need dummy variables or not.

So, what are dummy variables? And why do we need them?

Dummy variables are variables that are used when we have a categorical variable that we cannot do mathematical operations on.

For example, if one feature of a house is the presence of a garden, we can see that the possible values for this variable are either YES or NO. So, we create a dummy variable for this variable where YES is replaced by 1 and NO is replaced by 0.

This can be further extended for other variables that we cannot operate on, such as the blood type. In this case, what we do is convert this variable with one-hot encoding.

If we have three blood types only, then the first blood type will be replaced with 001, the second one will be replaced by 010 and the final one will be replaced by 100. This is one-hot encoding, and we can extend it further based on the number of possible values that this categorical variable can have.

So, we have to convert our categorical variables into dummy variables to make all of our variables contain only numbers that the machine learning algorithms can understand and work with.

We will see how to do so in the next tutorial.

3.3.5. Normalize Numerical Variables

Moving to the numerical variables, we have to do some preprocessing as well. The most important and basic preprocessing for the numerical variables is normalization.

Let's continue our discussion on the house prices dataset by examining the number of rooms and the area of this house. We can say, for example, that any practical house can have from one to ten or more rooms, while it could have an area of 100 square feet to thousands of square feet.

The problem exists here because the different variables normally have different scales. This will affect our algorithm as it would think that the area of the house matters more than the number of rooms, which we do not want to happen.

So, in order to make all our variables have the same scale, we normalize all of our numerical variables.

This can be done using different ways.

- Standard score: This is done by getting the mean of every variable and subtracting the examples from it and dividing by the standard deviation of this variable.

$$X = \frac{X - \mu}{\sigma}$$

This works well when the data are normally distributed.

- Min-Max Feature scaling: This is basically subtracting the minimum value and dividing by the maximum value minus the minimum value.

$$X = \frac{X - X_{\min}}{X_{\max} - X_{\min}}$$

There are different normalization methods, but these two are the most commonly used in machine learning.

Let us look at a complete project.

We start by importing the needed libraries, fixing the path, and loading the cars' dataset.

```
import numpy as np
import pandas as pd
import os
from sklearn.model_selection import train_test_split ## Splitting the data
from sklearn.preprocessing import StandardScaler, MinMaxScaler ## Normalizing the dataset
from sklearn.model_selection import cross_val_score ## K-Cross Validation
from sklearn import svm ## Support Vector Machine Algorithm ( will take about in chapter 5)
from sklearn.datasets import load_iris ## Toy dataset
```

```
os.chdir('D:')
os.getcwd()
```

```
cars_df=pd.read_excel('cars.xls')
```

Then, we convert the categorical variables into dummy variables

```
cars_df_dum=pd.get_dummies(cars_df.drop(columns='Model'))
```

```
print(cars_df.shape)
print(cars_df_dum.shape)
```

```
(392, 9)
(392, 10)
```

After that, we choose MPG as our target variable.

```
X=cars_df_dum.drop(columns='MPG')
y = cars_df_dum.MPG
```

In case you want to remember why we split our dataset; this image can help.

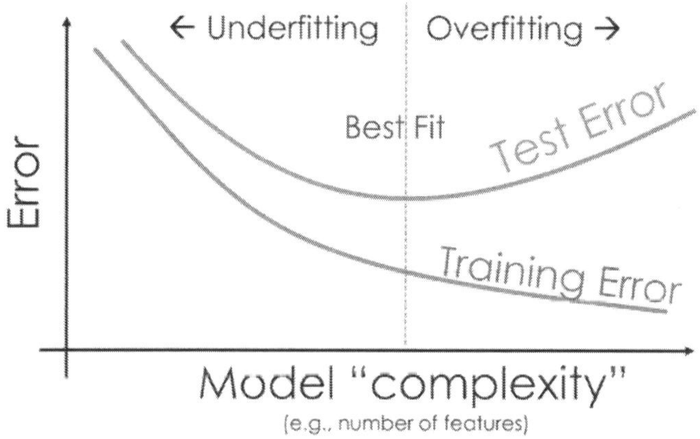


```
X_train,X_test,y_train,y_test=train_test_split(X,y,
                                  test_size=0.3,random_state=42)
```

Now, let us normalize our dataset.

```
scaler=StandardScaler()
```

```
X_train_n=pd.DataFrame(scaler.fit_transform(X_train),
                        columns=X_train.columns)
```

```
X_test_n=pd.DataFrame(scaler.transform(X_test),
                      columns=X_test.columns)
```

Hint: You can use MinMaxScaler and see which works better for you on the following algorithm.

After finishing this part, let us see how we can utilize cross-validation.

```
iris = load_iris()
```

```
clf = svm.SVC(kernel='linear', C=1)
scores = cross_val_score(clf, iris.data, iris.target, cv=5)
print(scores)
```

```
[0.96666667 1.         0.96666667 0.96666667
 1.        ]
```

These five numbers represent the cross-validation accuracy on each fold; we used five folds in this example.

Further Readings

If you are curious about other normalization techniques you can check here

https://www.studytonight.com/dbms/database-normalization.php

4

Statistics and Probability

In this chapter, we will talk in more depth about statistics and probability, which we introduced in the previous chapter.

4.1. Why Probability and Statistics?

Before we talk about the different aspects of probability and statistics, let us first get motivated about why we should learn about them.

As you know, there are very few things in the world that we can be sure about 100%. Most things we are sure about only to some extent. Thus, we need probability and statistics to provide a rational and scientific way to deal with this uncertainty.

Also, as we will see in the next chapters, all the machine learning algorithms are heavily based on probability and statistics theorems. So, in order to understand them correctly and know how to use them, we have to know the basis for these algorithms.

4.2. Data Categories

Data can be split into two major categories: Numerical data (quantitative data) and Categorical data (qualitative data).

We can say that the data are categorical if the different values that the data can have cannot be used in mathematical operations. Categorical data can be split even more into ordinal (ordered) data and nominal (unordered) data. The rating of a movie is an excellent example of ordinal categorical data, while blood type is a good example of nominal data.

On the other hand, numerical data can be used in mathematical operations. Numerical data can be split even more into discrete numerical data and continuous numerical data. Discrete numerical data can only have one of a pre-defined set of values. An example of that is the number of bedrooms in a house. Continuous data can have any value from negative infinity to infinity. An example of that is the speed of a car. But of course, depending on the nature of the variable in the data, even the continuous variables should be restricted by a range.

4.3. Summary Statistics

Given that we now understand how we can categorize our data, let's talk about how to perform statistical analysis on them.

The first step of your analysis no matter the dataset or the problem is to calculate key values called summary statistics. These values are used to describe the dataset observations by using four different classes of measures.

4.3.1. Measures of Central Tendency

The first class of measures is the measure of location, also called the central tendency. These measures are used to describe the data by identifying the central position. This identification can be made by using three measures, which are:

1. The **mean** which is equal to the sum of all the values divided by a number of values, which is simply taking the average.
2. The **median** which is calculated by sorting the dataset and getting the middle value.
3. The **mode** which is the most occurring value in the dataset.

Let us take a numerical example and calculate the three measures. Suppose our data is the following

{13,40,50,50,90,18,30,50,30,70}

So, first, we calculate the mean using the following equation

$$mean = \frac{13 + 40 + 50 + 50 + 90 + 18 + 30 + 50 + 30 + 70}{10} = 44.1$$

Then, we calculate the median by first sorting the data.

{13,18,30,30,40,50,50,50,70,90}

After that, we take the middle value as our median, which will be $\frac{40+50}{2} = 45$ as the number of examples is even, so we take the average of the two middle values.

Finally, we calculate the mode by observing the most occurring value, which is 50 in our case.

4.3.2. Measures of Asymmetry

The second class of measures is the measure of shape or symmetry. In this measure, we try to identify if the data is centered, which means the number of examples on the left side of the center is nearly equal to the number of examples on the right side of the center of now. The most used measure in this class is the skewness of the data distribution. We say that the data is positively skewed if the mean > median > mode, and negatively skewed if the mean<median<mode. By identifying any skewness in the data, we can use different preprocessing techniques to make the data symmetric.

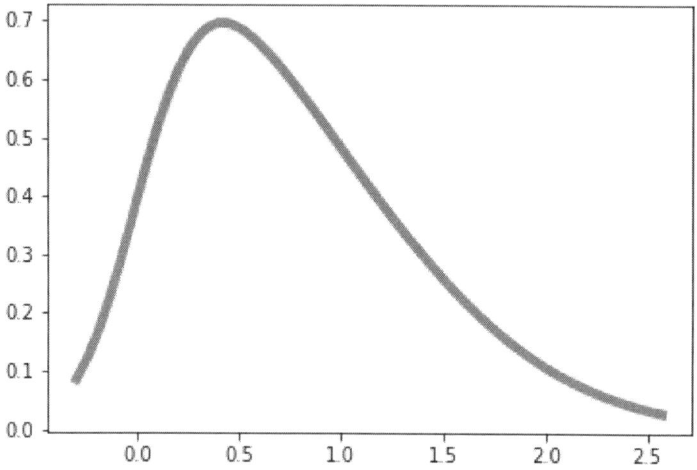

Figure 1- Right-Skewed (Positive Skewed)

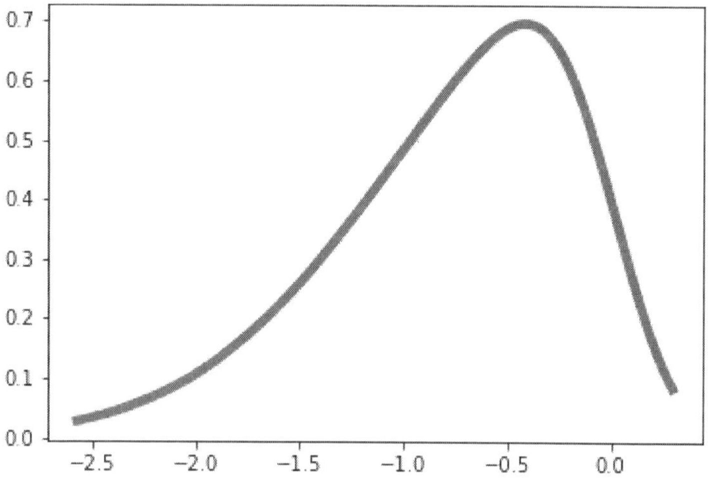

Figure 2- Left-Skewed (Negative Skewed)

4.3.3. Measures of Spread

The third class of measures is the measure of spread which is also called the measure of variability. There are many measures to achieve this task, but we will focus only on the most important three, which are:

1. **Range** is the difference between the smallest and the largest value of the data. Note that this does not consider all the values in the data, but, instead it takes only the minimum and the maximum values. For example, if we have {10,8,20,40,12,15,30,25} as our examples, then the range will be (8-40) only.
2. **Variance** measures how far the sum of the squared distances is from each point to the mean. This can indicate the dispersion around the mean as it is the average all squared deviation. The equation to calculate the variance is $\sigma^2 = \frac{\sum_{i=1}^{n} x_i - \mu}{n}$.
3. **Standard deviation,** the square root of the variance is the most commonly used measure as it has the same units as the data.

Here is a numerical example to show how we can calculate the measures of spread. Suppose that we have the following dataset.

{3,5,6,9,10}

$$mean = \frac{3+5+6+9+10}{5} = 6.6$$

$$Variance = \frac{(3-6.6)^2 + (5-6.6)^2 + (6-6.6)^2 + (9-6.6)^2 + (10-6.6)^2}{5} = 6.64$$

$$standard\ deviation = \sqrt{Variance} = 2.576$$

4.3.4. Measures of Relationship

These measures are mainly used to compare and find the relation between two or more different variables. There are two main measures to do so:

1. **Covariance** which measures the relationship between the variability of two or more different variables by calculating the effect of changing one variable's values to the other variables' values. We use this measure to have an idea about the direction of the relationship—whether the variables tend to move in tandem or show an inverse relationship. However, covariance does not indicate the strength of this relationship, nor the dependency between the variables as it is not normalized. The equation to calculate the covariance is the following:

$$Cov(X,Y) = \frac{\sum_{i=1}^{n}(X_i - \underline{X})(Y_i - \underline{Y})}{n}$$

2. **Correlation** which is the covariance after normalization. This normalization is done by calculating the standard deviation of both variables and dividing the covariance by them. By using correlation, we can measure the strength of the relationship between different variables. This is because the correlation is a pure value that does not have any units. The range of the correlation is from -1 to 1 as -1 indicates a pure negative correlation. This means that as one variable increases, the other variable decreases in the same way. If the correlation value is 1, then there is a pure positive correlation. Finally,

if the correlation is zero, then the two variables are independent of each other. The equation to calculate the correlation is the following:

$$\rho = \frac{Cov(X,Y)}{\sigma_x \sigma_y}$$

4.4. Bayes Rule

Bayes rule is one of the pioneering probability theorems that were used in machine learning applications.

Before we discuss it, we must understand three fundamental concepts in probability: marginal probability, joint probability and conditional probability.

In this chapter, we will discuss the most famous and used supervised learning algorithms. This is a significant chapter that you'll have to go through in detail to get the utmost benefit. We will first explore the most basic supervised learning algorithm.

4.4.1. Marginal Probability

If we have an event A, the marginal probability is the probability that this event will occur regardless of any other events. We use this notation to indicate marginal probability $P(A)$. For example, suppose that we have four red balls and four blue balls. Then, the marginal probability of picking a red ball is $(red) = 0.5$.

4.4.2. Joint Probability

The second fundamental probability concept is joint probability, which we notate as $P(A \cap B)$. This is the intersection between the two events, which means that the two events have to occur together. We can visualize it using a Venn diagram as follows.

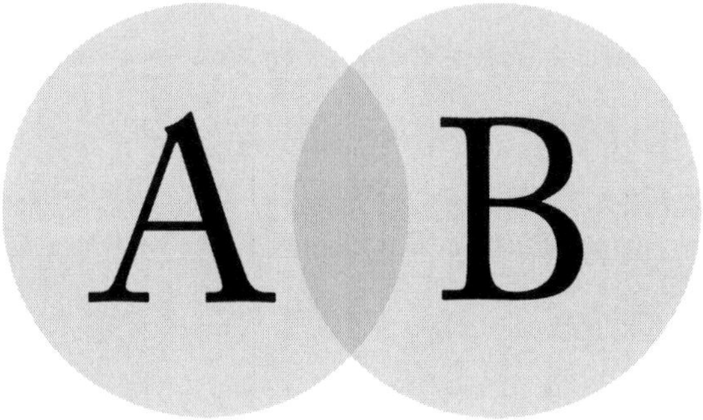

As we can see, the intersection between the two events is the joint probability. For example, if we have a traditional card deck with fifty-two cards, then the probability of choosing a black eight card is $P(black \cap 8) = \frac{2}{52}$ because there are only two cards that satisfy these two conditions.

4.4.3. Conditional Probability

Finally, conditional probability is a measure of the probability of an event given that some other event has occurred. We write this mathematically as follows $P(B)$, which is translated to the probability of event A given that event B has occurred. For example, the probability of picking up an eight from the deck given that it is a black card is $P(black) = \frac{1}{26}$, because given that it is a black card, we know that it must be one of the twenty-six black cards.

We can link the three concepts together as follows:

$$P(B) = \frac{P(A \cap B)}{P(B)}$$

The proof of this theorem is out of this book's scope, so we only need to understand that these three main probability concepts are interconnected.

4.4.4. Bayes Rule

Given that we now have some familiarity with different probability concepts, we can introduce Bayes rule. Bayes rule has the advantage of providing us with a method to update our beliefs based on new evidence.

Suppose for example that we want to estimate the probability that a given person will be accepted for graduate studies or not. If you only have his or her exam grades, you will provide a different probability than if you have additional evidence such as the number of published papers.

Bayes rule can be written as follows:

$$P(B) = \frac{P(A) * P(A)}{P(B)}$$

This rule combines both conditional probability and marginal probability. Also, it is derived from joint probability.

Here, we want to get the probability of event A given that B is the new evidence that we have. We call this the posterior, which would be "the probability of getting accepted given that this person has published papers".

We call $P(A)$ the likelihood, as it the probability of observing the new evidence, given our initial hypothesis. This can be translated for our example as follows "probability of having published papers given that the person gets accepted".

The marginal probability $P(A)$ is also called the prior, as it is the probability of our hypothesis without any additional prior information. Referring to our example, we can say that this maps to "the probability of getting accepted".

Finally, $P(B)$ is the marginal likelihood which could be translated to "the probability of having published papers".

In order to understand Bayes rule, let us look at a numerical example. Assume that the probability of getting accepted at this university is 10%. Assume also that the probability of publishing papers is 30%, which means that out of every ten people applying to this university, there are three people who have published papers. Also, assume that 20% of people that got accepted have published papers, so $(accepted) = 0.2$.

Without having the new evidence, which is the published papers, we would have said that the probability for being accepted is the prior probability which is $(accepted) = 0.1$. But now, using Bayes rule, we can have more precise calculation as follows:

$$P(published) = \frac{P(accepted) * P(accepted)}{P(published)} = \frac{0.2 * 0.1}{0.3} = 0.066$$

We will see in the following chapter that there is a whole algorithm called Naïve Bayes that is based entirely on Bayes rule.

5

Supervised Learning Techniques

In this chapter, we will discuss the most famous and used supervised learning algorithms. This is a crucial chapter to go through in detail in order to get the utmost benefit. We will first explore the most basic supervised learning algorithm called linear regression. Then, we will go through more advanced and complex algorithms which are logistic regression, support vector machines, decision trees, K-nearest neighbors and naïve Bayes. Finally, we will define the metrics that will help us evaluate any machine learning model.

Our discussion will be divided mainly into two main parts: how the algorithm works intuitively and mathematically, how to implement it in Python.

5.1. Linear Regression

5.1.1. Simple and Multiple Linear Regression Introduction

Suppose that you have a hypothesis that there is a linear relation between a person's income and the area of the house that this person lives in. To test your hypothesis, you collected a dataset or found one online, that contains two variables, which are the income and the area. Now, you want a mathematical model to fit this data and see if there is a linear relation or not. Let's suppose that it is really a linear relation, so we focus now on how to model this data. By doing so, we can predict the income of a new person just by knowing his/her house area.

If you remember from school, we can do this by using the following equation.

$$y = mx + b$$

In this equation, we can find the output `y` by multiplying the input `x` by the slope `m` and by adding this to the y-intercept `b`. We have the output and the input, but what about the slope and the intercept?

In fact, this is what we are trying to learn, because if we already have the slope and the intercept, then there is no problem to solve.

So, our goal is to find `m` and `b` which we will call the weights and the bias from now on.

This is the basic definition of linear regression. We can also summarize it by saying, "`In linear regression, our task is to model a relationship between target variable and input variables by fitting a line`".

If the input variables are more than one, then we call this a multiple linear regression problem, and if there is only one input variable, like our example, then we call it a simple linear regression problem.

Now we'll plot the data using some arbitrary numbers that we can assume for now are true.

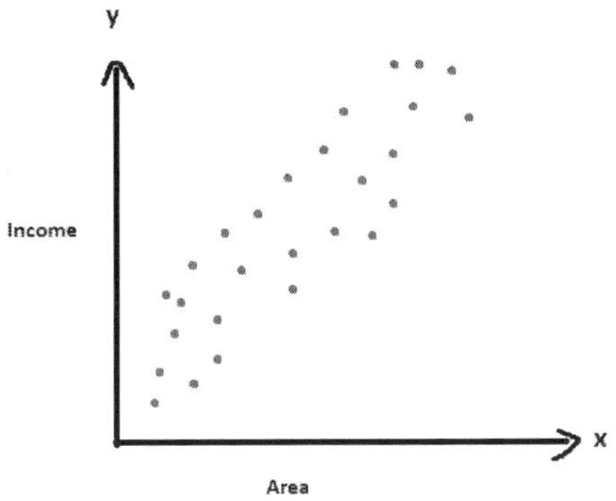

It's clear that we can fit our model using different lines by tweaking `m` and `b`.

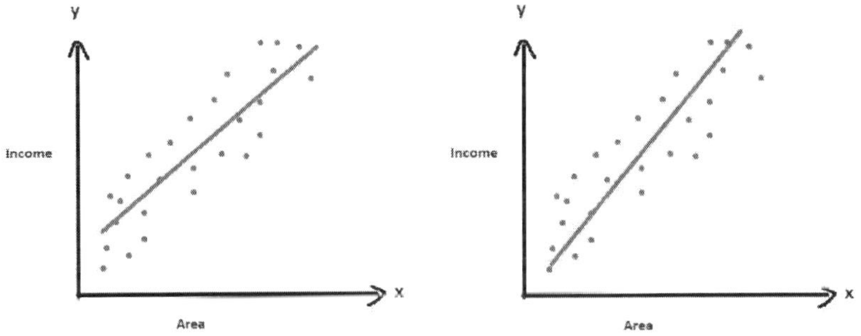

To stick to the machine learning notation, let's rename `b` to w_0 and `m` to w_1. So now, we can rewrite the equation this way

$$y = w_0 + w_1 * x$$

We can generalize this equation even further to be true for multiple regression.

$$y = \sum_{i=0}^{n} w_i x_i = w^T x$$

The T superscript that we use for w is called the transpose, and this equation is the same as the sum equation, but it is mainly used when we convert our variables into vectors and matrices. By converting them, we can avoid using loops which takes too much time to finish if we have a large number of inputs. Using vectors is always preferable as computers are optimized to perform matrix multiplication more than loops. We call this paradigm `vectorization`.

As we can see, there are infinite values for the weights, and we cannot really tell, until now, which set of weights gives the best performance.

There are two main methods to determine these weights. Both of them are based on minimizing the error. However, they differ in their approaches to do so, as the first method does this by getting a closed-form mathematical solution, while the second one is an iterative solution that tries to converge to the correct answer.

The first method is quite simple, as we say that the error is $\epsilon_i = y_i - \hat{y}_i$ where y_i is the true output for example `i`, and $\hat{y}_i$ is the estimated output for example `i`. So, the error, which is also called the residual, is the difference between them. Our objective is to minimize the sum of the squared prediction errors. We use the square because we want all our errors to be positive values and eliminate any negative values. We could also minimize the sum of the absolute prediction errors as this will also do the trick; however, using the squaring technique has some mathematical advantages over the absolute technique. Therefore, we will stick with the sum of the squared errors technique.

So, we can write this mathematically as follows.

$$E = \sum_{i=1}^{n} (y_i - \hat{y}_i)^2 = \sum_{i=1}^{n} (y_i - (w_0 + w_i x_i)^2$$

We can find `w` using some mathematical manipulation that we will not really be concerned about right now, but it has a closed-form solution that is applied.

The second method is an iterative method called the gradient descent. In this method, we have our cost function which is the same as the sum of the squared errors. Our objective again, is to find the weights that minimize the cost function as follows.

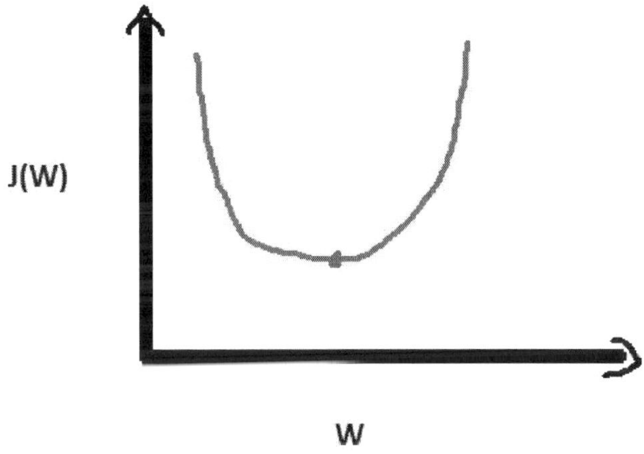

If you studied pre-calculus in high school, you will know that by saying `minimize` or `maximize` for a function, we mean getting the first derivative of this function and making this derivative equal to zero. The symbol that we will use for the derivative of the cost function is ∇J. The most common `optimization` algorithm used in machine learning for minimization is called `gradient descent`.

The intuition behind the gradient descent is very simple. You start by choosing random weights. Then you calculate the first derivative of the cost function. After that, you move in the opposite direction of this value, multiplying this number by a factor called the `learning rate`. Finally, we update the weights and repeat until convergence.

$$w = w - \alpha \nabla J(w)$$

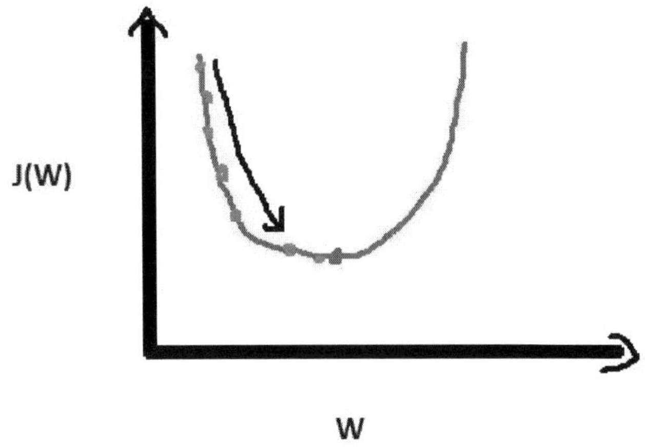

So, you might have two questions. The first one asks what the value of the learning rate should be. The answer is that it depends on the convergence rate. So, if we have an error that is far from the right answer, then we will want a bigger learning rate. However, once we start converging, this big learning rate will make it difficult for us to reach the minimum value as it may overshoot. Also, choosing a very small learning rate will make the model take too much time to converge and it may also get stuck in a local minimum and not reach the global minima. Nonetheless, people tend to use learning rate in the range of 10^{-2} - 10^{-5}. So, a good method to choose your learning rate is to start from 10^{-5} and increase it sharply as long as it gives you good results, then increase it carefully once you reach a critical value.

Note that the learning rate is not included in the trainable parameters of the model; thus, we call it a `hyperparameters`. As we will see in the next algorithms, there will be many hyperparameters which we will have full control of.

The second question is why we take the negative of the gradient. The answer is that the derivative is the slope at this point, and the direction of that slope is in the opposite direction of the correct answer. Therefore, we use the negative sign in our calculation of the new weights.

The algorithm that we have just discussed is called gradient descent, and it is used in many other machine learning algorithms as it is a very solid optimization algorithm. Note also that there are two variations of this algorithm which are stochastic gradient descent and mini-batch gradient descent. We will discuss them in detail in chapter 7. However, it is enough to know for now that stochastic gradient descent updates the weights based on a single example while mini-batch updates them based on several examples equal to the batch. There are pros and cons for the use of each of the three versions of the algorithm. Using vanilla gradient descent is adequate for now.

Also, it is preferable to use gradient-descent based learning than the closed-form solution when we have a large number of features because it becomes computationally expensive to find a closed-form solution.

5.1.2. Simple Linear Regression in Python

Let us now see how this can be converted into Python code.

The first step is to import all the libraries that we will need.

```
import pandas as pd
import os
import numpy as np
from sklearn.model_selection import train_test_split
from sklearn.linear_model import LinearRegression
from math import sqrt
from sklearn.metrics import mean_squared_error
import statsmodels.api as sm
import matplotlib.pyplot as plt
from sklearn.preprocessing import MinMaxScaler
import scipy as sp
```

Then, fix the directory and load the dataset.

```
os.chdir('D:')
os.getcwd()
cars_df=pd.read_excel('cars.xls')
cars_df.head()
```

We print some information about the dataset, and given that we preprocessed it in chapter 3, we won't need to do any preprocessing again.

```
cars_df.info()
```

```
<class 'pandas.core.frame.DataFrame'>
RangeIndex: 392 entries, 0 to 391
Data columns (total 9 columns):
Model           392 non-null object
MPG             392 non-null float64
Cylinders       392 non-null int64
Displacement    392 non-null float64
Horsepower      392 non-null int64
Weight          392 non-null int64
Acceleration    392 non-null float64
Year            392 non-null int64
Origin          392 non-null object
dtypes: float64(3), int64(4), object(2)
memory usage: 27.6+ KB
```

We choose MPG variable to be our output and the Horsepower variable to be our input.

```
y=cars_df.MPG
X=cars_df.Horsepower
```

We then split our dataset into a training dataset and testing dataset.

```
X_train,X_test,y_train,y_test=train_test_split(X,y,test_size=0.3,random_state=42
```

Then, we fit our dataset using sklearn linear regression function.

```
regressor = LinearRegression()
regressor.fit(X_train, y_train)
```

After that, we predict the output and measure the performance using the root mean square error metric (RMSE).

```
y_prediction = regressor.predict(X_test)
RMSE = sqrt(mean_squared_error(y_true = y_test, y_pred = y_prediction))
print(RMSE)
```

```
4.955413560049774
```

5.1.3. Multiple Linear Regression in Python

Now, let us do the same but using multiple linear regression.

The code will be the same until we choose our variables.

```
y=cars_df.MPG
X=cars_df.Horsepower
```

After looking at the input, we observe that it contains a categorical variable, so we convert it into dummy variables.

```
X=pd.get_dummies(X,drop_first=True)
```

We then split our dataset as usual.

```
X_train,X_test,y_train,y_test=train_test_split(X,y,test_size=0.3,random_state=42
```

Given that we have more than one input variable, we need to normalize our input.

```
scaler=MinMaxScaler()
X_train_sc=pd.DataFrame(scaler.fit_transform(X_train),columns=X_train.columns)
X_test_sc=pd.DataFrame(scaler.transform(X_test),columns=X_test.columns)
```

We finally fit and predict.

```
regressor = LinearRegression()
regressor.fit(X_train_sc, y_train)
```

```
y_prediction = regressor.predict(X_test_sc)
RMSE = sqrt(mean_squared_error(y_true = y_test, y_pred = y_prediction))
print(RMSE)
```

```
3.216235254988254
```

The error is less when we used a multiple linear regression model.

5.1.4. Linear Regression Coefficients

To perform the linear regression model more concretely, we use the coefficient of determination R^2.

$$R^2 = 1 - \frac{SS_{res}}{SS_{tot}}$$

Where,

$$SS_{res} = \sum_{i=1}^{n} r_i^2$$

$$SS_{tot} = \sum_{i=1}^{n} y_i^2$$

We know that r_i is the difference between the predicted value and the true value, also known as the residual. Therefore, we can say that R^2 is a measure of the reduction in the sum of squared values between the raw label values and the residuals. If $R^2 = 0$, then our model is useless and does not reduce the error. On the other hand, if $r_i = 0$, then $R^2 = 1$ which is our ultimate target.

Another variation of R^2 is R^2_{adj} which is the same except for the SS terms as the variance of the residual and the true labels.

We will now see how we can use SciPy to do the same tasks that we did on simple linear regression and multiple linear regression with the addition of calculating R^2 and R^2_{adj}.

```
X_multi=sm.tools.tools.add_constant(X_train, prepend=True, has_constant='skip')
```

```
# OLS Regression
mod = sm.OLS(y_train, X_multi)
res = mod.fit()
print(res.summary())
```

```
                            OLS Regression Results
==============================================================================
Dep. Variable:                    MPG   R-squared:                       0.626
Model:                            OLS   Adj. R-squared:                  0.625
Method:                 Least Squares   F-statistic:                     455.7
Date:                Thu, 30 May 2019   Prob (F-statistic):           4.55e-60
Time:                        01:39:08   Log-Likelihood:                -823.78
No. Observations:                 274   AIC:                             1652.
Df Residuals:                     272   BIC:                             1659.
Df Model:                           1
Covariance Type:            nonrobust
==============================================================================
                 coef    std err          t      P>|t|      [0.025      0.975]
------------------------------------------------------------------------------
const         41.0848      0.869     47.255      0.000      39.373      42.797
Horsepower    -0.1663      0.008    -21.348      0.000      -0.182      -0.151
==============================================================================
Omnibus:                       13.528   Durbin-Watson:                   2.150
Prob(Omnibus):                  0.001   Jarque-Bera (JB):               14.281
Skew:                           0.500   Prob(JB):                     0.000792
Kurtosis:                       3.499   Cond. No.                         327.
==============================================================================
```

We can see that R^2 and R^2_{adj} are 62.5% and 62.6% for simple linear regression.

```
X_multi=sm.tools.tools.add_constant(X_train, prepend=True, has_constant='skip')
# OLS Regression
mod = sm.OLS(y_train, X_multi)
res = mod.fit()
print(res.summary())
```

```
                            OLS Regression Results
==============================================================================
Dep. Variable:                    MPG   R-squared:                       0.826
Model:                            OLS   Adj. R-squared:                  0.821
Method:                 Least Squares   F-statistic:                     157.8
Date:                Thu, 30 May 2019   Prob (F-statistic):           3.78e-96
Time:                        01:39:09   Log-Likelihood:                -718.66
No. Observations:                 274   AIC:                             1455.
Df Residuals:                     265   BIC:                             1488.
Df Model:                           8
Covariance Type:            nonrobust
================================================================================
                   coef    std err          t      P>|t|      [0.025      0.975]
--------------------------------------------------------------------------------
const          -14.3960      5.861     -2.456      0.015     -25.935      -2.857
Cylinders       -0.3331      0.409     -0.814      0.416      -1.139       0.473
Displacement     0.0204      0.010      2.138      0.033       0.002       0.039
Horsepower      -0.0288      0.016     -1.747      0.082      -0.061       0.004
Weight          -0.0063      0.001     -8.003      0.000      -0.008      -0.005
Acceleration     0.0413      0.117      0.353      0.724      -0.189       0.271
Year             0.7782      0.066     11.766      0.000       0.648       0.908
Origin_Japan     0.0253      0.722      0.035      0.972      -1.397       1.447
Origin_US       -3.3369      0.727     -4.588      0.000      -4.769      -1.905
==============================================================================
Omnibus:                       17.206   Durbin-Watson:                   2.012
Prob(Omnibus):                  0.000   Jarque-Bera (JB):               20.888
Skew:                           0.510   Prob(JB):                     2.91e-05
Kurtosis:                       3.889   Cond. No.                     8.91e+04
==============================================================================
```

We can see that R^2 and R^2_{adj} are 82.6% and 82.1% for multiple linear regression, which is much better than simple linear regression.

Now, let us plot the residual while keeping in mind that the error should have a normal distribution.

```
# add your actual vs. predicted points
plt.scatter(y_test, regressor.predict(X_test))
# add the line of perfect fit
straight_line = np.arange(0, 60)
plt.plot(straight_line, straight_line)
plt.title("Fitted Values")
plt.show()
```

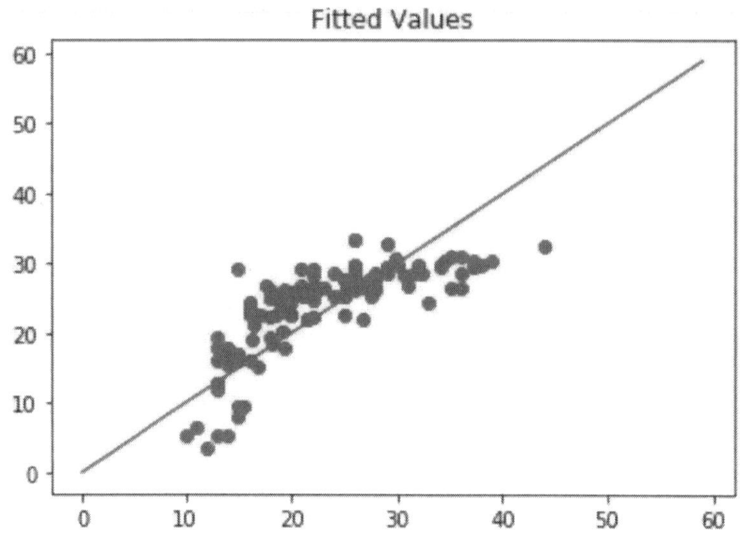

Let us now plot the residual for the training data.

```
pred_val1 = res.fittedvalues.copy()
residual_train = y_train - pred_val1
fig, ax = plt.subplots(figsize=(10,8))
_, (__, ___, r) = sp.stats.probplot(residual_train, plot=ax, fit=True)
r**2
plt.show()
```

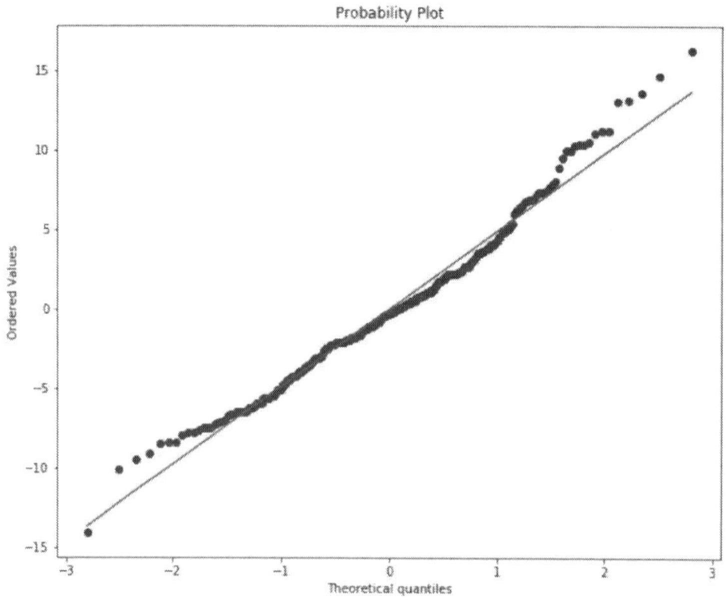

As we can see, it nearly fits on the red line corresponding to R^2

We can do the same on the test set.

```
X_test['const']=1
residual_test = res.predict(X_test)
fig, ax = plt.subplots(figsize=(10,8))
_, (__, ___, r) = sp.stats.probplot(residual_test, plot=ax, fit=True)
plt.show()
```

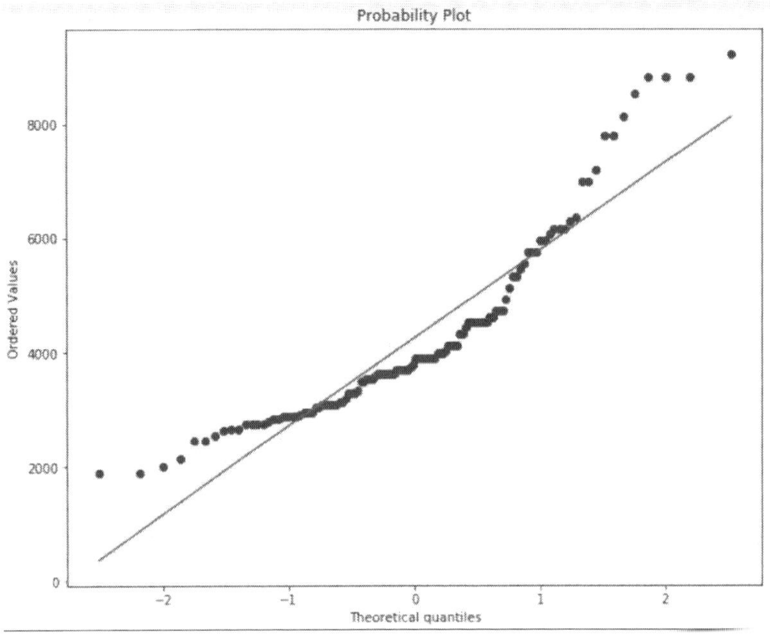

It didn't do well on the test set as linear regression has many limitations; one of them is that it cannot model non-linear functions.

Therefore, we will explore more complex algorithms that can handle nonlinear functions.

5.2. Logistic Regression

5.2.1. Logistic Regression Intuition

In linear regression, we saw how we can perform regression analysis using the linear regression equation with the gradient descent to update the weights. Now, we will do something very similar but for classification purposes.

The main difference between regression and classification is that in regression we want to estimate a value in continuous space with no restriction, while in classification our goal is also to estimate a value but within a discrete space with limited value. For example, in house price estimation, the house price can be any value, while in dog breed classification, for example, we want to predict to which breed the current image of a dog belongs. We know beforehand that it must be one of 100 possible values if we assume that there are only 100 dog breeds in the world.

To simplify the classification problem and focus only on the algorithm of logistic regression, we will assume, for now, that we have only two classes. We can treat our problem as a binary classification problem. For example, we would predict if a student will be accepted into a specific university or not.

Therefore, we can formalize our output as a probability from [0,1] and if it is above a certain threshold, 0.5 for example, then this student will get accepted, and if it is less than the threshold, then he will get rejected.

However, the equation that we used for linear regression is not limited by this constraint. So, we use a `logistic` function to transform our output to be in the range [0,1] so we can treat it as a probability. The most famous and currently used logistic function is the `sigmoid` which has the following equation.

$$y(z) = \frac{1}{1 + e^{-z}}$$

Where z is the linear equation that we used in linear regression

$$z = \sum_{i=0}^{n} w_i x_i = w^T x$$

To understand how the sigmoid function squashes our input into [0,1], we can plot it using Python, and we would get the following curve.

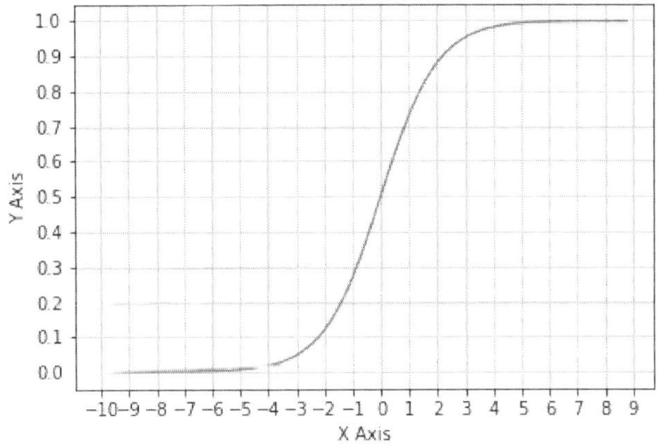

We can have this plot by writing the sigmoid as a Python function and then call this function with different values of input.

As you can see, the output, the Y-axis, can only take values in the range [0,1], and it reaches zero at negative infinity and reaches one and positive infinity. We can also see that the output is 0.5 when the input is zero. We can alter that by scaling the sigmoid function or changing the bias.

Moving to the loss function, we cannot use the same mean square error loss that we used for linear regression, as the numbers are all between 0 and 1 so the results will be significant. Thus, we need a loss function that is sensitive to small changes. To do so, we use the `negative log-likelihood` loss function which is defined as follows:

$$J(w) = -\sum_{i} (y^{i} \, log \, log \left(h_w(x^{i})\right) + (1 - y^{i}) \, log \, log \left(1 - h_w(x^{i})\right))$$

There is no closed-form solution to calculate the weights as in linear regression; therefore, the only possible way to estimate the weights is to use an iterative solution such as Gradient Descent.

The mathematics behind the final output is complex, so the only thing that you need to know is that gradient descent and other iterative optimization algorithms are the only way to update the weights in logistics regression and hence classify the output correctly.

5.2.2. Logistic Regression Regularization

One of the most frequent problems that many people face when they try to implement and run logistic regression is overfitting, so we use a technique called regularization to address this problem.

Regularization is a fancy word for the penalty, as we penalize the model if it is becoming more complex. We can understand this better by looking at how we update the weights when we introduce the regularization term.

$$w = w - \alpha \frac{\partial J(w)}{\partial x} - \lambda \alpha w$$

We say that α is the learning rate and λ is the penalization term. So, we see that the regularization term is added as a second term in the loss function. The purpose of this regularization term is to push the parameters towards smaller numbers, and thus, the model does not become more complex, and hence it doesn't overfit.

There are many different methods to implement the regularization term; however, the two most common ways are the Lasso method, also called "L1", and the Ridge method, which is also called "L2".

The main difference between the two methods is that the Lasso method tries to push all the parameters towards zero, while the Ridge method tries to push all the parameters towards very small numbers but not equal to zero. Both methods are used, and you have to experiment with both of them to know which one works best for each specific case.

5.2.3. Logistic Regression Pros and Cons

We can see that the main advantages of using logistic regression are that it is very easy to understand and interpret, very fast to train and predict and works well with sparse data if regularization is used.

The main disadvantages of using logistic regression are that it requires the data to be preprocessed and scaled, and it doesn't work very well compared to more complex algorithms if the data is complex by nature.

5.2.4. Logistic Regression in Python

Let us now see how we can implement logistic regression using Python.

The first step is, of course, importing the needed libraries.

```
from sklearn.linear_model import LogisticRegression
from sklearn.model_selection import train_test_split
from sklearn.preprocessing import StandardScaler,MinMaxScaler
from sklearn import metrics
from sklearn.metrics import accuracy_score
import pandas as pd
import numpy as np
import os
import matplotlib.pyplot as plt
import seaborn as sns
```

Then, we fix the path as the one containing our dataset.

```
os.chdir('D:')
os.getcwd()
```

In this exercise, we will be using German credit dataset which contains different features that are used to decide whether a person should be accepted for a loan, or not, based on his credit score.

```
credit=pd.read_csv('german_credit.csv')
```

After loading the dataset, we print some information about the dataset.

```
credit.info()
```

```
<class 'pandas.core.frame.DataFrame'>
RangeIndex: 1000 entries, 0 to 999
Data columns (total 22 columns):
Customer_ID                 1000 non-null int64
checking_account_status     1000 non-null object
loan_duration_mo            1000 non-null int64
credit_history              1000 non-null object
purpose                     1000 non-null object
loan_amount                 1000 non-null int64
savings_account_balance     1000 non-null object
time_employed_yrs           1000 non-null object
payment_pcnt_income         1000 non-null int64
gender_status               1000 non-null object
other_signators             1000 non-null object
time_in_residence           1000 non-null int64
property                    1000 non-null object
age_yrs                     1000 non-null int64
other_credit_outstanding    1000 non-null object
home_ownership              1000 non-null object
number_loans                1000 non-null int64
job_category                1000 non-null object
dependents                  1000 non-null int64
telephone                   1000 non-null object
foreign_worker              1000 non-null object
bad_credit                  1000 non-null int64
dtypes: int64(9), object(13)
memory usage: 172.0+ KB
```

As we see in the following figure, there are twenty-two columns, twenty-one of them are features and the last one is our target. Also, only nine of them are numerical, so we need to convert the other thirteen from categorical to numerical using dummy variables.

```
Y=credit['bad_credit']
```

We choose the column with the name bad credit to be our output.

```
Y.value_counts()
```

```
0    700
1    300
Name: bad_credit, dtype: int64
```

As we can see, the data is unbalanced as 70% of the output is good and 30% is bad. Right now, we cannot really do anything about it, but in the deep learning chapter of this eBook, we will see how we can do data augmentation to solve this crucial problem.

```
credit=pd.get_dummies(credit)
```

We convert our categorical features into numerical features using the get dummies function in Pandas.

```
credit.columns
```

```
Index(['Customer_ID', 'loan_duration_mo', 'loan_amount', 'payment_pcnt_income',
       'time_in_residence', 'age_yrs', 'number_loans', 'dependents',
       'bad_credit', 'checking_account_status_0 - 200 DM',
       'checking_account_status_< 0 DM',
       'checking_account_status_> 200 DM or salary assignment',
```

We now have dozens of features' columns, so we print their names.

```
X=credit[['loan_duration_mo', 'loan_amount', 'payment_pcnt_income',
       'time_in_residence', 'age_yrs', 'number_loans', 'dependents',
       'checking_account_status_0 - 200 DM',
       'checking_account_status_< 0 DM',
       'checking_account_status_> 200 DM or salary assignment',
```

We copy and paste the names of these columns, so we can assign them to our input matrix.

```
X_train,X_test,Y_train,Y_test=train_test_split(X,Y,test_size=0.3,random_state=42
```

Then, we split our dataset into training and testing dataset.

```
scaler=MinMaxScaler()
X_train=pd.DataFrame(scaler.fit_transform(X_train),columns=X_train.columns)
X_test=pd.DataFrame(scaler.transform(X_test),columns=X_test.columns)
```

After that, we perform normalization and scaling on all features.

```
logreg=LogisticRegression()
mod1=logreg.fit(X_train,Y_train)
```

Our data can now be trained using a logistic regression model.

```
pred1=logreg.predict(X_test)
accuracy_score(y_true=Y_test, y_pred=pred1)
```

```
0.77
```

We test our model and get 77% which is not that good. However, you can do the same steps with the normalization and see how this score drops dramatically.

```
plt.figure(figsize=(15,10))
plt.bar(X_train.columns.tolist(),logreg.coef_[0])
plt.xticks(rotation=90,size=10)
plt.show()
```

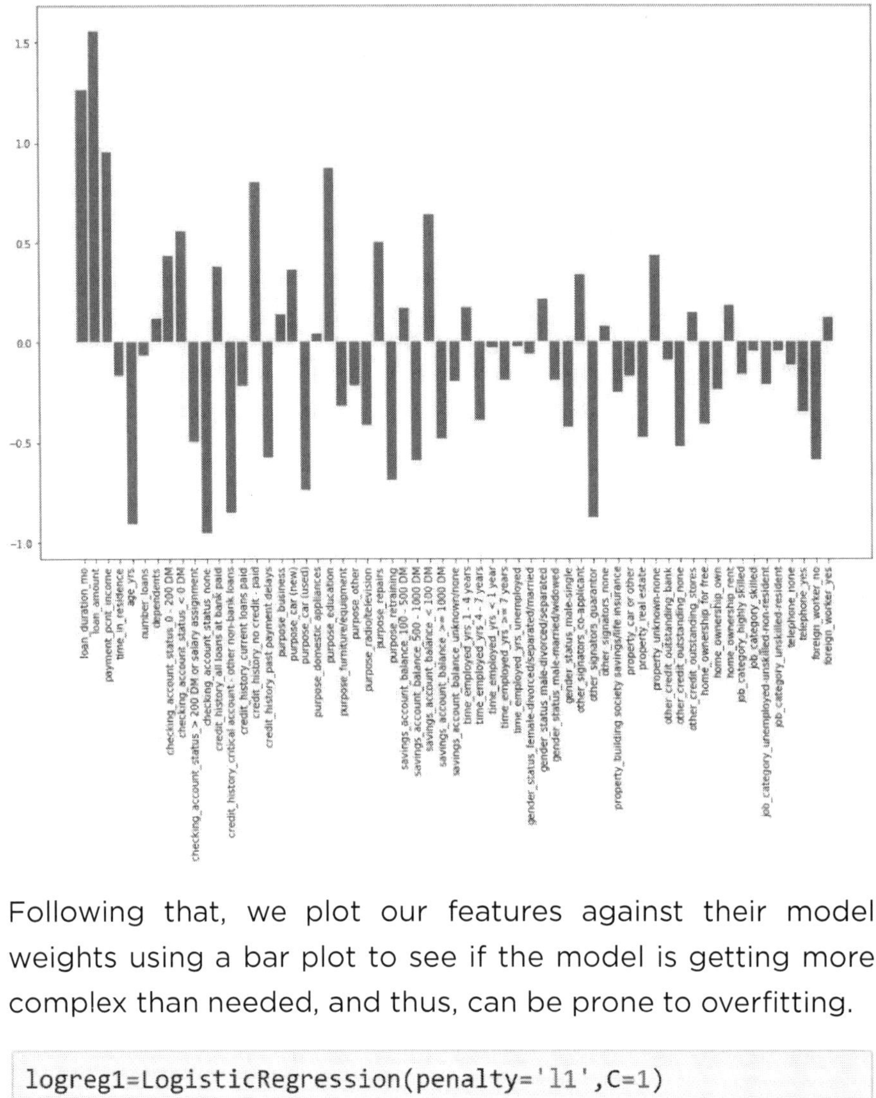

Following that, we plot our features against their model weights using a bar plot to see if the model is getting more complex than needed, and thus, can be prone to overfitting.

```
logreg1=LogisticRegression(penalty='l1',C=1)
mod2=logreg1.fit(X_train,Y_train)
pred2=logreg1.predict(X_test)
accuracy_score(y_true=Y_test, y_pred=pred2)
```

```
0.7566666666666667
```

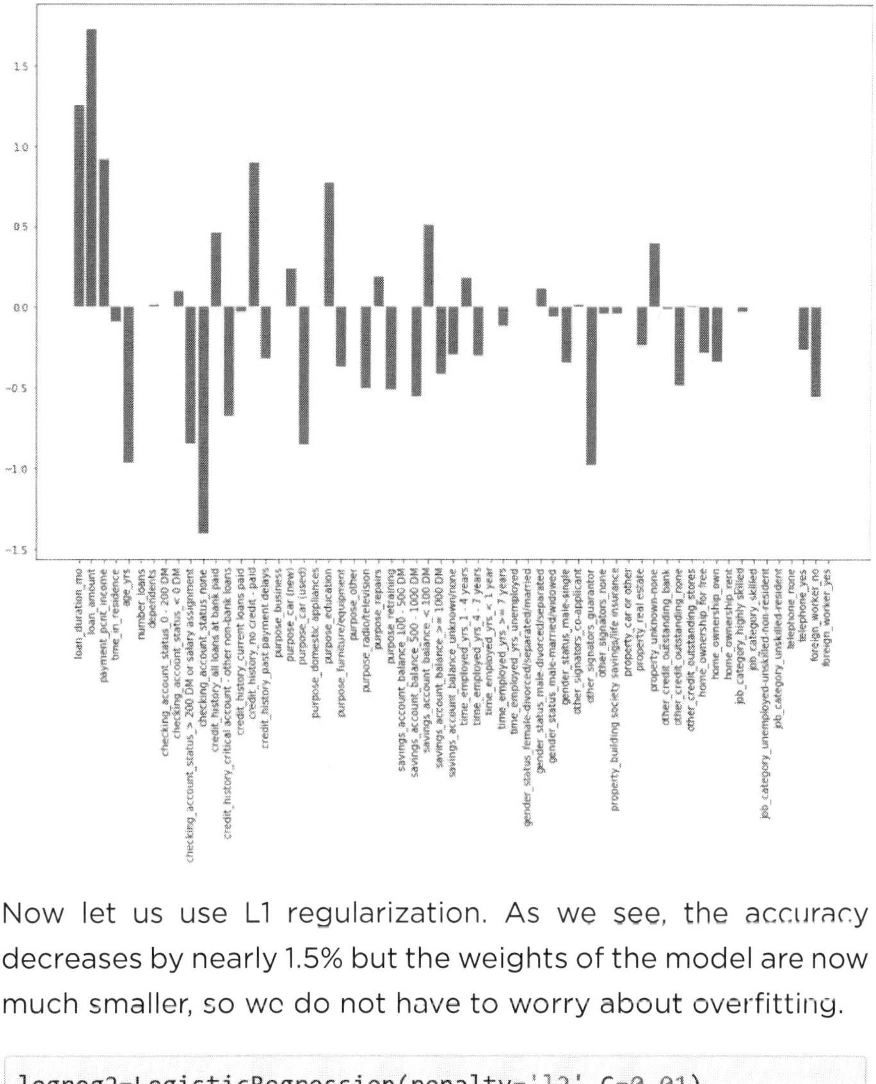

Now let us use L1 regularization. As we see, the accuracy decreases by nearly 1.5% but the weights of the model are now much smaller, so we do not have to worry about overfitting.

```
logreg2=LogisticRegression(penalty='l2',C=0.01)
mod3=logreg2.fit(X_train,Y_train)
pred3=logreg2.predict(X_test)
accuracy_score(y_true=Y_test, y_pred=pred3)
```

```
0.7
```

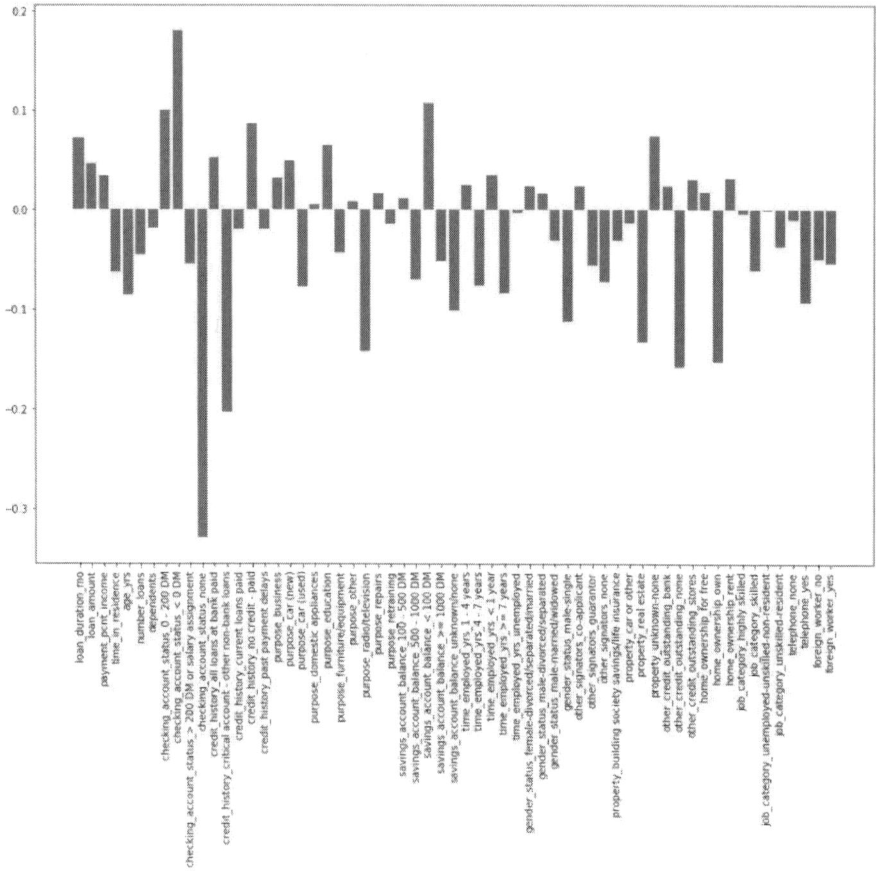

We do the same using L2 regularization, and we can see that the results in this specific case are much worse. Note that this is not the general case, and you must experiment with both techniques to decide which is better in that case.

5.3. Support Vector Machines

5.3.1. SVM Intuition

Support Vector Machines (SVM) are complex and give better results than linear regression in almost all cases. Also, the same algorithm can be used either for classification or regression, which makes it preferable for many people. As we will see, it is very memory efficient and works extremely well even in high dimensional space.

Suppose for example, that we want to separate the following points for a classification purpose.

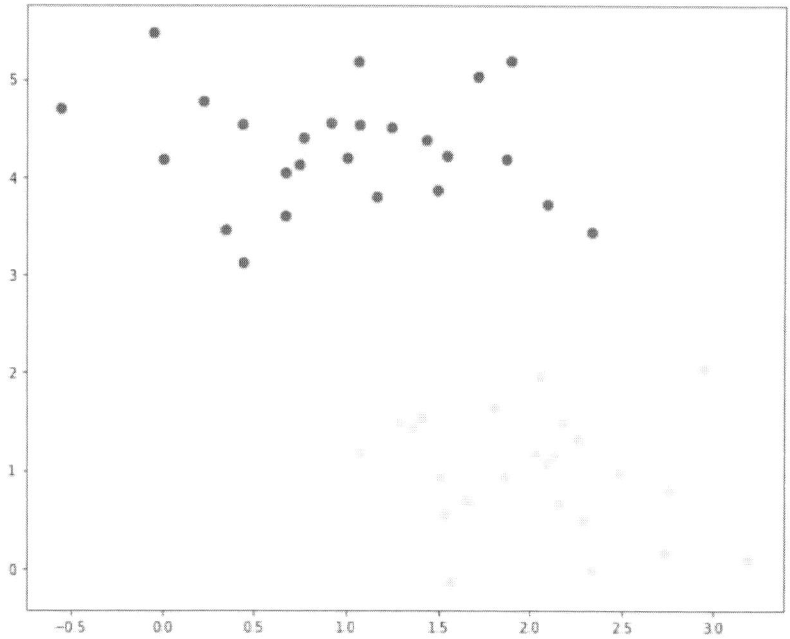

What is the best separator for these points?

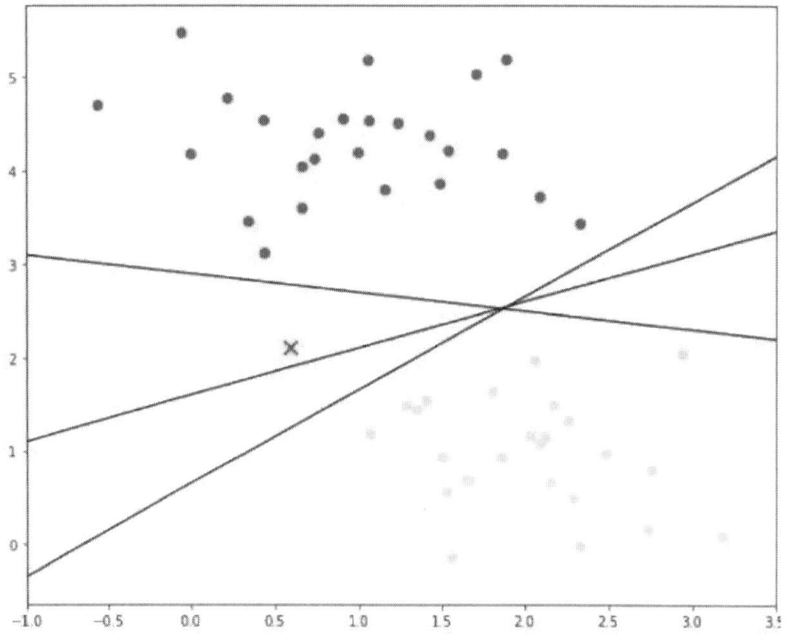

As we can see, the three lines separate the dataset correctly. However, when we test our models, each one of them will classify the test data differently.

So, our target is not only to find a line that separates the dataset correctly, but also to maximize the margin between the different classes. By doing so, there is a higher chance that the test dataset will be classified correctly.

We define the margin to be twice the distance between the hyperplane, which is just a line on our case, and the nearest points to the hyperplane. These points are called the `support vector`

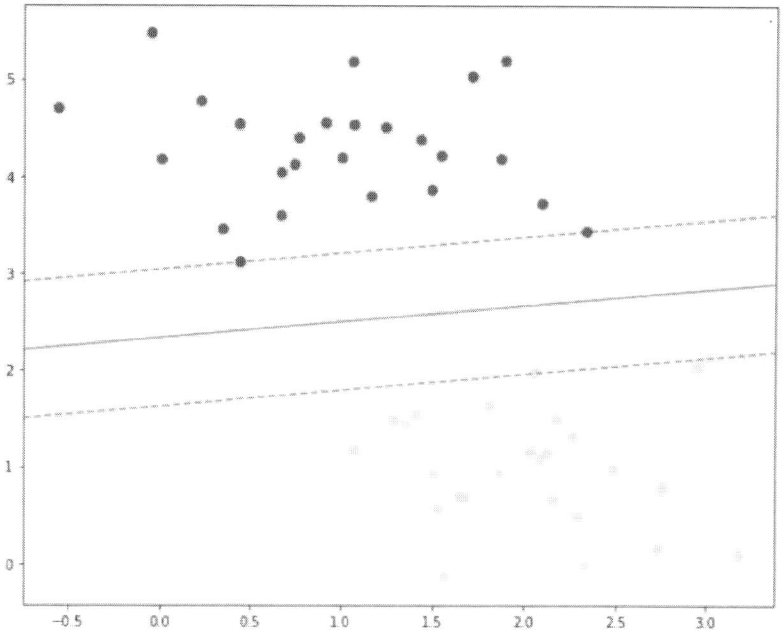

Here, we have the four support vectors as two of them correspond to the red class and two to the yellow class.

We can use the same linear regression model $w^T x$ for the support vector, and by doing so we can write $w^T(x_+ - x_-) = 2$, where x_+ corresponds to the red support vectors and x_- corresponds to the yellow support vectors. Also, we got 2 because of subtracting the two equations $w^T x_+ = 1$ and $w^T x_- = -1$ from each other.

After normalization, we have $\frac{2}{||w||}$ as our margin, which we try to maximize. You can find some people minimizing the reciprocal $\frac{||w||}{2}$ instead to have one minimization problem. Therefore, our cost function now has two terms, one for minimizing the classification error, and one for minimizing the reciprocal of the margin.

We may add also a penalization term C, which allows the examples to be classified wrongly but assign them a penalty proportional to the distance required to move them back on the correct side. Using small C means that we focus more on maximizing the margin than on classifying all outputs correctly while using large C means the opposite. So, `C` hyperparameter affects the trade-off between training accuracy and margin maximization.

Therefore, our objective function (cost function) is now:

$$J(w) = \frac{||w||}{2} + C\sum_{i=0}^{n} w_i^T x_i$$

Suppose now that we want to separate these points.

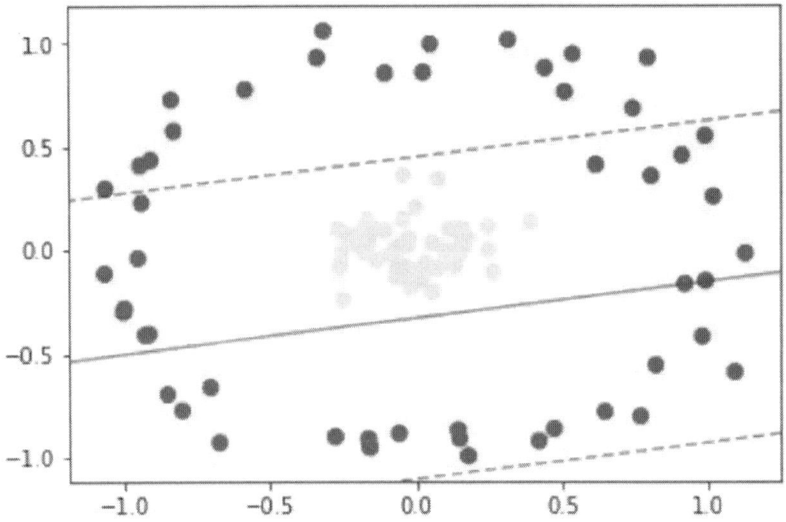

It is clear that we cannot do so using any linear hyperplane.

To solve this problem, SVM uses the `kernel trick`, which is nothing but a set of functions that takes low-dimensional input space and transforms it into a higher dimensional input space where the data can be separated. Some of the most commonly used kernels are Radial Basis Functions, Sigmoid Kernel and Polynomial Kernel. Explaining the math behind each of these kernels is beyond the scope of this book and can be found in many academic statistics references. However, you can experiment with all kernels using sklearn very easily and compare the results to know which is better for this specific dataset.

So, overall, there are three main hyperparameters which are the kernel, the C penalty, and Gamma hyperparameter. We discussed the first two, but we did not discuss the third one. Gamma is a hyperparameter for deciding to what extent do the far away points affect the overall decision of the separation line. So, we say that a large gamma value means that close points have the most influence on the decision, while a small gamma value means that the far points have the most influence on the decision.

5.3.2. SVM Pros and Cons

SVM is considered one of the most powerful traditional machine learning algorithms, thanks to the kernel trick. Also, it was empirically proven that it performs well on different datasets from different fields. Moreover, it works exceptionally well on both high-dimensional data and low-dimensional data.

However, it suffers from not scaling very well as the number of samples increases exponentially. In addition to that, it needs extensive preprocessing before we can leverage its true power. Finally, it requires exhaustive hyperparameter tuning.

5.3.3. SVM in Python

Let's now see how we can use Python to train the SVM classifier.

We first import all the libraries that we will use.

```
import matplotlib.pyplot as plt
import numpy as np
from sklearn.model_selection import train_test_split
from sklearn.svm import SVC # "Support vector classifier"
from sklearn.datasets.samples_generator import make_blobs
from sklearn.metrics import accuracy_score
from sklearn.model_selection import train_test_split
```

We will be using synthetically generated data.

```
X, y = make_blobs(n_samples=1000, centers=2,
                  random_state=0, cluster_std=0.60)
```

Then, we split our dataset.

```
X_train, X_test, y_train, y_test = train_test_split(X, y,
                          random_state=42, test_size=0.3)
```

Finally, we fit the model and test it.

```
model = SVC(kernel='linear', C=1E10)
model.fit(X, y)
```

```
accuracy_score(y_test, model.predict(X_test))
```

```
1.0
```

It classifies the data perfectly.

Let's see one more example of using a cancer dataset and observe how changing `C` hyperparameter changes the accuracy.

```
from sklearn.datasets import load_breast_cancer
cancer= load_breast_cancer()
```

```
X_train, X_test, y_train, y_test = train_test_split(cancer.data,
                                        cancer.target, random_state=0)
svc = SVC()
svc.fit(X_train, y_train)
print("Accuracy on training set: {:.2f}".format(svc.score(X_train, y_train)))
print("Accuracy on test set: {:.2f}".format(svc.score(X_test, y_test)))
```

```
Accuracy on training set: 1.00
Accuracy on test set: 0.63
```

This low accuracy on the test set is a result of not doing normalization before training, so let us fix that.

```
# compute the minimum value per feature on the training set
min_on_training = X_train.min(axis=0)
# compute the range of each feature (max - min) on the training set
range_on_training = (X_train - min_on_training).max(axis=0)
# subtract the min, and divide by range
# afterward, min=0 and max=1 for each feature
X_train_scaled = (X_train - min_on_training) / range_on_training
X_test_scaled = (X_test - min_on_training) / range_on_training
```

Let us try to fit the model again now.

```
svc = SVC()
svc.fit(X_train_scaled, y_train)
print("Accuracy on training set: {:.3f}".format(
svc.score(X_train_scaled, y_train)))
print("Accuracy on test set: {:.3f}".format(svc.score(X_test_scaled, y_test)))
```

```
Accuracy on training set: 0.948
Accuracy on test set: 0.951
```

Using the SVC as it is with its default hyperparameters, which you can find on sklearn official documentation, gives us great results.

```
svc = SVC(C=1000)
svc.fit(X_train_scaled, y_train)
print("Accuracy on training set: {:.3f}".format(
svc.score(X_train_scaled, y_train)))
print("Accuracy on test set: {:.3f}".format(svc.score(X_test_scaled, y_test)))
```

```
Accuracy on training set: 0.988
Accuracy on test set: 0.972
```

Tweaking the `C` hyperparameter gives us even better results.

Let us now see how can we use SVM for regression.

We will be using the same car dataset, so the first few steps are exactly the same.

```
clf = svm.SVR()
clf.fit(X_train_sc, y_train)
```

These are the default values for all the hyperparameters available for SVM.

```
y_prediction = clf.predict(X_test_sc)
RMSE = sqrt(mean_squared_error(y_true = y_test, y_pred = y_prediction))
print(RMSE)
```

```
3.6560625557615127
```

The results are comparable to linear regression.

```
parameters=[{'C':[1,10,100,1000],'kernel':['linear']},
            {'C':[1,10,100,1000],'kernel':['rbf'],'gamma':[0.5,0.1,0.01,0.001,0.0001]},
            {'C':[1,10,100,1000],'kernel':['sigmoid'],'gamma':[0.5,0.1,0.01,0.001,0.0001]}]
grid_search=GridSearchCV(estimator=clf,param_grid=parameters,
                         cv=10,n_jobs=-1)
```

We can use grid search to find the best combination of C, Kernel and gamma—learning rates that will result in the best accuracy score.

```
grid_search=grid_search.fit(X_train_sc,y_train)
```

```
y_prediction_gr=grid_search.predict(X_test_sc)
RMSE = sqrt(mean_squared_error(y_true = y_test, y_pred = y_prediction_gr))
print(RMSE)
```

```
2.627683452694091
```

We got 2.6 which is much better than the best result—3.21—that we got from linear regression.

5.4. Decision Trees and Random Forests

5.4.1. Decision Trees Intuition

We'll now tackle another widely used supervised machine learning algorithm, which is decision trees and its modification called random forests.

As the name infers, the random forests algorithm is based on being random and having forests, which means that we use decision trees to build forests randomly. Therefore, if you understand the decision trees thoroughly, it will be very easy to understand random forests also.

To make any decision, we ask ourselves some questions and based on their answers, we choose what we want to do. For example, suppose that you want to go to the cinema and watch a movie. Your decision to do this or not can be visualized as follows:

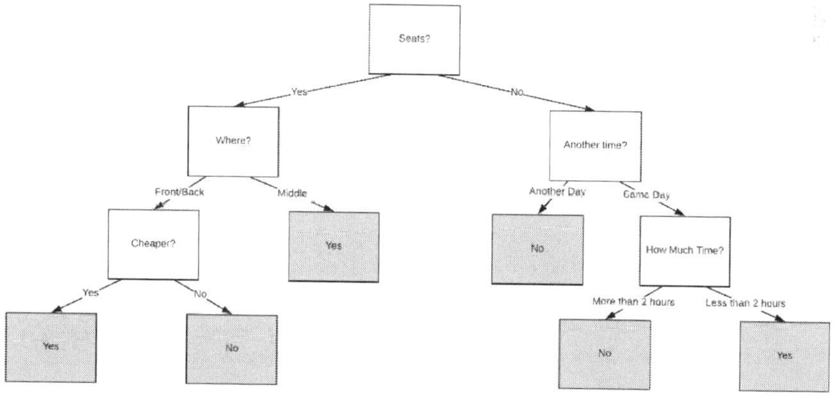

So, if there is a seat, then you will ask about the position of this seat. Let us assume that you prefer to set in the middle, so if a seat in the middle is available, then you will book it. Otherwise, you can settle for another place in case it is cheaper. But, if you did not find a seat, you will ask if there is a seat on the same day. Based on that, you will wait only in case it will take less than two hours.

We can see that this is how we think and rationalize about many of our decisions. In our example, we can treat the booking problem as a classification problem. We can also use decision trees for regression by asking some questions and having paths that lead to different outputs.

We call the questions that we ask the nodes of the tree with each node corresponding to a specific question which we call an attribute A_i. The answers to these questions, or attributes, are called the branches of the tree v_{ij}. Also, we call the last nodes with the final answers the leaf nodes or simply the leaves. These are the classes in case of classification and the predicted values in case of regression.

Therefore, our objective is to find the best path to get the output.

Let us assume that we have a Boolean, only 0 or 1 set of functions of n attributes. Then, the maximum number of possible classes is 2^n and the maximum number of functions or truth tables that we can make out of this is 2^{2^n}. Of course, if we have more attributes then our problem will be even more complex to solve. So, you can see that the problem, although solvable theoretically, requires a lot of computational power that is sometimes not even possible practically.

Thus, our objective is now to find the best path to get the output in an effective and practical manner. So, we should construct a decision tree that is as small as possible yet contains the maximum useful information.

To do so, we use a greedy algorithm called divide and conquer. Using this algorithm has proven to get us a small enough tree but not guaranteed to get us the smallest tree. The algorithm has three main steps which we will mention here and study them in detail, shortly.

First, we start with an empty tree. After that, we divide the problem into many sub-problems to test the most important and useful attributes in our decision. Finally, we use recursion which is applying the second step again iteratively from the root of the tree to the final leaves.

You might be thinking about how we decide the most important attributes. The answer is that we can think of them as being the ones that make the most difference in our decision while training. In other words, they are the ones that reduce the uncertainty about the decision better than the other attributes.

However, you might also have another question in mind; how to measure this uncertainty. This is done by calculating a famous quantity called **Entropy**. This quantity was coined by Shannon, one of the most influential scientists in the field of information theory, in the last century.

To understand what entropy represents, let us take some examples. Suppose that you have a fair coin with equal probability of having heads or tails. We will see right now that the entropy of this coin is 1 bit. The bit is the unit to represent the entropy because it was originally developed to work with bits. The entropy of an unfair coin that either always comes up as heads or tails is zero. So, we can say that entropy represents how much uncertainty we have about our problem. Therefore, it equals zero if the coin comes up always as heads or tails as there no surprise in that. On the other hand, if we have a fair coin, then the entropy will be the maximum because we have an equal probability for each event to happen. The formula that Shannon developed the entropy is the following

$$H(x) = -\sum_{i=1}^{n} P_i log_2 P_i$$

Let us calculate the entropy of an unfair coin that comes up tails 99% of the time.

$$H(99\%\ heads) = -0.99 * log_2 P(0.99) - 0.01 * log_2 P(0.01)$$
$$= 0.08\ bit$$

We can see that the result is nearly zero because there is nearly any surprise in this problem.

The following plot visuals how the entropy changes with the probability. It is maximized when we have equal probabilities.

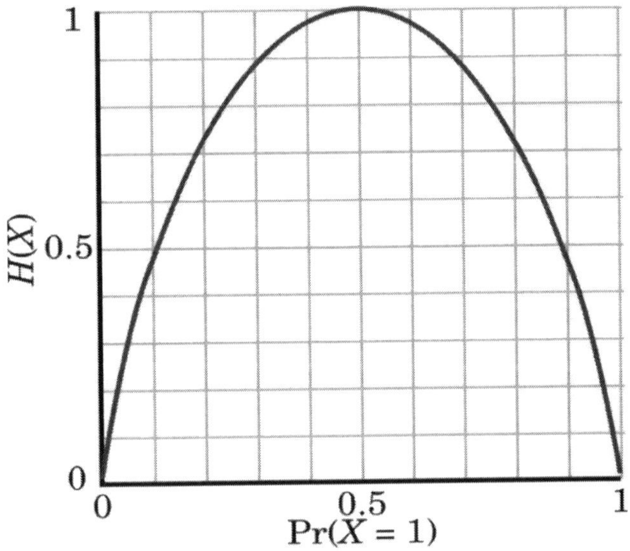

Another quantity that can be used to calculate the uncertainty is the **Gini Index** which is very similar to the entropy. The formula of it is as follows:

$$Gini(x) = 1 - \sum_{i=1}^{n} P_i^2$$

Both of them are used extensively in practice. While using Gini impurity index is computationally better because it does not require computing any logarithmic functions, entropy is more commonly used so we will stick with it for the rest of this section.

Our problem right now is to reduce the entropy due to a specific attribute and do this recursively. This is the definition of **Information Gain:**

$$IG(X) = H(Y) - H(Y|X)$$

It can be translated to "the information gain of event Y given that event X happened is the entropy of Y after subtracting the entropy of Y given that event X happened". So, if X is completely informative about Y, then the information gain is equal to the entropy of Y. While if X is completely uninformative about Y, then the information gain is equal to zero.

So, let us now write the algorithm in detail:

1. Create a root node for the tree
2. If all examples are positive, return leaf node 'positive'
3. Or, if all examples are negative, return leaf node 'negative'
4. Calculate the entropy of current state $H(Y)$
5. For each attribute, calculate the entropy with respect to the attribute 'x' denoted by $H(Y|X)$
6. Select the attribute which has the maximum value of $IG(Y|X)$

7. Remove the attribute that offers the highest IG from the set of attributes
8. Repeat until we run out of all attributes, or the decision tree has all leaf nodes.

5.4.2. Decision Trees Example

The best way to understand this algorithm is to see how it works using a numerical example. So, let us suppose that we want to decide if your friend is going to play golf or not tomorrow. To do so, you observed and documented his decision in the last fourteen days while taking into consideration four attributes: the outlook, the temperature, the humidity and the wind strength. Finally, you come up with the following table.

Day	Outlook	Temperature	Humidity	Wind	Play Golf
D1	Sunny	Hot	High	Weak	No
D2	Sunny	Hot	High	Strong	No
D3	Overcast	Hot	High	Weak	Yes
D4	Rain	Mild	High	Weak	Yes
D5	Rain	Cool	Normal	Weak	Yes
D6	Rain	Cool	Normal	Strong	Yes
D7	Overcast	Cool	Normal	Strong	No
D8	Sunny	Mild	High	Weak	Yes
D9	Sunny	Cool	Normal	Weak	No
D10	Rain	Mild	Normal	Weak	Yes
D11	Sunny	Mild	Normal	Strong	Yes
D12	Overcast	Mild	High	Strong	Yes
D13	Overcast	Hot	Normal	Weak	Yes
D14	Rain	Mild	High	Strong	No

We apply the algorithm by first calculating the entropy.

$$H(x) = -\frac{9}{14}log_2\left(\frac{9}{14}\right) - \frac{5}{14}log_2\left(\frac{5}{14}\right) = 0.94$$

We got $\frac{9}{14}$ because our friend played golf nine days out of the fourteen days, while he did not play only five days out of the fourteen days; hence the second term.

Then, we calculate the attribute that gives us the highest information gain. Let us start with the wind attribute. We have eight days with strong wind and six days with weak wind. There were only two out of the eight days with a weak wind that our friend decided not to play, and six days that he decided to play. On the other hand, he played on three days when the wind was strong and did not play on three days also.

$$H(weak) = -\frac{6}{8}log_2\left(\frac{6}{8}\right) - \frac{2}{8}log_2\left(\frac{2}{8}\right) = 0.81$$

$$H(strong) = -\frac{3}{6}log_2\left(\frac{3}{6}\right) - \frac{3}{6}log_2\left(\frac{3}{6}\right) = 1$$

$$IG(wind) = H(x) - P(weak) * H(weak) - P(strong) * H(strong)$$

$$IG(wind) = 0.94 - \frac{8}{14}(0.81) - \frac{6}{14}(1) = 0.048$$

You can do the same with other attributes as practice, and you will get the following results.

$$IG(outlook) = 0.247$$

$$IG(temperature) = 0.029$$

$$IG(Humidity) = 0.151$$

Based on that, we choose outlook to be the root of our tree as it gives us the maximum information gain. Our tree now looks as follows:

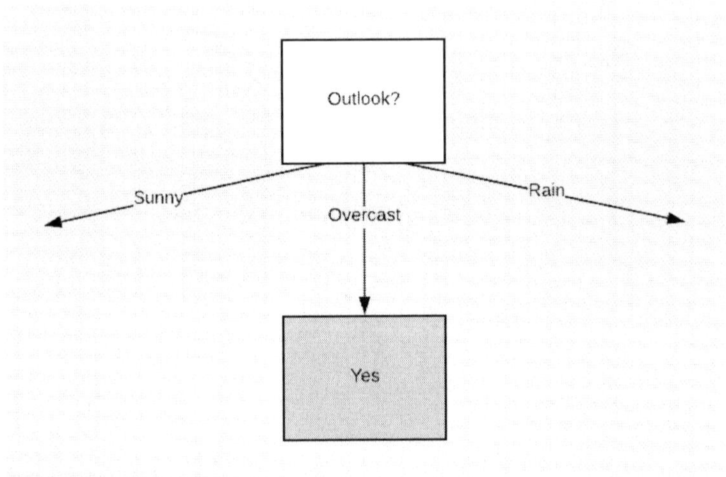

So, if the outlook is overcast, then we know for sure that our friend is going to play golf, and if not, then we repeat the algorithm: with the remaining attributes. Therefore, our table now looks like this:

Temperature	Humidity	Wind	Play Golf
Hot	High	Weak	No
Hot	High	Strong	No
Mild	High	Weak	No
Cool	Normal	Weak	Yes
Mild	Normal	Strong	Yes

If we go through the algorithm steps again, we will get the following entropy:

$$H(x) = -\frac{3}{5}log_2\left(\frac{3}{5}\right) - \frac{2}{5}log_2\left(\frac{2}{5}\right) = 0.96$$

Then, the information gains obtained with the remaining attributes are as follows:

$$H(Humidity) = 0.96$$

$$H(temperature) = 0.57$$

$$H(wind) = 0.019$$

Therefore, our final tree will be like this.

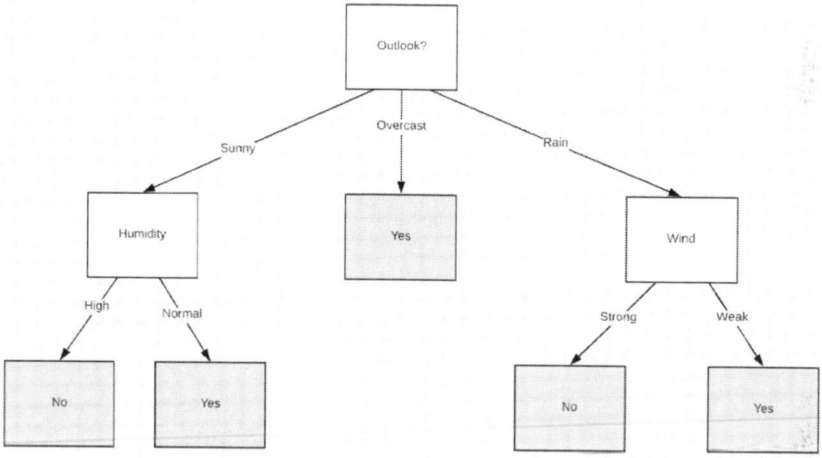

5.4.3. Decision Trees Pros and Cons

Decision trees are extremely easy to interpret and understand from a human perspective. Also, they have the advantage of being easy to visualize. Moreover, it does not require any preprocessing on the dataset like linear regression or many other algorithms. Finally, decision trees can be used for both regression and classification problems.

However, decision trees have a very high probability of overfitting very easily. This is because they can grow exponentially to get the best results on the training set, so the output is crafted for the training set only but fails dramatically on any test set. One workaround is to use a technique called pruning in which we stop the decision tree from growing further once the validation error increases. After performing the pruning operation, we would have different possible trees, so we compute the cost and the complexity of each one to choose the best one.

5.4.4. Decision Trees in Python

In this subsection, we will implement two decision trees, one for classification and one for regression. Let's start with the classification decision tree.

As usual, we start by importing all the libraries we will use in the exercise.

```
import numpy as np
import pandas as pd
from sklearn.model_selection import train_test_split
from sklearn.tree import DecisionTreeClassifier,DecisionTreeRegressor
from sklearn.linear_model import LinearRegression
from sklearn.metrics import accuracy_score
from sklearn import tree
import matplotlib.pyplot as plt
import os
from sklearn.externals.six import StringIO
from IPython.display import Image
from sklearn.tree import export_graphviz
import pydotplus
```

Then we fix the path as usual to the one containing our datasets.

```
os.chdir('D:')
os.getcwd()
```

We import our dataset which is like the one we used before in logistic regression, with the purpose of classification if we are going to give a loan to someone based on his credit score, or not.

```
credit=pd.read_csv('credit.csv',sep=',')
```

```
credit.info()
```

```
<class 'pandas.core.frame.DataFrame'>
RangeIndex: 700 entries, 0 to 699
Data columns (total 9 columns):
age          700 non-null int64
ed           700 non-null object
employ       700 non-null int64
address      700 non-null int64
income       700 non-null int64
debtinc      700 non-null float64
creddebt     700 non-null float64
othdebt      700 non-null float64
default      700 non-null object
dtypes: float64(3), int64(4), object(2)
memory usage: 49.3+ KB
```

We see that the dataset also suffers from the imbalance problem that we will ignore for now and focus on in chapter 7.

```
credit['default'].value_counts()
```

```
No     517
Yes    183
Name: default, dtype: int64
```

Then, we split our dataset.

```
X=credit[['age', 'ed', 'employ', 'address', 'income', 'debtinc', 'creddebt',
      'othdebt']]
Y=credit['default']
X_train,X_test,Y_train,Y_test=train_test_split(X,Y,test_size=0.3,random_state=43
```

After that, we convert all the categorical features into dummy variables.

```
X_train=pd.get_dummies(X_train)
X_test=pd.get_dummies(X_test)
```

We create our model and specify four hyperparameters. The first one is the criterion which we will use as the entropy but feel free to choose Gini and observe the difference. The second one, the random seed, is needed to replicate the results afterward because it will choose the same initial random weights if the same seed is used every time the code is executed. The third one is the maximum depth of the tree, which is a very crucial hyperparameter, that is needed to prevent the tree from being so deep and thus being more prone to overfitting. The final one is the minimum samples in each leaf which pushes the tree to be balanced. Another hyperparameter worth mentioning that we did not specify and left with its default value is the maximum leaf nodes which if defined limits the number of leaf nodes that the tree can have. This can help in reducing the computational complexity but at the expense of decreasing the accuracy.

```
mod1=DecisionTreeClassifier(criterion='entropy',random_state=42,
                            max_depth=4,min_samples_leaf=10)
```

We then train our model.

```
mod1.fit(X_train,Y_train)
```

By testing our model, we see it achieved an accuracy score of 75%.

```
Y_pred=mod1.predict(X_test)
accuracy_score(Y_test,Y_pred)
```

```
0.7523809523809524
```

We can visualize the decision tree using this template code.

```
feature_names=list(X_train.columns)
dot_data = StringIO()
export_graphviz(mod1, out_file=dot_data,
                feature_names=feature_names,
                filled=True, rounded=True,
                special_characters=True)
graph = pydotplus.graph_from_dot_data(dot_data.getvalue())
Image(graph.create_png())
```

As we can see, the visualization is very easy to follow and understand.

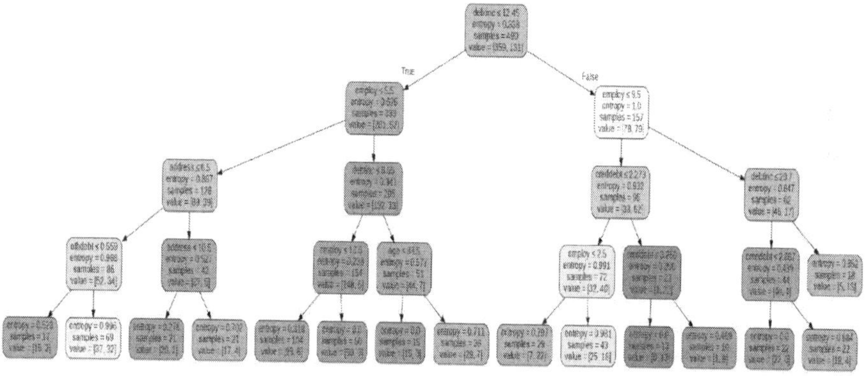

We can also print the importance of each feature.

```
print("Feature importances:\n{}".format(mod1.feature_importances_))
```

```
Feature importances:
[0.02508255 0.32778496 0.06341027 0.          0.43756197 0.10934599
 0.03681426 0.         0.         0.          0.         0.        ]
```

Moreover, we can plot the features against their importance as a bar plot as we did in logistic regression.

```
def plot_feature_importances(model):
    n_features = X_train.shape[1]
    plt.barh(range(n_features), model.feature_importances_, align='center')
    plt.yticks(np.arange(n_features), X_train.columns)
    plt.xlabel("Feature importance")
    plt.ylabel("Feature")
    plt.show()
```

As we can see, there are four features that did not contribute at all to the final output. This can be very insightful when performing feature selection.

```
plot_feature_importances(mod1)
```

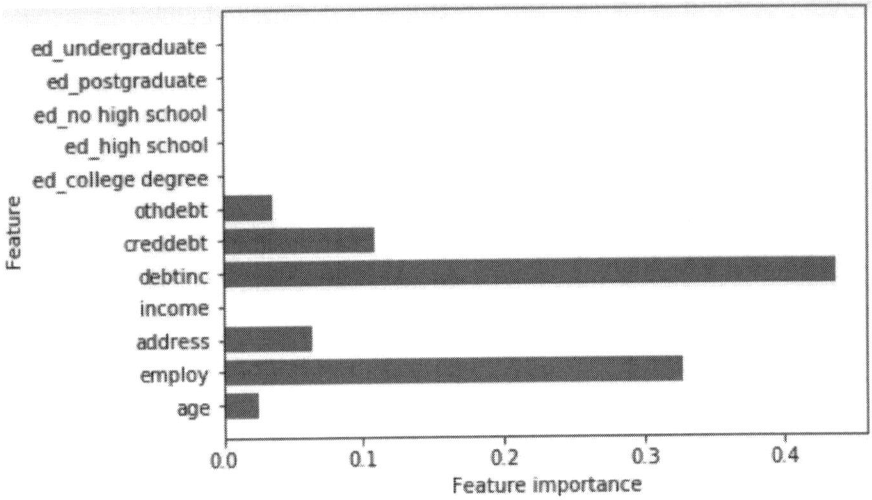

Now, let us move to a regression example. We start by importing the dataset which is two columns, one representing a single feature which is the year that the RAM was sold in, and the other one representing the price of the RAM based on that feature. Then we plot the input vs output.

```
ram_prices = pd.read_csv("ram_price.csv")
plt.figure(figsize=(15,10))
plt.semilogy(ram_prices.date, ram_prices.price)
plt.xlabel("Year")
plt.ylabel("Price in $/Mbyte")
plt.show()
```

As we see, the data can be modeled using a simple line nearly perfect.

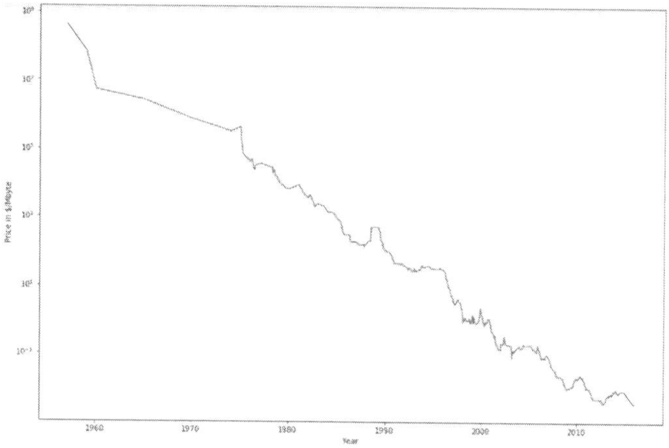

We then split our dataset while performing a logarithmic transformation on the output to narrow down the range of the prices to be more interpretable.

```
# use historical data to forecast prices after the year 2000
data_train = ram_prices[ram_prices.date < 2000]
from sklearn.ensemble import RandomForestClassifier,RandomForestRegressor

data_test = ram_prices[ram_prices.date >= 2000]
# predict prices based on date
X_train = data_train.date[:, np.newaxis]
# we use a log-transform to get a simpler relationship of data to target
y_train = np.log(data_train.price)
```

Now, let us create our decision tree regressor, while also creating a linear regression model, so we can compare their performance on this linearly separable dataset.

```
tree = DecisionTreeRegressor().fit(X_train, y_train)
linear_reg = LinearRegression().fit(X_train, y_train)
```

We then test our two models and retransform them using an exponential, which is the inverse of the logarithm.

```
X_all = ram_prices.date[:, np.newaxis]
pred_tree = tree.predict(X_all)
pred_lr = linear_reg.predict(X_all)
```

```
price_tree = np.exp(pred_tree)
price_lr = np.exp(pred_lr)
```

Finally, we plot our training data, our test data, our linear prediction and our tree prediction using the same graph.

```
plt.figure(figsize=(15,10))
plt.semilogy(data_train.date, data_train.price, label="Training data")
plt.semilogy(data_test.date, data_test.price, label="Test data")
plt.semilogy(ram_prices.date, price_tree, label="Tree prediction")
plt.semilogy(ram_prices.date, price_lr, label="Linear prediction")
plt.legend()
plt.show()
```

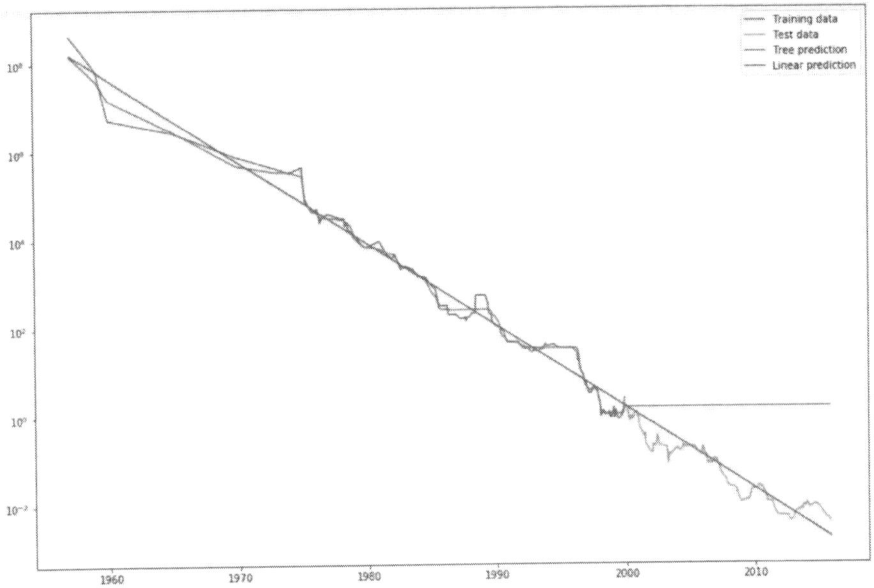

The linear model approximates the data with a line, as we knew it would. This line provides quite a good forecast for the test data (the years after 2000) while glossing over some of the finer variations in both the training and the test data. The tree model, on the other hand, makes perfect predictions on the training data; we did not restrict the complexity of the tree, so it learned the whole dataset by heart. However, once we leave the data range for which the model has data, the model keeps predicting the last known point. The tree has no ability to generate "new" responses, outside of what was seen in the training data. This shortcoming applies to all models based on trees.

5.4.5. Random Forests Intuition

Given that we now have a solid understanding of decision trees, understanding random forests is quite easy. Random forests are one of the ensemble methods which operate by constructing many different decision trees while training. They were proposed to tackle the problem of overfitting that decision trees suffer from. Therefore, we can think of the random forest as a majority voting algorithm where it creates different decision trees with a different set of features in each tree, and then it takes the average of their output.

Creating different decision trees with a different set of features in each tree is referred to as **Bagging,** which is a category of ensemble methods. Another source of randomness in the random forest is feature selection at each node, as now we have different features in each tree, so the splitting based on the information gain calculation will differ in each tree.

There are many different hyperparameters for random forests which are the following

- The Number of estimators: Specify the number of decision trees.
- The Maximum number of features: Specify the maximum number of features when splitting a node.
- Maximum Depth: Maximum depth in each decision tree.
- Minimum Samples per split: Minimum number of examples that each node should have.

5.4.6. Random Forests Pros and Cons

Similar to decision trees, random forests do not require any preprocessing and can be used for both classification and regression. Moreover, they are more immune to overfitting than the decision trees.

However, random forests suffer from being slower while training than decision trees. Also, random forests have many hyperparameters, and grid search or random search is a must. Finally, because random trees are random, we cannot really be absolutely confident about their results as the results may change from time to time.

5.4.7. Random Forests in Python

We can use random forests for both regression and classification, so let us start with classification.

We will do the usual few first steps of importing the libraries, fixing the path, and importing the dataset.

```
import os
import pandas as pd
from sklearn.ensemble import RandomForestClassifier,RandomForestRegressor
from sklearn.model_selection import train_test_split
import matplotlib.pyplot as plt
from sklearn.metrics import accuracy_score,mean_squared_error
from math import sqrt
from sklearn import tree
```

```
os.chdir("D:")
os.getcwd()
```

```
credit=pd.read_csv('credit.csv',sep=',')
```

Then, we will split the credit dataset, which we also used in decision trees.

```
X=credit[['age', 'ed', 'employ', 'address', 'income', 'debtinc', 'creddebt',
       'othdebt']]
Y=credit['default']
X_train,X_test,Y_train,Y_test=train_test_split(X,Y,test_size=0.3,random_state=43)
```

After that, we convert the categorical features to numerical features using pandas get dummies function.

```
X_train=pd.get_dummies(X_train)
X_test=pd.get_dummies(X_test)
```

Following that, we create our random forest classifier with 500 decision trees and a maximum depth of 4. The number of jobs is specifying how many CPU cores that we want to train on. So, by choosing -1, then we use the maximum number of CPU cores available.

```
rf = RandomForestClassifier(n_estimators=500,max_depth=4,random_state=42,
                            n_jobs=-1)
```

We then train our model and test it.

```
rf.fit(X_train, Y_train)
```

```
RandomForestClassifier(bootstrap=True, class_weight=None, criterion='gini',
            max_depth=4, max_features='auto', max_leaf_nodes=None,
            min_impurity_decrease=0.0, min_impurity_split=None,
            min_samples_leaf=1, min_samples_split=2,
            min_weight_fraction_leaf=0.0, n_estimators=500, n_jobs=-1,
            oob_score=False, random_state=42, verbose=0, warm_start=False)
```

```
y_pred_test = rf.predict(X_test)
y_pred_train = rf.predict(X_train)
print(accuracy_score(Y_train,y_pred_train))
print(accuracy_score(Y_test,y_pred_test))
```

```
0.8571428571428571
0.7714285714285715
```

As we see, it got us better results on the same dataset than decision trees.

Now, we can visualize the importance of each feature in making our decisions.

```
importances_rf = pd.Series(rf.feature_importances_,
index = X_train.columns)
sorted_importances_rf = importances_rf.sort_values()
sorted_importances_rf.plot(kind='barh')
plt.show()
```

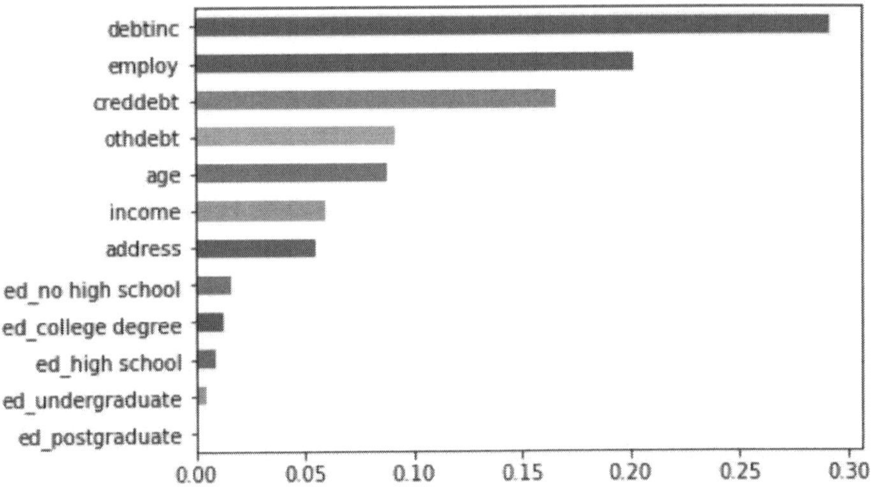

Let us now see how we can utilize random forests for a regression task.

Again, we start by importing the dataset and splitting it.

```
cars_df=pd.read_excel('cars.xls')
```

```
y=cars_df.MPG
X=cars_df[['Cylinders', 'Displacement', 'Horsepower', 'Weight',
       'Acceleration', 'Year', 'Origin']]
X=pd.get_dummies(X,drop_first=True)
X_train,X_test,y_train,y_test=train_test_split(X,y,test_size=0.3,random_state=42
```

Then, we create our random forest regression, train it, and test it.

```
rf = RandomForestRegressor(n_estimators=100,max_depth=4,random_state=42,
                           n_jobs=-1)
rf.fit(X_train, y_train)
```

```
RandomForestRegressor(bootstrap=True, criterion='mse', max_depth=4,
           max_features='auto', max_leaf_nodes=None,
           min_impurity_decrease=0.0, min_impurity_split=None,
           min_samples_leaf=1, min_samples_split=2,
           min_weight_fraction_leaf=0.0, n_estimators=100, n_jobs=-1,
           oob_score=False, random_state=42, verbose=0, warm_start=False)
```

```
y_pred=rf.predict(X_test)
RMSE = sqrt(mean_squared_error(y_true = y_test, y_pred = y_pred))
print(RMSE)
```

```
2.7928446988819404
```

Finally, we can also visualize feature importance.

```
importances_rf = pd.Series(rf.feature_importances_,
index = X_train.columns)
sorted_importances_rf = importances_rf.sort_values()
sorted_importances_rf.plot(kind='barh')
plt.show()
```

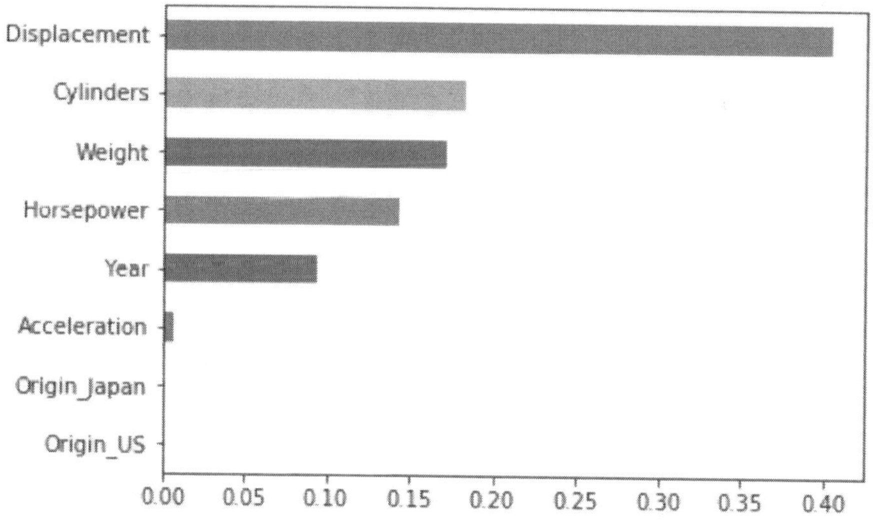

5.5. K-Nearest Neighbor

5.5.1. K-Nearest Neighbor Intuition

So far, we have discussed different machine learning algorithms that are based on the same method of calculating the error and training the classifier or regressor to minimize this error to get better results. Moving to K-Nearest Neighbor, or KNN for short, we will see a different method for training, which is no training at all.

KNN is a data-driven algorithm rather than a model-driven algorithm like the algorithms we've discussed so far. This means that the output is based on the distribution of the dataset itself, rather than having weights and calculating the error. Therefore, we say that KNN is a **non-parametric** model because there are no weights, and the outputs are obtained without any training.

So, you are now wondering, how does KNN work? Basically, in the case of classification, we classify the current example based on its proximity, or distance, to other examples. By looking at the name of the model, we observe that it has "K" in it. This "K" can be any number as we will see, and depending on this number, we make our decision. So, suppose that K=3, and we want to classify the current example where there are only two possible classes, then we compute the distance from the current example to all examples and get the nearest three examples. After that, we look at the class of these three examples, and we classify our current example into the same class as the dominant class. So, if two examples belong to the first class, and one example belongs to the second class, then our example will belong to the first class. We call this simple algorithm **Majority Voting**.

5.5.2. K-Nearest Neighbor Hyperparameters

So, we have only two things to consider when using KNN: the "K" parameter and the distance function.

For the "K" value, if we set it very low, the model will be more sensitive to noise. Also, it may lead to overfitting and non-smooth decision boundaries, as we will see. On the other hand, if we set it very large, then we might include examples from other classes which will also yield incorrect results. Thus, we can choose grid search or cross-validation with different values of "K" starting from 3 to 13 for examples and find the one that gives us the best test accuracy. Another good starting value for "K" is the square root of the number of examples in the dataset. This was found by experimentation, so it is not guaranteed to work every time.

Regarding the distance function, there is a general formula for numerical data to find the distance from a query point x_q to an example point x_j

$$L^p(x_i, x_j) = (\sum_i |x_{j,i} - x_q|^p)^{\frac{1}{p}}$$

If we set p=2, then we have our familiar Euclidean distance. We use it when the features of the data measure similar properties.

If we set p=1, then we have the Manhattan distance. We use this mainly when the features are not similar.

If we have categorical features, then we use another distance called the hamming distance which calculates the distance based on the similarity of the words.

Further Readings

If you want to know more about the different distance measures, you can take a look here

https://towardsdatascience.com/importance-of-distance-metrics-in-machine-learning-modelling-e51395ffe60d

5.5.3. Dimensionality Problem

So far in all the algorithms that we discussed before KNN, we did not really care about the number of features, because they were all parametric models which have a specific number of weights which are not extremely big in most cases. But right now, we are dealing with an algorithm which depends directly on the number of features, or the dimensions in the dataset. Thus, we need to restrict our dataset from containing too many features or the algorithm itself will perform very badly. We can do so manually to get insights about the most influential features as we did before in decision trees and random forests and work only on these features. Also, we can do this automatically using one of the unsupervised learning algorithms that are used for dimensionality reduction, such as PCA or GMM, which we will discuss in the next chapter.

5.5.4. Feature Normalization

We have been performing feature normalization in almost all the algorithms that we've tackled. We also emphasized the importance of feature normalization in chapter 3. However, feature normalization in KNN is a must, because as we said, it is a data-driven model, so if the features are not on the same scale, then the model will fail. There are different methods to perform feature normalization but let us revisit the two most used ones in practice, which are the min-max normalization and the z-score normalization, also called the standard-score normalization.

If you remember, we performed min-max normalization using the following formula:

$$X = \frac{X - X_{\min}}{X_{\max} - X_{\min}}$$

For the z-score normalization, we used the following formula:

$$X = \frac{X - \mu}{\sigma}$$

5.5.5. K-Nearest Neighbor Pros and Cons

KNN is very fast and intuitive to understand, especially when we are working with a small number of features. Also, it does not require any weights to be calculated, so this can be a huge advantage if the memory is a concern.

However, KNN performs very badly on sparse and high-dimensional datasets. Also, as we said, feature normalization is a must when working with KNN.

5.5.6. K-Nearest Neighbor in Python

Now, let's see how we can use KNN for either regression or classification.

The first step is, as usual, importing the libraries that we will use.

We will use a helper library called mglearn, which can help us with visualizing KNN in more depth.

```
import pandas as pd
import math
import numpy as np
from sklearn.preprocessing import StandardScaler
from sklearn.neighbors import KNeighborsClassifier
from sklearn.model_selection import train_test_split
from sklearn.metrics import accuracy_score
import os
import mglearn
from sklearn.neighbors import KNeighborsRegressor
import matplotlib.pyplot as plt
```

Then, we will use mglearn library to plot some arbitrary data and perform KNN classification with K=1.

```
mglearn.plots.plot_knn_classification(n_neighbors=1)
plt.show()
```

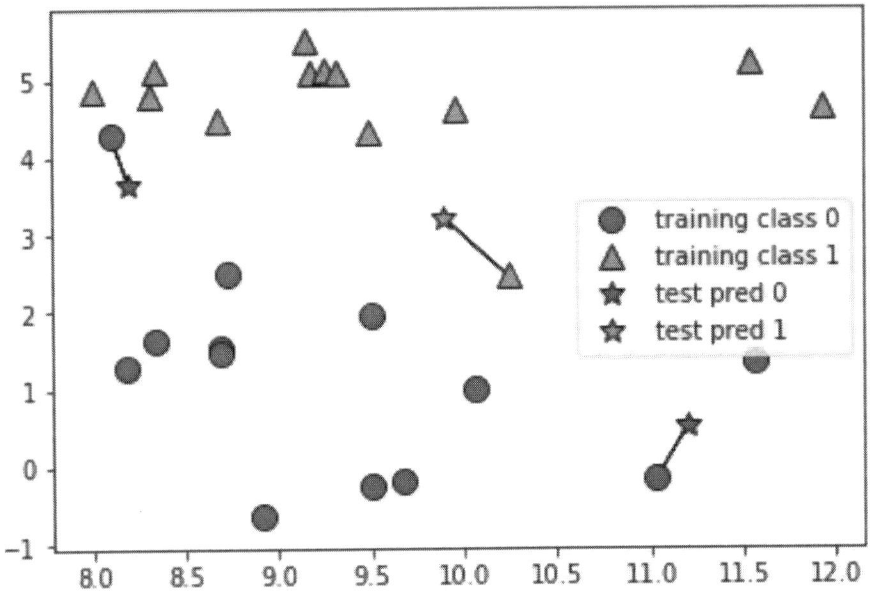

Let's do the same but using K=3.

```
mglearn.plots.plot_knn_classification(n_neighbors=3)
plt.show()
```

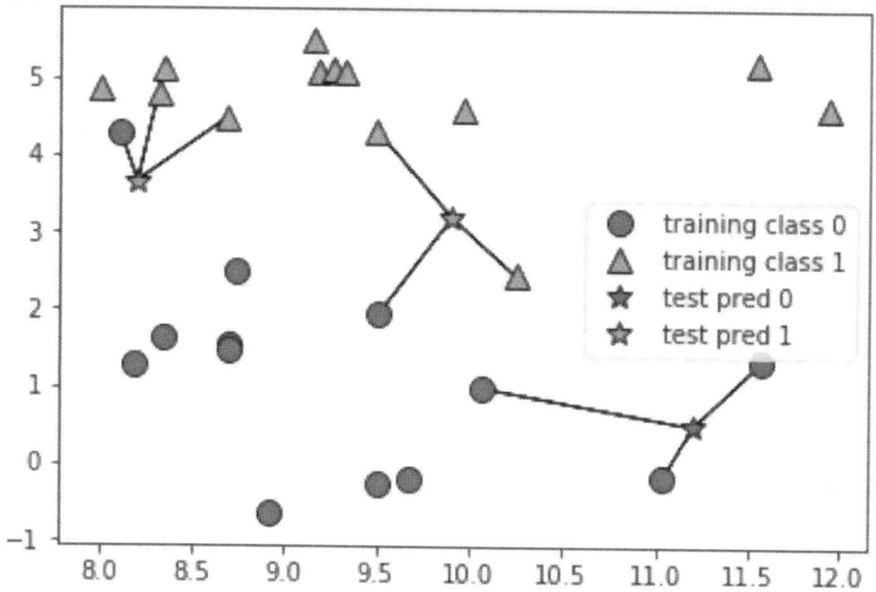

Our decision varies depending on the K value, as in the first case we classified two of the test points as class zero, while in the second case we classified only one of them as class zero.

Now, let us work with a real dataset called diabetes. In this dataset, we want to predict if the person has diabetes or not based on different features.

```
os.chdir('D:')
os.getcwd()
```

```
diabetes=pd.read_csv('diabetes.csv')
```

```
print(diabetes.head())
```

```
   NTS  PGC  DBP  TSFT  INS   BMI    DPF  Age Class
0    6  148   72    35    0  33.6  0.627   50   Yes
1    1   85   66    29    0  26.6  0.351   31    No
2    8  183   64     0    0  23.3  0.672   32   Yes
3    1   89   66    23   94  28.1  0.167   21    No
4    0  137   40    35  168  43.1  2.288   33   Yes
```

There is a huge problem of missing data in our dataset. We talked about this problem before in chapter 3, so let us now see how we can solve it practically.

```
zero_not_accepted=['PGC','DBP','TSFT','INS','BMI']
```

```
for column in zero_not_accepted:
    diabetes[column]=diabetes[column].replace(0,np.NaN)
    mean=int(diabetes[column].mean(skipna=True))
    diabetes[column]=diabetes[column].replace(np.NaN,mean)
```

As we see, we looped through the different features that have this issue and replaced each missing instance with a Nan with is short for Not a Number. Then, we got the mean of this current feature while not taking the missing instances into consideration. Finally, we replaced the missing instances with the mean of the feature.

```
diabetes.head()
```

	NTS	PGC	DBP	TSFT	INS	BMI	DPF	Age	Class
0	6	148.0	72.0	35.0	155.0	33.6	0.627	50	Yes
1	1	85.0	66.0	29.0	155.0	26.6	0.351	31	No
2	8	183.0	64.0	29.0	155.0	23.3	0.672	32	Yes
3	1	89.0	66.0	23.0	94.0	28.1	0.167	21	No
4	0	137.0	40.0	35.0	168.0	43.1	2.288	33	Yes

We then split our dataset into training and testing sets.

```
X=diabetes.iloc[:,0:8]
Y=diabetes.iloc[:,8]
X_train,X_test,Y_train,Y_test=train_test_split(X,Y,test_size=0.3,random_state=42
```

Then, performing feature normalization is a must. We use standard normalization, which is the same as z-score, but feel free to use min-max normalization.

```
sc_X=StandardScaler()
X_train=sc_X.fit_transform(X_train)
X_test=sc_X.transform(X_test)
```

We then use K as the square root of the number of examples in our dataset, as we discussed earlier.

```
math.sqrt(len(Y_test))
```

```
15.198684153570664
```

Then we use the Euclidean distance as the distance function for our model, and we train it.

```
classifier=KNeighborsClassifier(n_neighbors=15,
                                metric='euclidean')
classifier.fit(X_train,Y_train)
```

We then test our model and report the accuracy.

```
Y_pred=classifier.predict(X_test)
print(accuracy_score(Y_test,Y_pred))
```

```
0.7402597402597403
```

Let us now use KNN for regression.

We will use mglearn to visualize the effect of changing K on our predicted value.

```
mglearn.plots.plot_knn_regression(n_neighbors=1)
plt.show()
```

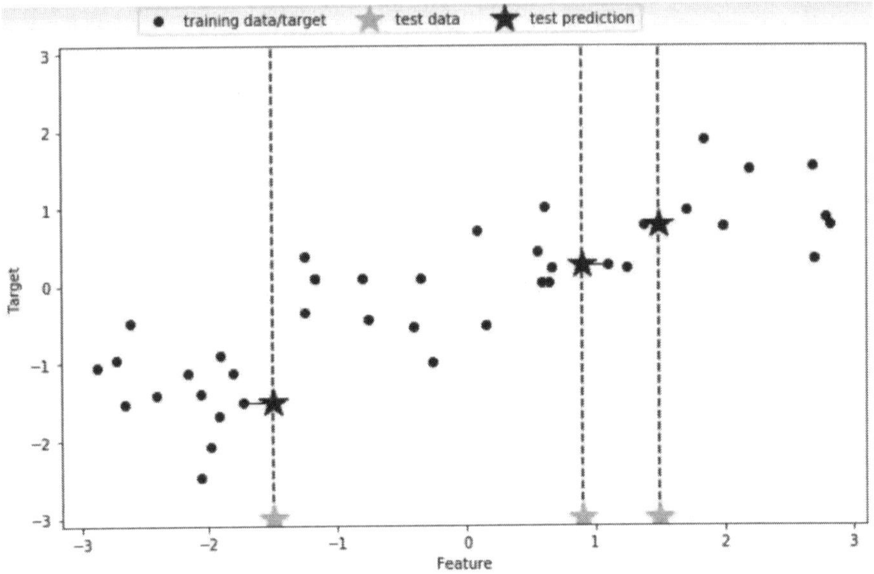


```
mglearn.plots.plot_knn_regression(n_neighbors=3)
plt.show()
```

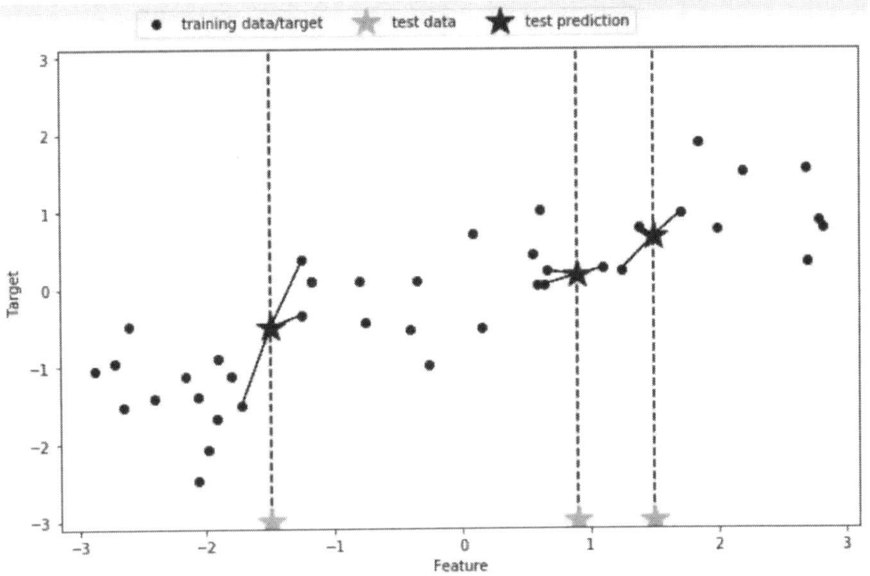

Then, we will use an artificially-made dataset from mglearn to train a KNN regressor.

```
X, y = mglearn.datasets.make_wave(n_samples=40)
# split the wave dataset into a training and a test set
X_train, X_test, y_train, y_test = train_test_split(X, y, random_state=0)
```

```
print("Test set R^2: {:.2f}".format(reg.score(X_test, y_test)))
```

```
Test set R^2: 0.65
```

```
reg = KNeighborsRegressor(n_neighbors=3)
reg.fit(X_train, y_train)
```

We then use the following loop to visualize the effect of changing K on both the train and test scores.

```
fig, axes = plt.subplots(1, 3, figsize=(15, 4))
# create 1,000 data points, evenly spaced between -3 and 3
line = np.linspace(-3, 3, 1000).reshape(-1, 1)
for n_neighbors, ax in zip([1, 3, 9], axes):
    # make predictions using 1, 3, or 9 neighbors
    reg = KNeighborsRegressor(n_neighbors=n_neighbors)
    reg.fit(X_train, y_train)
    ax.plot(line, reg.predict(line))
    ax.plot(X_train, y_train, '^', c=mglearn.cm2(0), markersize=8)
    ax.plot(X_test, y_test, 'v', c=mglearn.cm2(1), markersize=8)
    ax.set_title(
        "{} neighbor(s)\n train score: {:.2f} test score: {:.2f}"
        .format(n_neighbors, reg.score(X_train, y_train),
        reg.score(X_test, y_test)))
    ax.set_xlabel("Feature")
    ax.set_ylabel("Target")
axes[0].legend(["Model predictions", "Training data/target",
    "Test data/target"], loc="best")
plt.show()
```

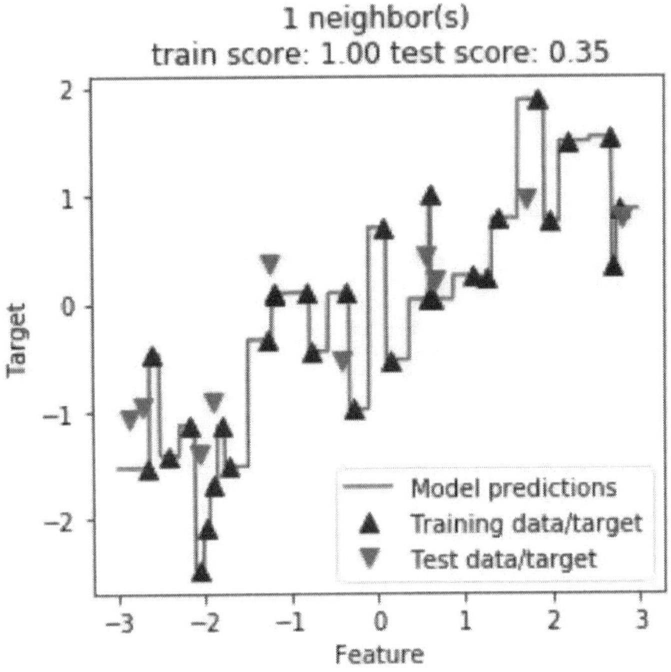
1 neighbor(s)
train score: 1.00 test score: 0.35
Target
Feature
Model predictions
Training data/target
Test data/target
2
1
0
−1
−2
−3
−2
−1
0
1
2
3

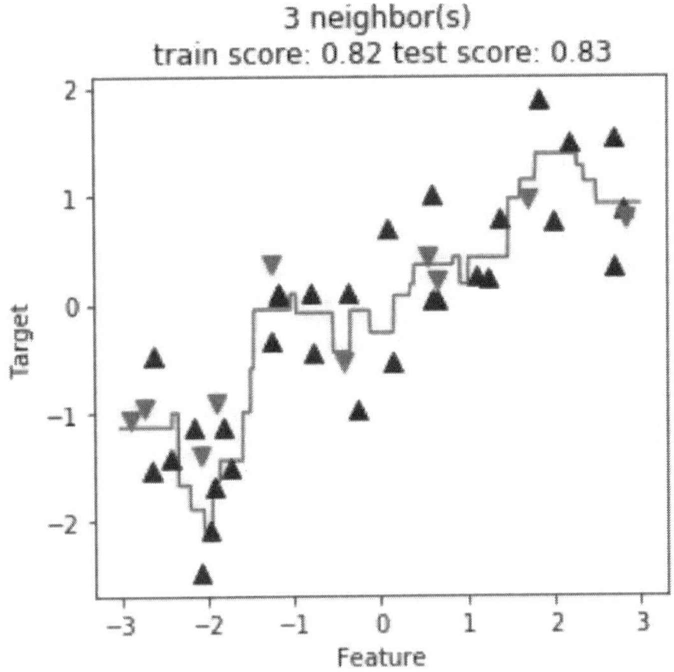
3 neighbor(s)
train score: 0.82 test score: 0.83
Target
Feature
2
1
0
−1
−2
−3
−2
−1
0
1
2
3

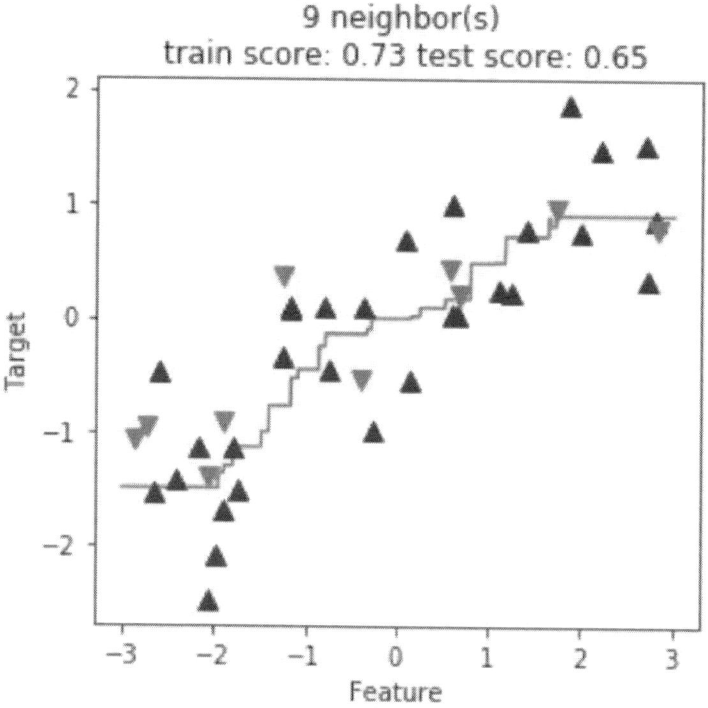

As we see, using K=1 resulted in an overfitted model with a perfect score while training but with a very bad score while testing. Also, using K=9 did not result in a good test score because the decision is based on distant points. On the other hand, using K=3 resulted in a good test score.

5.6. Naïve Bayes

5.6.1. Bayes Theory Revision

If you have reached this part, then I would like to say congratulations! This is the last supervised learning algorithm that we are going to discuss. In fact, we tackled it theoretically in the last section of chapter 4, which is the Naïve Bayes Theorem.

So, before we start seeing the algorithm in action and how it can be used in Python, let us revise the theory quickly with an example.

First, let us write the formula of Bayes Theorem.

$$P(B) = \frac{P(A) * P(A)}{P(B)}$$

If you remember, we said that the conditional probability $P(A)$ is called the `likelihood` which is the probability of observing the new evidence, given our initial hypothesis. We also said that the marginal probability $P(A)$, which is called the `prior`, is the probability of our hypothesis without any additional prior information. Finally, we said that $P(B)$ is the `marginal probability`.

So, using Bayes Rule, we can update our beliefs when new information or evidence is found. You can revisit the cancer example that we tackled in the previous chapter.

5.6.2. Naïve Bayes Intuition

You might be wondering how we can use Bayes Rule in machine learning, and why the algorithm is called "Naïve" Bayes. The answer to these questions can be obtained by looking at a classification problem and following the steps of the algorithm accordingly.

But before that, we should know that it is called "Naïve" mainly because it assumes that the features are independent, which means that the presence of one feature does not affect the others.

Knowing that, let us revisit the golf example that we discussed in the decision tree section.

Day	Outlook	Temperature	Humidity	Wind	Play Golf
D1	Sunny	Hot	High	Weak	No
D2	Sunny	Hot	High	Strong	No
D3	Overcast	Hot	High	Weak	Yes
D4	Rain	Mild	High	Weak	Yes
D5	Rain	Cool	Normal	Weak	Yes
D6	Rain	Cool	Normal	Strong	Yes
D7	Overcast	Cool	Normal	Strong	No
D8	Sunny	Mild	High	Weak	Yes
D9	Sunny	Cool	Normal	Weak	No
D10	Rain	Mild	Normal	Weak	Yes
D11	Sunny	Mild	Normal	Strong	Yes
D12	Overcast	Mild	High	Strong	Yes
D13	Overcast	Hot	Normal	Weak	Yes
D14	Rain	Mild	High	Strong	No

We will assume that all the features are independent, which means that if the wind is weak, for example, then this does not imply anything about the outlook of this day. Another assumption is that all the features contribute equally to the prediction.

These assumptions are, of course, invalid in most cases. This is because the features, by nature, have some dependency on each other, while some of the features are more important in predicting the output than the others. However, these two assumptions are crucial to derive the naïve Bayes classifier as we will see.

Let us rewrite the Bayes Rule again

$$P(X) = \frac{P(Y) * P(Y)}{P(X)}$$

where $X = (x_1, x_2, x_3, \ldots., x_n)$ which represents the different features. If the features are independent, we can then write the Bayes Rule again as follows:

$$P(x_1, x_2, x_3, \ldots., x_n) = \frac{P(Y) * P(Y) * \ldots * P(Y) * P(Y)}{P(x_1) * P(x_2) * \ldots * P(x_n)}$$

We can obtain all the values by looking at the dataset and substitute them into the equation. Let us do so for the outlook column as an example.

Outlook	Play Golf
Sunny	No
Sunny	No
Overcast	Yes
Rain	Yes
Rain	Yes
Rain	Yes
Overcast	No
Sunny	Yes
Sunny	No
Rain	Yes
Sunny	Yes
Overcast	Yes
Overcast	Yes
Rain	No

We can then get the frequency table as follows:

Weather	Yes	No
Overcast	4	-
Rainy	2	3
Sunny	3	2

Then we can get the likelihood table as follows:

Weather	Probability
Overcast	0.29
Rainy	0.36
Sunny	0.36

Now, let us assume we want to know the probability that our friend will play if the weather is sunny. We can convert this to:

$$P(Sunny) = \frac{P(Yes) * P(Yes)}{P(Sunny)}$$

From our likelihood table, we got $P(Sunny) = 0.36$, and from the frequency table we got that $(Yes) = \frac{9}{14}$. Also, we can get that $P(Yes) = \frac{3}{9}$ because we have 9 Yeses and only 3 of them were Sunny. Therefore, we can get $(Sunny) = 0.6$.

We observe that the denominator does not change because all the features are independent. As a result, we can remove it and add a proportionality instead

$$P(x_1, x_2, x_3, \dots, x_n) \propto P(Y) * \prod_{i=1}^{n} P(x_i|Y)$$

where the Π represents the multiplication of the probability.

We can manipulate this even further by saying that we want to find the class y which gives us the maximum probability. This was fairly easy in case of a binary classification problem like the golf problem because if we got $P(Sunny) = 0.6$, then $P(Sunny)$ will be 0.4 and we really do not need to calculate it. However, if the classification problem is multivariate, then we need a formula for that.

$$y = argmax_y P(y) \prod_{i=1}^{n} P(x_i|Y)$$

By getting this formula we can classify the output, which is our goal.

As you can see, Naïve Bayes is also a data-driven algorithm like KNN and does not require the calculation of any weights or defining any loss functions.

Finally, Naïve Bayes has only one hyperparameter, which is called alpha. Increasing the value of this hyperparameter smoothes the naïve Bayes model, which makes it even more naïve. Decreasing it will make the model result in fewer assumptions resulting in more accuracy. However, changing the value of this hyperparameter has little influence on the overall performance of the algorithm.

There are three main variations of naïve Bayes that are used in practice: Multinomial Naïve Bayes, Complement Naïve Bayes and Bernoulli Naïve Bayes.

Further Readings

If you want to know more about the different variations of Naïve Bayes, you can take a look here

https://scikit-learn.org/stable/modules/naive_bayes.html

5.6.3. Naïve Bayes Pros and Cons

As we've seen, naïve Bayes does not require any training, so it is very fast to implement compared to other algorithms. It also gives good results even for high-dimensional data as opposed to KNN. Thus, we usually treat this algorithm as our baseline model to compare the other algorithms with.

Based on these advantages, Naïve Bayes has many different applications including real-time prediction, text classification and recommendation systems.

On the other hand, the assumptions that this algorithm is making are not realistic in many cases, which harms the performance dramatically. Also, it requires data preprocessing in contrast with decision trees and random forests.

5.6.4. Naïve Bayes in Python

Let us see how to train and use a Naïve Bayes classifier.

First, we import the needed libraries. We will use a real-world dataset from sklearn called 20newsgroups which contains 18846 examples in text form belonging to twenty different classes. You can check more about this interesting dataset here. We will also use a function called TfidfVectorizer which is used to get something like the frequency table that we used in the golf example, but for text. We will also evaluate our model using something called the confusion matrix, which we will see shortly.

```
% matplotlib inline
import numpy as np
import matplotlib.pyplot as plt
import seaborn as sns; sns.set()
from sklearn.datasets import fetch_20newsgroups
from sklearn.feature_extraction.text import TfidfVectorizer
from sklearn.naive_bayes import MultinomialNB
from sklearn.pipeline import make_pipeline
from sklearn.metrics import confusion_matrix
```

Then, we will load the dataset and split it into a training set and a test set.

```
data=fetch_20newsgroups()
```

```
train=fetch_20newsgroups(subset='train')
test=fetch_20newsgroups(subset='test')
```

We then create our multinomial Naïve Bayes classifier and train it. Then, we test it and store the predicted outputs.

```
model=make_pipeline(TfidfVectorizer(),MultinomialNB())
model.fit(train.data,train.target)
labels=model.predict(test.data)
```

Given that we have a multi-class classification problem, we need a more informative score that accuracy. Thus, we use the confusion matrix, which tells us the true labels and the predicted labels for each class, so we can find the most frequent mistakes, which may enable us to perform more hyperparameters tuning on our model or use a different model to avoid these mistakes. We will explore the confusion matrix, as well as different model evaluation metrics in the next sections.

```
mat=confusion_matrix(test.target,labels)
plt.figure(figsize=(15,30))
sns.heatmap(mat.T,square=True,annot=True,fmt='d',
            cbar=False,cmap='RdYlGn',
           xticklabels=train.target_names,
           yticklabels=train.target_names)
plt.xlabel('true label')
plt.ylabel('predcited label')
```

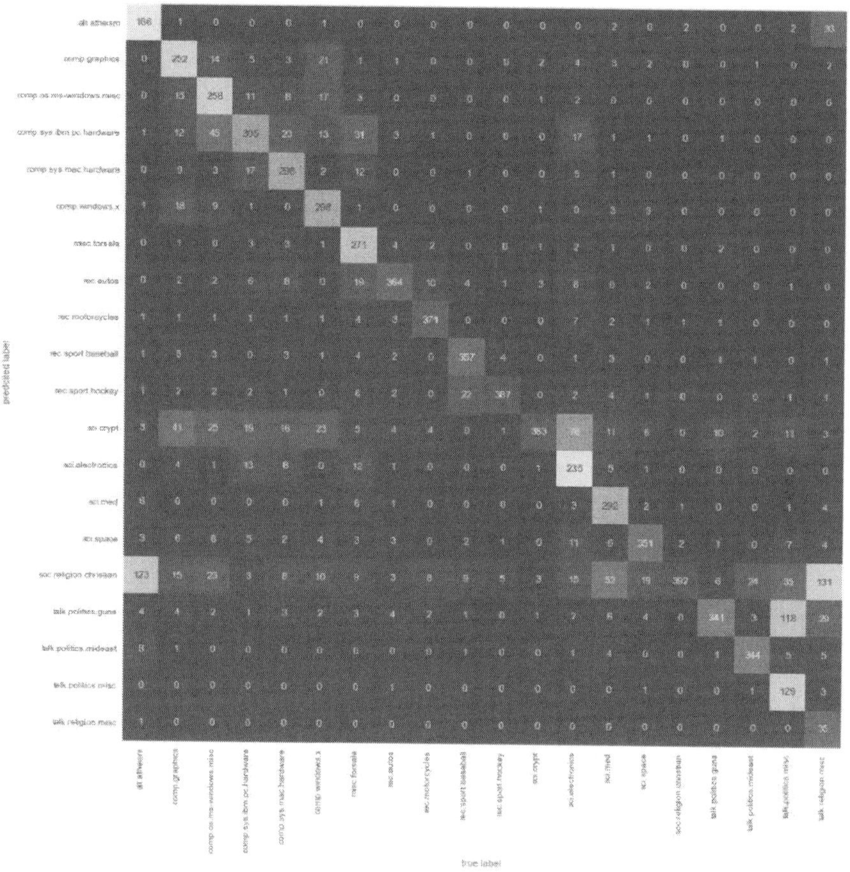

Finally, we can create a simple function that gives us the predicted class, and we use it to predict a given text.

```
def predict_category(s,train=train,model=model):
    pred=model.predict([s])
    return train.target_names[pred[0]]
```

```
predict_category('Jesus Christ')
```

```
'soc.religion.christian'
```

```
predict_category('Bush')
```

```
'talk.politics.misc'
```

5.7. Model Evaluation and Selection

If you have followed all the sections in all the chapters, then this section will be mostly revision for you, with some additional insights and tips.

5.7.1. Splitting the Dataset

We discussed in chapter 2 the problem of overfitting and why it happens. We also said then that we need to split our dataset into a training set and a test set to prevent our model from cheating. We then introduced the concept of hyperparameters, and we should understand by now the importance of this concept and why we must consider it. Thus, to experiment with different hyperparameters' combinations, we saw the need of further splitting our dataset. We called this third split the validation set.

5.7.2. Cross-Validation

However, there was a huge drawback to using a static validation set; we can only experiment with only one3 combination of hyperparameters. Also, if we split our dataset even further, then our training set might get too small and then our model will not be representative. Thus, we introduced the k-fold cross-validation technique which is based on using the same validation set but with the effect of having different validation sets.

We split our dataset into k separate parts, and the training process is repeated k times. Each time, the training set equals "100-K percent" of the dataset, and the validation set is "K percent" of the dataset. To have the effect of different validation sets, we choose these datasets, the training, and the validation randomly each time.

Finally, we calculate the overall accuracy of our model by taking the average accuracies of the "K" different iterations.

5.7.3. Evaluation Metrics

Moving to the evaluation metrics, we mentioned many of them through this chapter, but we now need to summarize all of them and introduce other important ones that we did not have the chance to encounter.

For regression problems, we have four main different metrics to evaluate our model, which we covered in the linear regression section of this chapter.

In summary, these metrics are:

- R^2: The coefficient of determination which we discussed, in detail, in the linear regression section of this chapter.
- MSE: The Mean Square Error
- RMSE: The Root Mean Square Error
- MAE: The Mean Absolute Error

For the classification problems, we have different evaluation metrics, of which we didn't tackle them all.

The first and the most intuitive one is the accuracy, where we report the number of predicted outputs that match the true outputs.

The second metric, with which we can deduce many different metrics, is called the confusion matrix, which we saw in action while working with Naïve Bayes. We can see the confusion matrix in the following figure.

		True condition	
	Total population	Condition positive	Condition negative
Predicted condition	Predicted condition positive	**True positive**	**False positive,** Type I error
	Predicted condition negative	**False negative,** Type II error	**True negative**

From the confusion matrix, we get the accuracy which is:

$$Accuracy = \frac{TP + TN}{P + N}$$

Also, we can get another two metrics called the precision and the recall.

$$Precision = Positive\ Predictive\ Value = \frac{TP}{TP + FP}$$

$$Recall = Sensitivity = True\ Positive\ Rate = \frac{TN}{TP + FN}$$

And we can also get a combination of the precision and the recall called the F-score as follows:

$$F = \frac{2}{\frac{1}{Recall} + \frac{1}{Precision}}$$

So, why don't we just get the accuracy? Why do we need precision and recall?

To answer this question, let's look at two different classification problems and see if the accuracy is the best evaluation metric to use.

Suppose that you have a spam classification problem where you classify emails to be either spam or ham. So, we have two different kinds of errors: false positives and false negatives. The false positives occur when we misclassify a ham email as a spam email, and the false negatives occur when we misclassify a spam email as a ham email. Which of these two errors are more critical? I think you'll agree with me that putting an important email into the spam folder is more crucial than getting annoyed with a spam email into your main email folder. Of course, both are considered types of errors, but in our problem, we care more about having the minimum number of false positives. Thus, we use precision as our metric when evaluating the model.

For the second problem, suppose we have a cancer detection problem to classify the patients into those who either have cancer, or not. Again, we have two types of errors, which are predicting that a healthy patient has cancer and predicting that a sick patient does not have cancer. In contrast to the first example, we here care more about the false negatives because of the nature of the problem itself. We really do not want a cancer patient to be classified as healthy, but we can accept that some of our healthy patients are misclassified because then they will do more tests and they will find themselves healthy afterward. Thus, we use recall as our evaluation metric.

If we want a harmonic mean between accuracy and recall, then we use the F-score.

We can also deduce another metric that is used when evaluating machine learning models. This is the ROC curve, where ROC is short for Receiver Operating Characteristic. The ROC curve is a plot of the False Positive Rate against the True Positive Rate. It is used mainly to select the optimum model which should have an area under the curve—AUC—equal to or near 1. This is because the True Positive Rate should be equal to or near 1, while the False Positive Rate should be equal to or near 0. Moreover, a random classifier is found to have an AUC of 0.5.

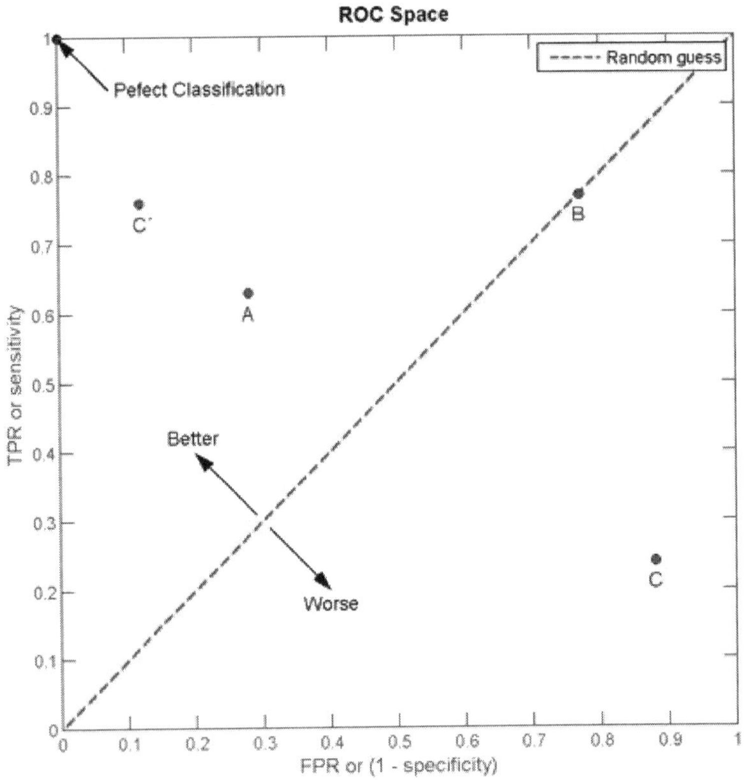

5.7.4. Hyperparameters Tuning

To perform hyperparameters tuning, there are two main techniques that are used in practice—the grid search and the random search.

For the grid search, we choose candidate values for each one of the hyperparameters in our classifier or regressor. Then we train on every possible combination of these hyperparameters, and then we use the combination that gave us the best performance on the test set.

For the random search, we specify a range for each one of the different hyperparameters along with the number of iterations. Then, our model is trained for that specific number of iterations, while using a different random combination of the hyperparameters for each iteration. Then, we also use the combination that got us the best performance on the test set.

So, we say that grid-search is a discrete conclusive search over all the points, but it is computationally expensive. On the other hand, random search is a continuous non-conclusive search that is computationally efficient.

5.7.5. Grid Search in Python

Let us now see how we can perform grid search using Python.

First, we import the libraries that we will use.

```
import pandas as pd
import numpy as np
import matplotlib.pyplot as plt
import os
from sklearn.model_selection import train_test_split
from sklearn.preprocessing import StandardScaler
from sklearn.svm import SVC
from sklearn.metrics import confusion_matrix
from sklearn.model_selection import cross_val_score
from sklearn.model_selection import GridSearchCV
%matplotlib inline
```

We then fix the path that contains the dataset and load the dataset.

```
os.chdir("D:")
os.getcwd()
```

```
dataset=pd.read_csv('ads.csv')
dataset.head()
```

	User ID	Gender	Age	EstimatedSalary	Purchased
0	15624510	Male	19	19000	0
1	15810944	Male	35	20000	0
2	15668575	Female	26	43000	0
3	15603246	Female	27	57000	0
4	15804002	Male	19	76000	0

We then split our dataset as usual.

```
X=dataset.iloc[:,[2,3]].values
y=dataset.iloc[:,4].values
X_train,X_test,y_train,y_test=train_test_split(X,y,
                                               test_size=0.3,random_state=42)
```

After that, we perform feature normalization.

```
sc=StandardScaler()
X_train=sc.fit_transform(X_train)
X_test=sc.transform(X_test)
```

Then, we train a support vector classifier with a radial basis function kernel.

```
classifier=SVC(kernel='rbf',random_state=42)
classifier.fit(X_train,y_train)
```

We can now use the classifier on the test set to make predictions.

```
y_pred=classifier.predict(X_test)
cm=confusion_matrix(y_test,y_pred)
accuracies=cross_val_score(estimator=classifier,
                           X=X_train,y=y_train,cv=10)
print(cm)
print(accuracies.mean())
print(accuracies.std())
```

```
[[68  5]
 [ 2 45]]
0.8922459405218026
0.04844494533063745
```

As we see, we got 60 TP, 45 TN, 2 FN and 5 FP. Also, we got an average of 89% accuracy using 10-fold cross-validation.

Following that, we use grid search to tune our hyperparameters. We choose the first set to be four different values for the C hyperparameter with a linear kernel and the second set to be four different values for the C hyperparameter with an RBF kernel and five different values for gamma.

```
parameters=[{'C':[1,10,100,1000],'kernel':['linear']},
           {'C':[1,10,100,1000],'kernel':['rbf'],
            'gamma':[0.5,0.1,0.01,0.001,0.0001]}]
grid_search=GridSearchCV(estimator=classifier,
                         param_grid=parameters,
                        scoring='accuracy',cv=10,n_jobs=-1
grid_search=grid_search.fit(X_train,y_train)
best_accuracy=grid_search.best_score_
best_accuracy
```

```
0.8928571428571429
```

We got 89% also using 10-fold cross-validation with nearly no improvement. However, we can benefit from what we did by getting the best hyperparameters combination that gave us this result and tune them even further.

```
best_parameters=grid_search.best_params_
best_parameters
```

```
{'C': 1, 'gamma': 0.5, 'kernel': 'rbf'}
```

As we can see, we got the best gamma equals 0.5, so we can experiment with different values of gamma near this value with different values of C.

```
parameters=[{'C':[1,10,100,1000],'kernel':['linear']},
           {'C':[1,10,100,1000],'kernel':['rbf'],
            'gamma':[0.1,0.2,0.3,0.4,0.5,0.6,0.7,0.8,0.9]}]
grid_search=GridSearchCV(estimator=classifier,
                         param_grid=parameters,
                        scoring='accuracy',cv=10,n_jobs=-1)
grid_search=grid_search.fit(X_train,y_train)
best_accuracy=grid_search.best_score_
print(best_accuracy)
best_parameters=grid_search.best_params_
print(best_parameters)
```

```
0.9
{'C': 100, 'gamma': 0.6, 'kernel': 'rbf'}
```

Finally, we get 90% accuracy. We can repeat this process as many times as we want until the grid search does not give us different values for the hyperparameters.

6

Unsupervised Learning Techniques

In the previous chapter, we discussed the most used supervised learning algorithms. In this chapter, we will discuss some of the most used unsupervised ones. By the end of this chapter, if you followed it thoroughly, you can confidently say that you understand how both the supervised learning algorithms and the unsupervised learning algorithms work.

Unlike supervised learning algorithms, in unsupervised learning scenarios, we do not have labels for the output. Thus, our goal is not to perform regression or classification, but instead, it will be to cluster the output together and to reduce the dimensionality of the features as we briefly mentioned in the previous chapter.

We will see two fundamental algorithms, k-means and hierarchical clustering that are used for clustering. Also, we will explore the most famous algorithm, Principal Component Analysis which is used for dimensionality reduction.

As in the previous chapter, our discussion will be divided into two main parts of how the algorithm works intuitively and mathematically, and how to implement it in Python.

6.1. K-Means Clustering

6.1.1. K-Means Intuition

Look at the sky in the morning and focus a little bit. Sometimes, you can cluster different clouds together and form a shape in your mind. None of the clouds had any information of their own. But when clustered together, you extracted useful information.

So, how did you cluster the clouds together to form some shapes?

You did that by noticing the similarity within each group of clusters while also noticing the dissimilarity between each group and the other ones. This is equivalent to finding high intra-class similarity and low inter-class similarity. To find the similarity either within each group or between the different groups, you estimated the distance between the different clusters.

Market segmentation is another interesting use for clustering, where we have different features for each client, and we want to cluster similar clients together, so we can have an oriented market campaign tailored for them.

K-means is a well-known clustering algorithm that is used today in many applications. Like K-nearest neighbor, we have a hyperparameter called "K" which in this algorithm specifies the number of clusters that we want. Note also that this algorithm assumes that the data are divided equally among the clusters.

The algorithm has four main steps as follows:

1. Select initial centroids at random
2. Assign each object in the dataset to the cluster with the nearest centroid
3. Recalculate the positions of the centroids to be the mean of the objects assigned to them.
4. Repeat steps two and three until there is no change in the centroids' positions.

Along with these steps, the algorithm calculates two distances: the inter-class distance and the intra-class distance. The first distance is also called Within Group Sum of Squares, or SSW, while the second distance is called Between Groups Sum of Squares or SSB. The Total Sum of Squares, or SST, is the result of adding the two distances together.

$$SST = \sum_{j=1}^{m} \sum_{i=1}^{n} (y_{i,j} - \bar{y}_m)^2$$

$$SSB = \sum_{l=1}^{k} \sum_{j=1}^{m} (y_{k,m} - \bar{y}_m)^2$$

$$SSW = \sum_{l=1}^{k} \sum_{j=1}^{m} \sum_{i=1}^{n} (y_{i,j} - \bar{y}_m)^2$$

Where `i` represents data points, `j` represents the features, and k represents the number of clusters.

The following figures from Wikipedia explain the K-means algorithm perfectly.

We choose K to be 3 in our case and initialize the centroids randomly.

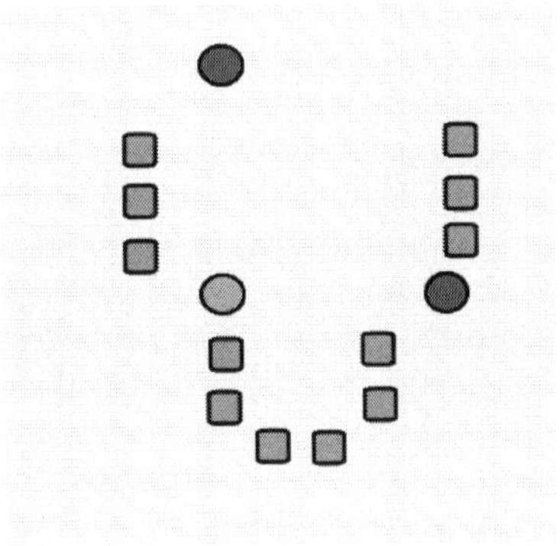

Then, we assign the different data points to the three clusters according to the SST and the SSB distances.

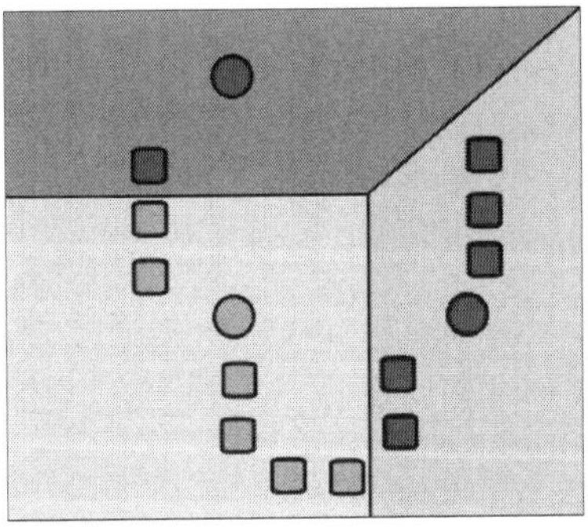

After that, we recalculate the centroids' positions to be the mean of the assigned data points.

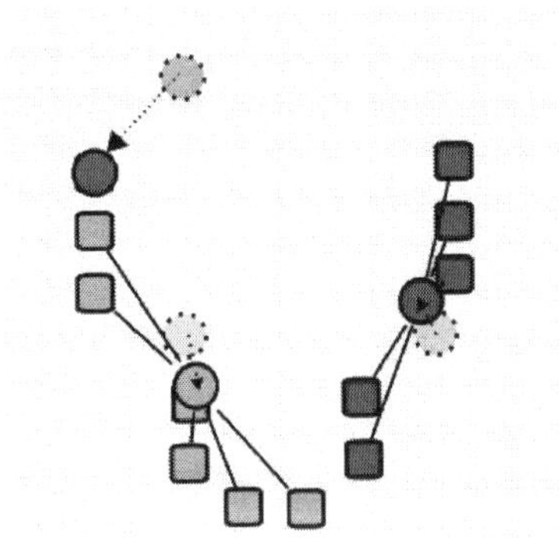

Finally, we repeat the second and the third steps until convergence.

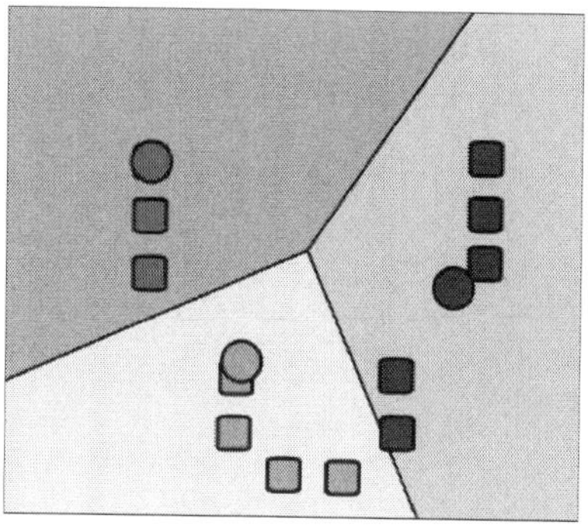

6.1.2. K-Means Initialization Trap

The two main issues that the K-means algorithm has are how should we initialize the centroids and the choice of the hyperparameter K.

The first issue is tricky because the initialization can alter the overall output of the algorithm dramatically. Tackling this issue is not easy and is still an active area of research. One practical method that is implemented in many frameworks such as sklearn is to set the centroids as far as possible to each while they are still within the distribution of the dataset.

6.1.3. Selecting the Number of Centroids

The second issue can be resolved by visualizing the dataset, if possible and estimating the value of K. This is a manual solution which is not feasible if the dataset contains more than three features, which is the case in most datasets.

Another possible workaround is to use grid search as we did in KNN. This can be slow sometimes and isn't considered the best solution.

A third solution is to use a technique called the elbow method. In this method, we plot the Sum of Squared Errors against the number of clusters and take the elbow of this plot as follows.

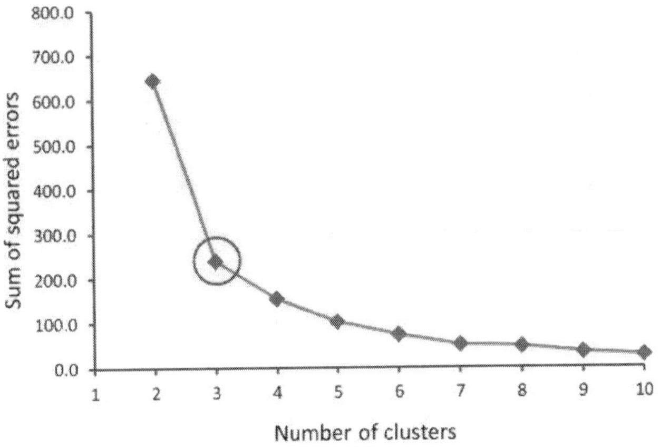

Finally, we can use the Silhouette Method, in which we plot the Silhouette coefficient against the number of clusters. This coefficient is calculated using the mean intra-class distance and the mean nearest-cluster distance for each example. The formula to calculate it is as follows:

$$S = \frac{b - a}{max\ (a, b)}$$

where bb is the mean nearest-cluster distance and aa is the mean intra-class distance.

6.1.4. K-Means Failure Cases

Because K-means assumes that the data are distributed equally among the centroids, the algorithm fails when this assumption is not present. The following figure shows that in more detail.

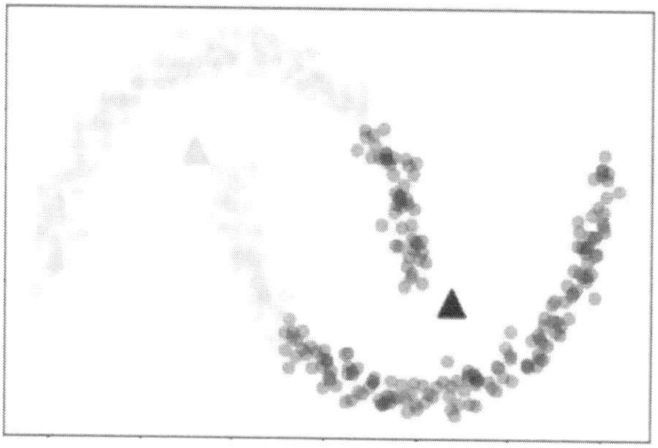

To solve this problem, we cannot use any techniques like we did with the initialization and the choice of the number of clusters. This is because it is a problem in the core of the algorithm itself. So, the only solution is to use another more complex algorithm that does not have the K-means assumptions. This is exactly what we will do in the next section.

6.1.5. K-Means Pros and Cons

As we've seen, K-means is a very intuitive and easy-to-follow algorithm. So, like Naïve Bayes, we can use K-means as a baseline model to which we can compare the performance of more complex algorithms.

On the other hand, we noticed three issues with K-means: the sensitivity to the choice of the number of clusters, the initialization problem, and the poor results on complex data.

Further Readings

If you want to play with and visualize K-means in dozens of scenarios, you can check <u>here</u>

https://www.naftaliharris.com/blog/visualizing-k-means-clustering/

6.1.6. K-Means in Python

Let us now see how we can deal with K-means in practice.

First, we will work with a real dataset and see how we can use the different techniques that we discussed to choose the value of K.

As usual, we import the needed libraries as an initial step.

```
from sklearn.preprocessing import StandardScaler
from sklearn.cluster import KMeans
import utils
import pandas as pd
import numpy as np
from itertools import cycle, islice
import matplotlib.pyplot as plt
from pandas.plotting import parallel_coordinates
from sklearn.metrics import silhouette_score
import os
%matplotlib inline
```

Then, we will fix the path and import the dataset which we will use in this part. This will be the daily weather dataset that contains different features regarding the weather for more than 1000 consecutive days.

```
os.chdir('D:')
os.getcwd()
```

```
data=pd.read_csv('daily_weather.csv',index_col=['number'])
```

We then drop the days that contain any missing values.

```
data.dropna(inplace=True)
```

After that, we can calculate some summary statistics which can provide us with insights if we want to do any further analysis.

```
data.describe().transpose()
```

	count	mean	std	min	25%	50%	75%	max
air_pressure_9am	1064.0	918.903180	3.179040	907.990000	916.595376	918.942281	921.169054	929.320000
air_temp_9am	1064.0	65.022609	11.168033	36.752000	57.398000	65.778479	73.530872	98.906000
avg_wind_direction_9am	1064.0	142.306756	69.149472	15.500000	65.979244	165.937461	191.100000	343.400000
avg_wind_speed_9am	1064.0	5.485793	4.534427	0.693451	2.245529	3.869906	7.264463	23.554978
max_wind_direction_9am	1064.0	148.480424	67.154911	28.900000	76.335351	176.350000	201.125000	312.200000
max_wind_speed_9am	1064.0	6.999714	5.590790	1.185578	3.064608	4.943637	8.747888	29.840780
rain_accumulation_9am	1064.0	0.182023	1.534493	0.000000	0.000000	0.000000	0.000000	24.020000
rain_duration_9am	1064.0	266.393697	1503.092216	0.000000	0.000000	0.000000	0.000000	17704.000000
relative_humidity_9am	1064.0	34.077440	25.356668	6.090000	15.093365	23.135000	44.660000	92.620000
relative_humidity_3pm	1064.0	35.148381	22.365475	5.300000	17.360468	24.371286	51.922500	92.250000

Also, as usual, we normalize our features using the standard scaler.

```
X = StandardScaler().fit_transform(data)
```

Now, to select the best number of clusters, we use the elbow method which we've discussed. We can do so by calculating the distances for a range of numbers and take the elbow of the curve.

```
K=range(2,15)
np.random.seed(42)
sse={}
for k in K:
    cluster_wine=KMeans(k,n_jobs=-1)
    cluster_wine.fit_predict(X)
    sse[k] = cluster_wine.inertia_
```

```
plt.figure()
plt.plot(sse.keys(),sse.values(), marker="o") #sse is dictionary
plt.xlabel("Number of cluster")
plt.ylabel("SSE")
plt.show()
```

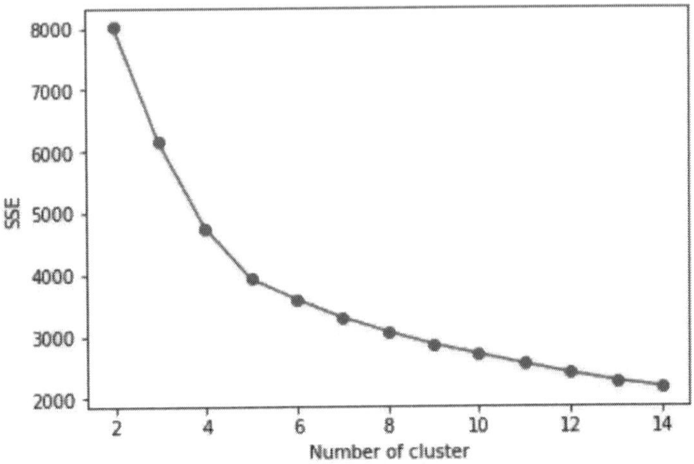

The second method is to use the silhouette score from the sklearn library, and we take the value with the highest score.

```
np.random.seed(42)
sil_coef={}
for k in range (2,15):
    cluster_wine=KMeans(k,n_jobs=-1)
    cluster_wine.fit_predict(X)
    sil_coef[k]=silhouette_score(X,cluster_wine.labels_,metric='euclidean')

#Higher Silhouette Coefficient score relates to a model with better defined clusters
sil_coef
```

```
plt.figure()
plt.plot(sil_coef.keys(),sil_coef.values(), color='#840101',linewidth=2,marker='o')
plt.xlabel("Number of cluster")
plt.ylabel("Silhouette Score")
plt.show()
```

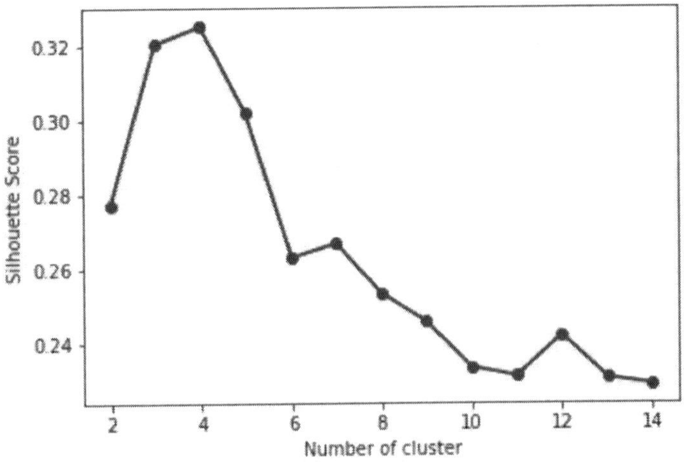

As we see, both methods provided us with 4 as the best number of clusters.

Now, let us work with a synthetic dataset which can help us to see the algorithm step-by-step and the problems of K-means.

We start by importing the libraries.

```
import numpy as np
import numpy.random as npr
from sklearn.metrics.pairwise import euclidean_distances
import matplotlib.pyplot as plt
from sklearn.datasets import make_blobs
from sklearn.datasets import make_moons
from matplotlib.patches import Ellipse
from sklearn.mixture import GaussianMixture
%matplotlib inline
```

Then, we will define some helper functions for plotting and generating the data itself.

```
def plot_clust(X,W=None,z=None):
    if z is not None:
        if np.any(z<0):
            plt.scatter(X[z<0,0], X[z<0,1], marker="o", facecolors='none', edgecolor='black', alpha=0.3);
        if np.any(z>=0):
            plt.scatter(X[z>=0,0], X[z>=0,1], marker="o", c=z[z>=0], alpha=0.3);
    else:
        plt.scatter(X[:,0], X[:,1], marker="o", c='black', alpha=0.3);
    if W is not None:
        plt.scatter(W[:,0], W[:,1], marker="^", s=200, c=np.arange(W.shape[0]));
    else:
        plt.title("number of clusters = %d" % len(set(np.unique(z))-set([-1])));
    plt.show()
```

```
def generate_data(data_type = 1, n_samples = 1500, random_state = 170, k=3):
    n = 100
    d = 2

    if data_type == 1:
        X, z_true = make_blobs(n_samples=n_samples, random_state=random_state, centers=k)
    elif data_type == 2: #ellipsoidal data
        X, z_true = make_blobs(n_samples=n_samples, random_state=random_state, centers=k)
        transformation = [[0.60834549, -0.63667341], [-0.40887718, 0.85253229]]
        X = np.dot(X, transformation)
    elif data_type == 3: #unequal variance
        X, z_true = make_blobs(n_samples=n_samples, cluster_std=[1.0, 2.5, 0.5], random_state=random_state)
    elif data type == 4: #nonconvex cluster
        X, z_true = make_moons(n_samples, noise=.05, random_state=random_state)
    return X, z_true
```

Now, let us generate 300 examples which are clustered into three clusters.

```
X, z_true = generate_data(data_type = 1, random_state = 170, n_samples = 300, k = 3)
n = len(X)
plot_clust(X,z=z_true)
```

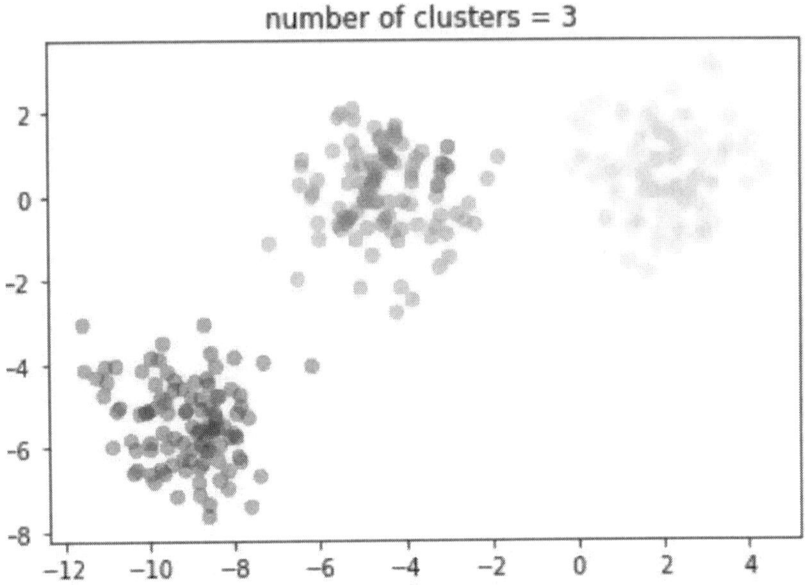

Let us look at the algorithm step-by-step. The first step is to choose the number of clusters and initialize them randomly.

```
k = 3
npr.seed(2)

W = X[npr.choice(n, k, replace=False)]

plot_clust(X,W)
```

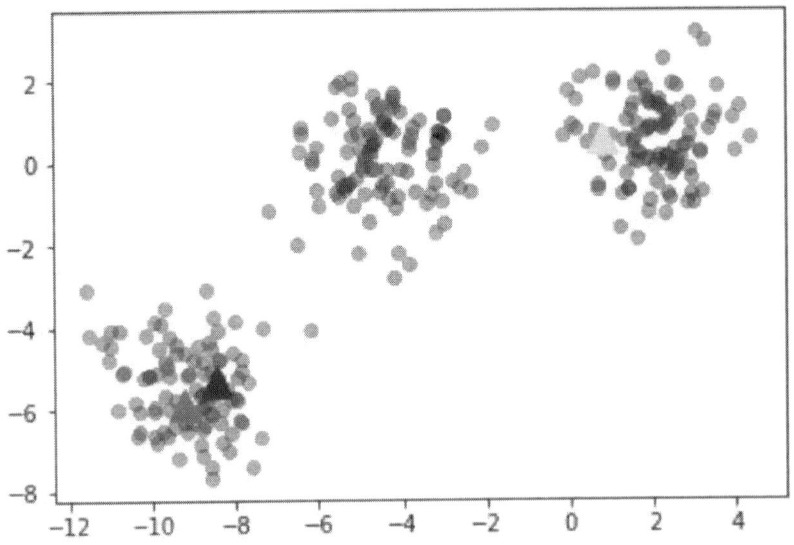

The second step is to assign each example into one of the centroids.

```
def update_z(X,W):
    dist2 = euclidean_distances(X, W)
    return np.argmin(dist2, axis=1)

z = update_z(X,W)
plot_clust(X,W,z)
```

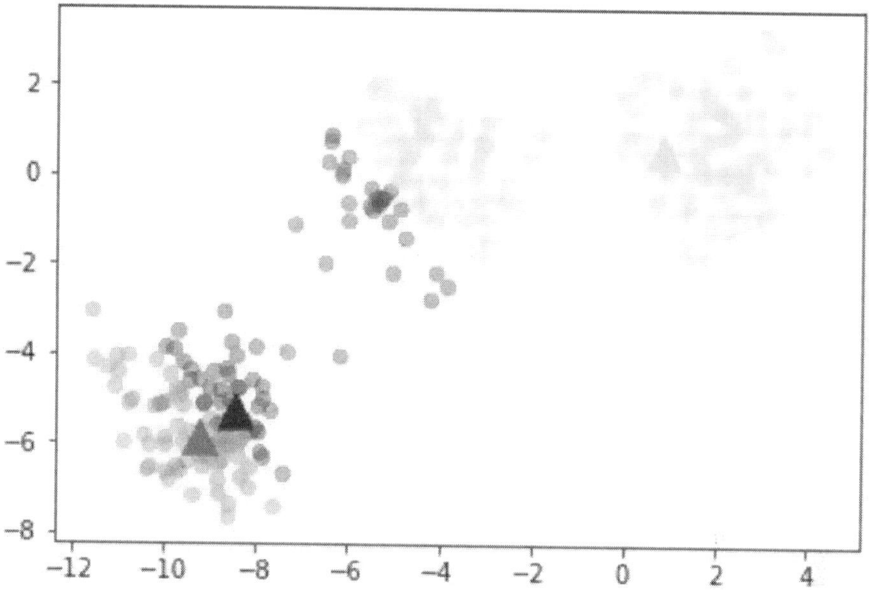

The third step is to update the centroids' positions to be the mean of the assigned values.

```
def update_W(X,z,W_old):
    # just being a bit careful about the case of a cluster with no points in it
    W = W_old.copy()
    for kk in range(k):
        W[kk] = np.mean(X[z==kk],axis=0)
    return W

W = update_W(X,z,W)
plot_clust(X,W,z)
```

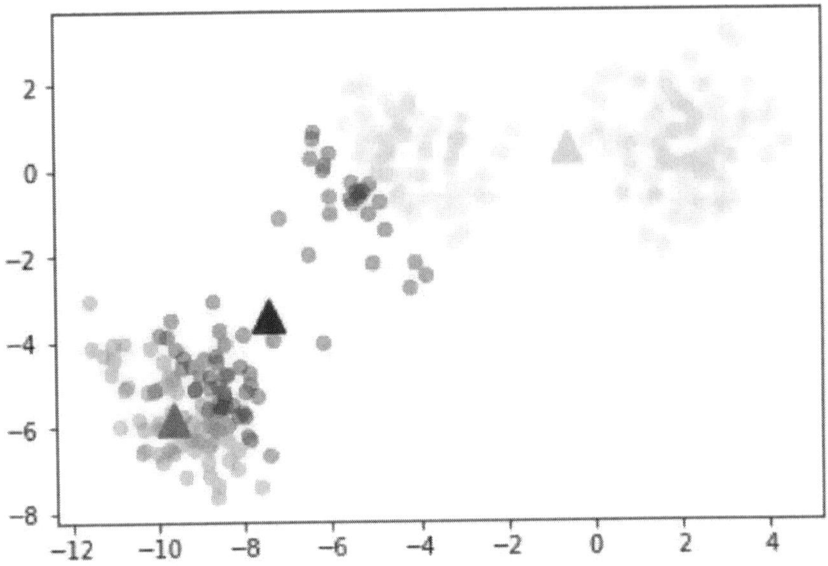

The final step is to repeat the process until convergence. Let us assume that this will happen after 100 iterations.

```
# better: loop until np.all(z_new == z)
for itr in range(100):
    z = update_z(X,W)
    W = update_W(X,z,W)
plot_clust(X,W,z)
```

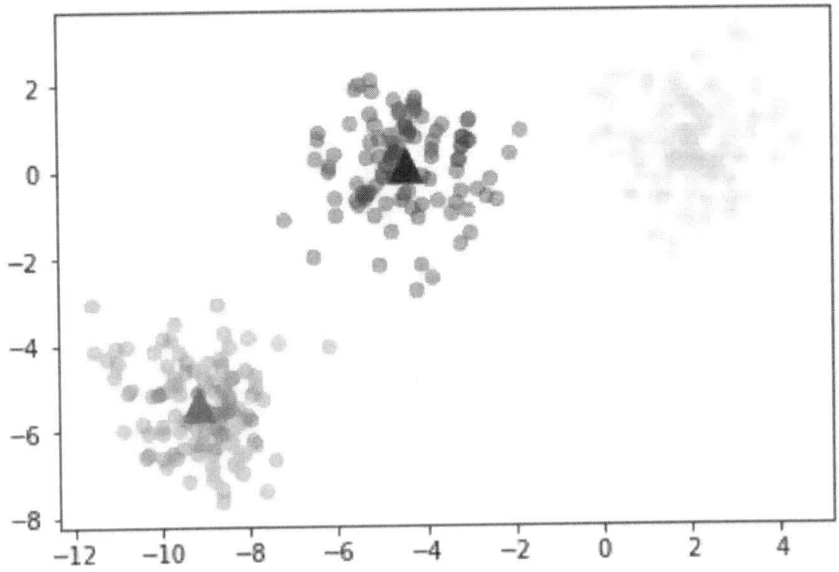

What we have seen is an ideal case, so let us see what will happen if any of the problems that we discussed occur.

The first problem is the initialization problem. So, we will use the same code for generating the data with the same number of clusters, but we will change the seed in order to initialize the weights differently.

```
npr.seed(5)

X, z_true = generate_data(data_type = 1, random_state = 170, n_samples = 300, k = 3)
n = len(X)
k = 3
W = X[npr.choice(n, k, replace=False)]
plot_clust(X,W)

for itr in range(100):
    z = update_z(X,W)
    W = update_W(X,z,W)

plot_clust(X,W,z)
```

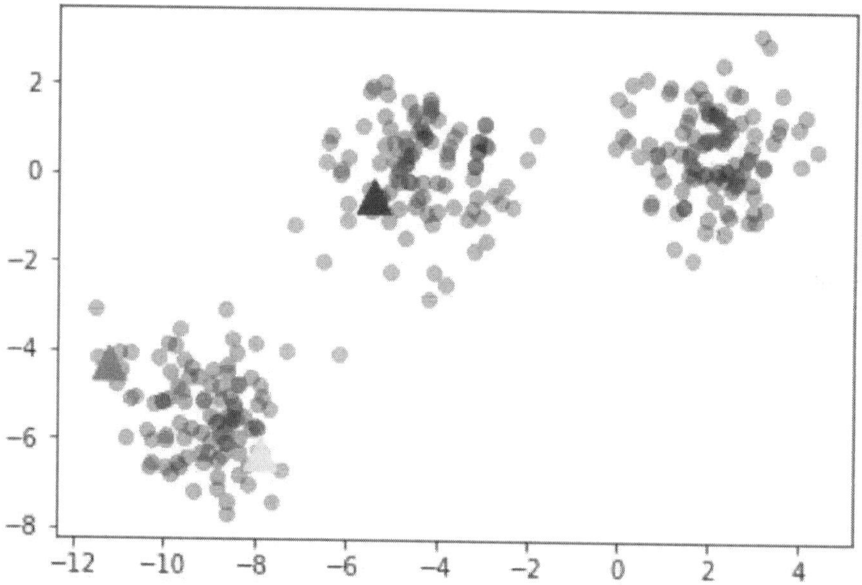

As we can see, two different centroids were initialized near each other which will lead to a failure case.

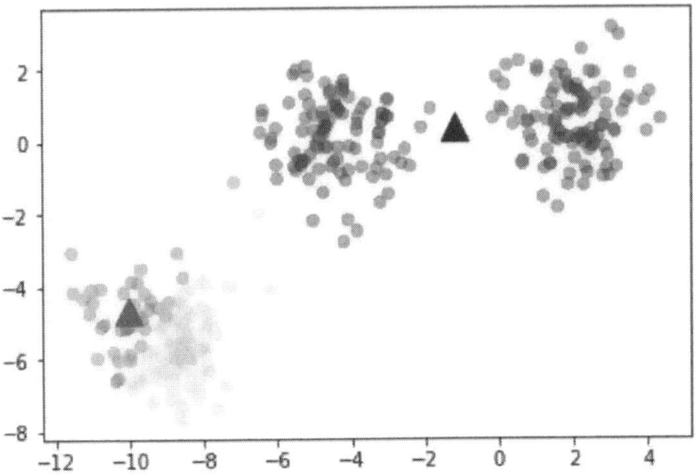

The second problem is the choice of the number of clusters. In order to simulate this, let's create the same clusters but assign only two centroids.

```
npr.seed(2)

X, z_true = generate_data(data_type = 1, random_state = 170, n_samples = 300, k = 3)
n = len(X)
k = 2
W = X[npr.choice(n, k, replace=False)]
plot_clust(X,W)

for itr in range(100):
    z = update_z(X,W)
    W = update_W(X,z,W)

plot_clust(X,W,z)
```

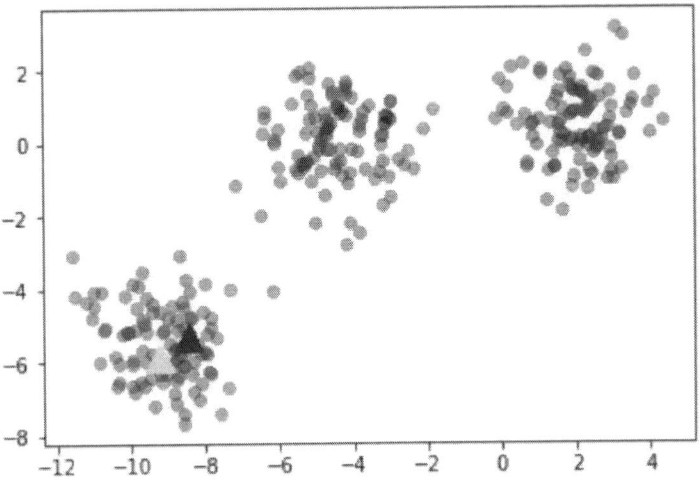

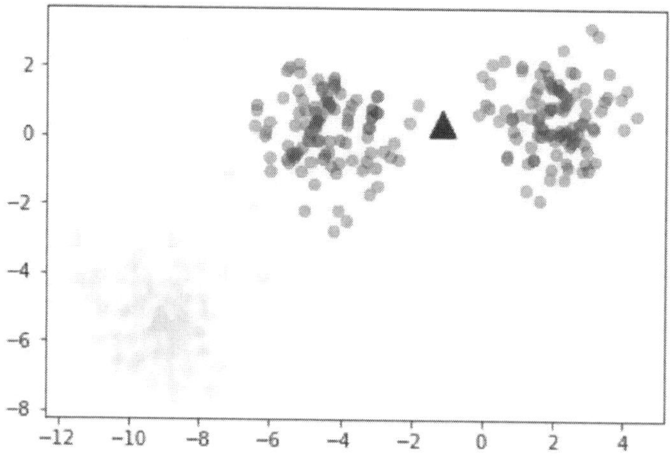

As we see, this also resulted in a failure in the algorithm.

The third problem is the distribution of the data themselves. Let us assume that the clusters are not isotropic, which means that we cannot represent them as circles.

```
npr.seed(1)

X, z_true = generate_data(data_type = 2, random_state = 170, n_samples = 300, k = 3)
n = len(X)
k = 3
W = X[npr.choice(n, k, replace=False)]
plot_clust(X,W)

for itr in range(100):
    z = update_z(X,W)
    W = update_W(X,z,W)

plot_clust(X,W,z)
```

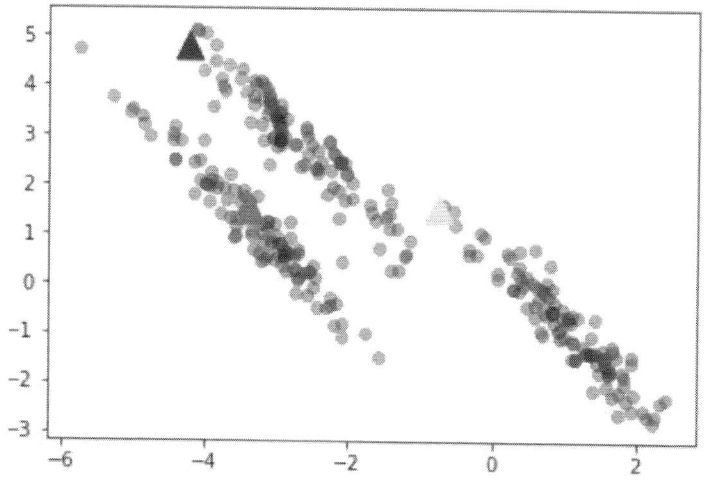

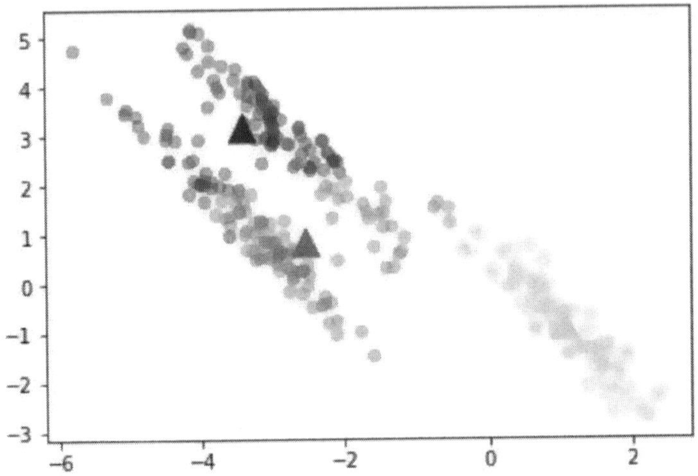

Again, the algorithm cannot cluster the data successfully.

Another problem with the data occurs when we do not have equal variances. We can simulate this by the following code.

```
npr.seed(1)

X, z_true = generate_data(data_type = 3, random_state = 170, n_samples = 400, k = 3)
n = len(X)
k = 3
W = X[npr.choice(n, k, replace=False)]
plot_clust(X,W)

for itr in range(100):
    z = update_z(X,W)
    W = update_W(X,z,W)

plot_clust(X,W,z)
```

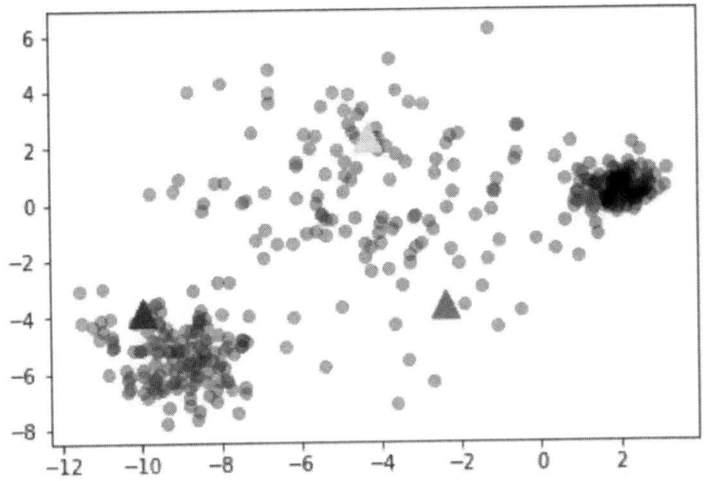

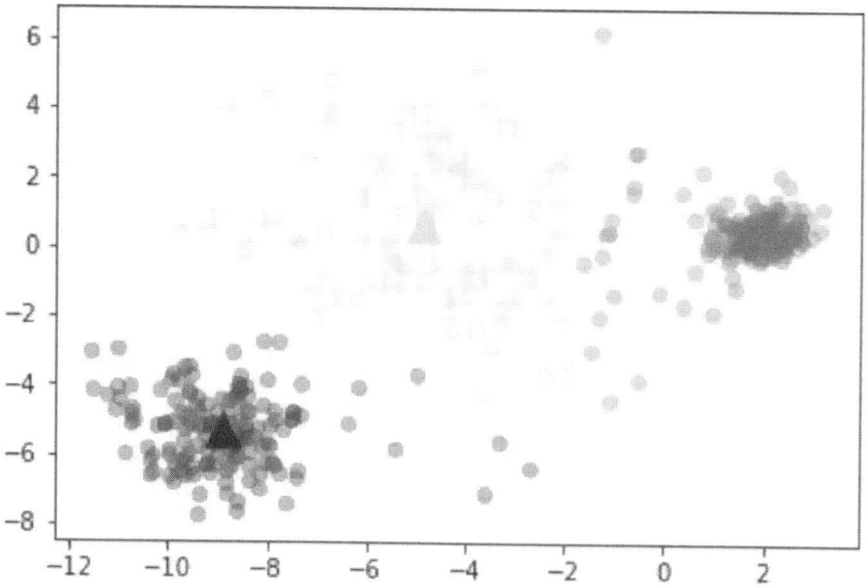

The algorithm did its best to cluster the data, but there is no metric that we can use to evaluate if this is the optimum clustering or not.

Finally, if the data do not have convex clusters, then the algorithm will not work as well.

```
npr.seed(1)

X, z_true = generate_data(data_type = 4, random_state = 170, n_samples = 400, k = 2)
n = len(X)
k = 2
W = X[npr.choice(n, k, replace=False)]
plot_clust(X,W)

for itr in range(100):
    z = update_z(X,W)
    W = update_W(X,z,W)

plot_clust(X,W,z)
```

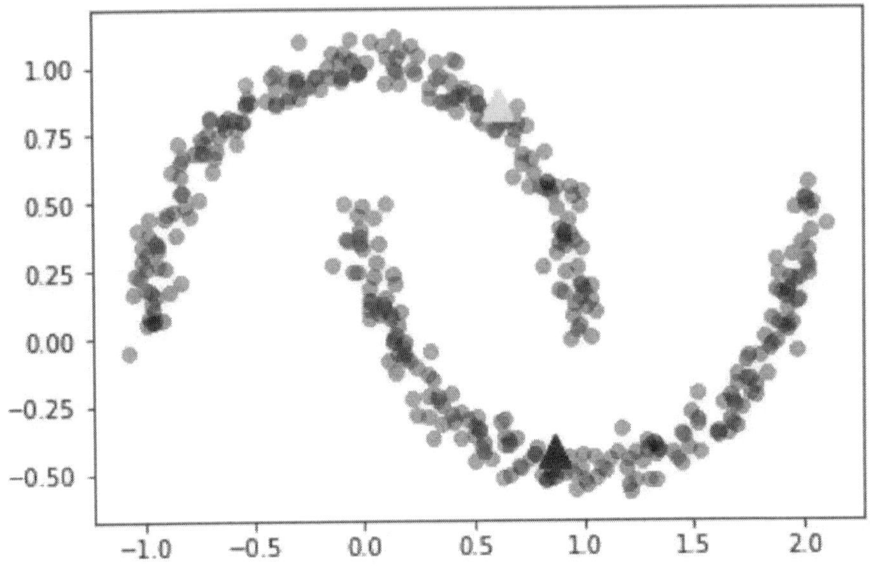
1.00
0.75
0.50
0.25
0.00
−0.25
−0.50
−1.0
−0.5
0.0
0.5
1.0
1.5
2.0

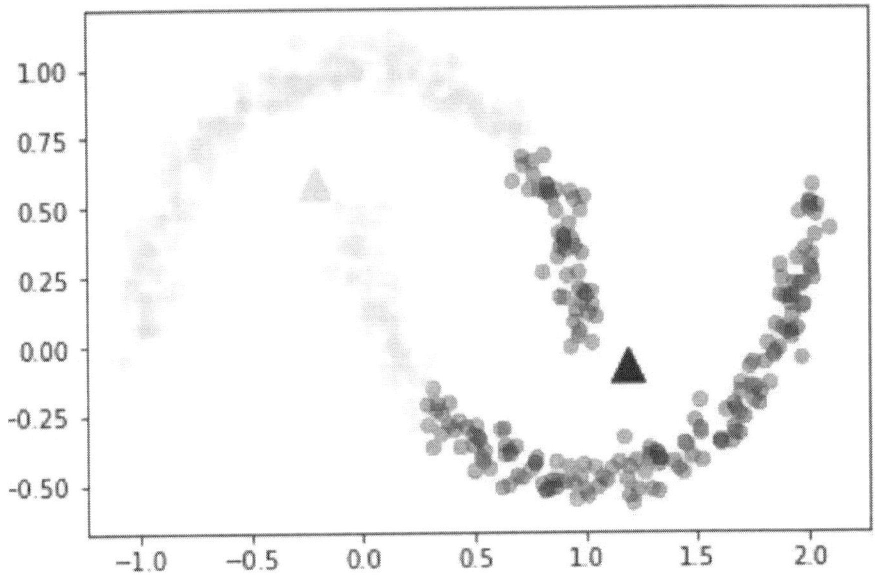
1.00
0.75
0.50
0.25
0.00
-0.25
-0.50
−1.0
−0.5
0.0
0.5
1.0
1.5
2.0

6.2. Hierarchical Clustering

6.2.1. Hierarchical Clustering Intuition

Although k-means is a very useful algorithm that can help us understand the idea behind clustering, it suffers from many problems.

To address these problems and solve them, we need another algorithm called hierarchical clustering.

The idea behind this algorithm is very intuitive. It assumes that every example in our dataset is a cluster by itself, and then combines different clusters based on the distances into one cluster. This is called the agglomerative method.

While this is the most popular method, some people use it in reverse, as they treat the whole dataset as one cluster, and split it into smaller clusters also based on the distances. This is, on the other hand, called the divisive method.

To compute the distance, we need to compute the distance between different examples and the distance between the different clusters. If you remember, to compute the distance between different examples, we used the general Minkowski distance and its special cases when we substitute $p = 2$ which is the Euclidean distance or when we substitute $p = 1$ which is the Manhattan distance. Feel free to revisit this part from the k-means section.

Computing the second distance, on the other hand, is trickier. While there are dozens of distance metrics used for this task, only five of them are currently used in real-world situations.

The first metric is called the single link, which is the smallest distance between one example in one cluster and another example in the other cluster. This can be written as follows:

$$dis(K_i, K_j) = min\ (K_{ip}, K_{jq})$$

The second metric is the complete link metric, which is the largest distance between one example in one cluster and another example in the other cluster. This can be written as follows:

$$dis(K_i, K_j) = max\ (K_{ip}, K_{jq})$$

The third metric is the average link metric, which is the average distance between one example in one cluster and another example in the other cluster. This can be written as follows:

$$dis(K_i, K_j) = avg\ (K_{ip}, K_{jq})$$

The fourth metric is the centroid metric, which is the distance between the centroids of two clusters. This can be written as follows:

$$dis(K_i, K_j) = dis\ (C_i, C_j)$$

The final metric is the medoid metric, which is the distance between the medoids, which are chosen examples in the middle of the clusters, of two clusters. This can be written as follows:

$$dis(K_i, K_j) = dis\ (M_i, M_j)$$

After choosing both metrics, we can visualize the hierarchical relationships between the different examples using a dendrogram. We will discuss how to construct and interpret the dendrogram in the Python section.

6.2.2. Hierarchical Clustering Pros and Cons

As we've seen, using hierarchical clustering solved many of the issues that we suffered from while using k-means, as it can handle complex data with no problems, while also providing insightful visualizations that can help us draw some conclusions about the dataset. Moreover, we do not really have to choose the value of "k" as the algorithm is based on another concept which either treats the whole dataset as one cluster and splits it into smaller clusters or treats each example as a different cluster and merges the similar examples or clusters them together.

However, as a trade-off, hierarchical clustering suffers from the problem of time complexity. This time complexity increases as the number of features increases.

6.2.3. Hierarchical Clustering in Python

The first step is to import the libraries. We will use SciPy modules, linkage and dendrogram for hierarchical clustering. Other than these two new modules, we will use the usual libraries such as NumPy, pandas, preprocessing from sklearn, and matplotlib.

```
import numpy as np
import pandas as pd
from scipy.cluster.hierarchy import linkage, dendrogram
from sklearn.preprocessing import normalize
import matplotlib.pyplot as plt
import os
```

Then, we will fix the path and load our dataset for this exercise. We will work with a dataset called stock movements which cannot be clustered with k-means algorithm because the dataset is not equally distributed.

```
os.chdir('D:')
os.getcwd()
```

```
movements=pd.read_csv('stock_movements.csv',index_col=0)
```

After that, we will normalize our features to use the clustering algorithm.

```
normalized_movements = normalize(movements)
```

Now, we choose the method for linking to be complete. Then, we visualize the constructed dendrogram. The horizontal axis of the diagram represents the features, while the vertical axis represents the cluster distance. As we can see, companies like McDonalds and MasterCard are considered more related to each other than McDonalds and Apple, for example. We do not use dendrogram to choose the number of clusters, as in fact, we do not really have an optimum number of clusters. Instead, dendrogram helps us in knowing how our dataset will be clustered if we have two or three clusters, for example, or any number.

Suppose that we want to have three clusters, then our first cluster will include all the features from Apple to Exxon, our second cluster will contain all the features from Home Depot to Procter Gamble, while the third one will contain all the features from Walgreen to McDonalds. We did this clustering based on the cluster distance, as the first cluster is the one with the least cluster distance, and so on.

```
margings = linkage(normalized_movements,method='complete')
plt.figure(figsize=(15,10))
dendrogram(margings,
           labels=movements.index.values,
           leaf_rotation=60,
           leaf_font_size=8)
plt.show()
```

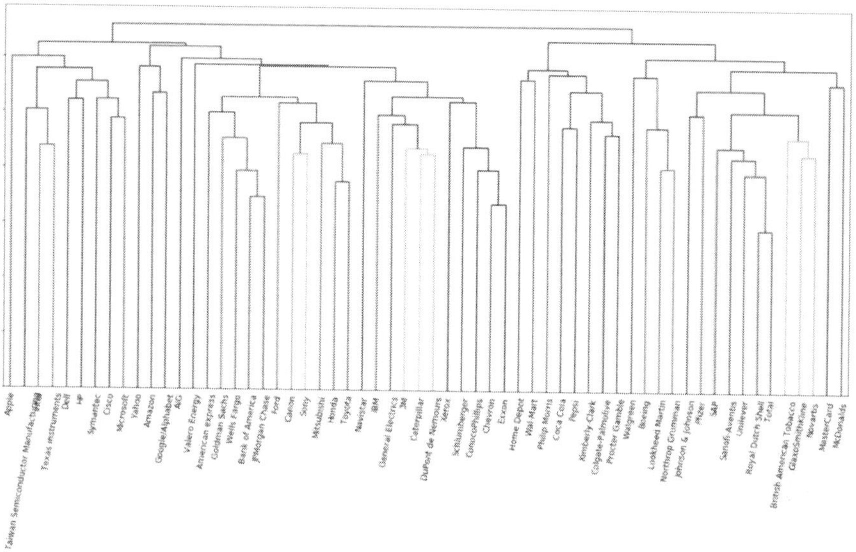

If we do the same visualization of the dendrogram but using a different linkage method such as the single method or the complete method, we see that the results change dramatically.

```
margings = linkage(normalized_movements,method='single')
plt.figure(figsize=(15,10))
dendrogram(margings,
           labels=movements.index.values,
           leaf_rotation=80,
           leaf_font_size=8)
plt.show()
```

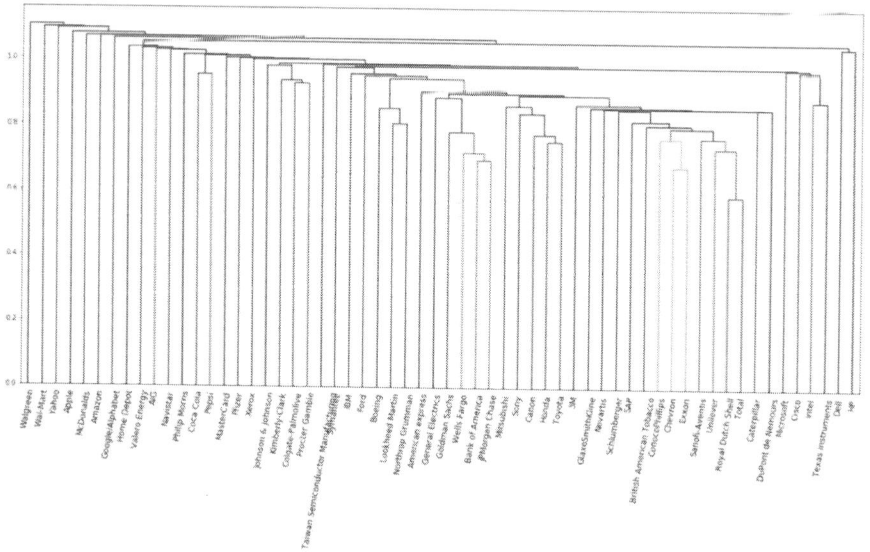

```
mergings = linkage(normalized_movements,method='average')
plt.figure(figsize=(15,10))
dendrogram(mergings,
           labels=movements.index.values,
           leaf_rotation=90,
           leaf_font_size=8)
plt.show()
```

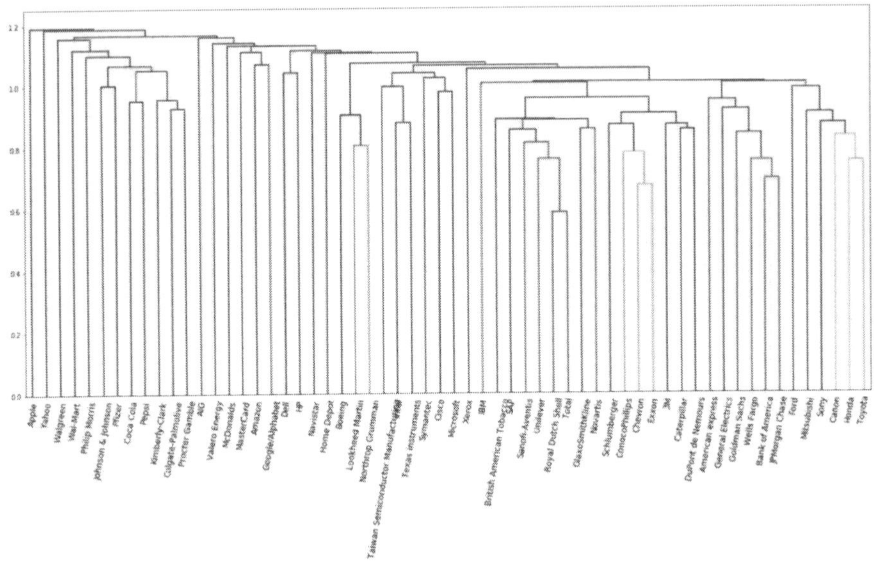

6.3. Principal Component Analysis

6.3.1. PCA Intuition

Finally, we have reached our last, but not least, traditional machine learning algorithm in this eBook.

If you remember, throughout our journey so far, we have come across many datasets which contained dependent features. Sometimes, it was easy to perform feature selection by hand after calculating some summary statistics. However, on many occasions, this was a really hard task. We said back then that we would see an unsupervised machine learning algorithm that was developed just for this specific-use case.

The time has come to discuss this algorithm, which is called principal component analysis. The goal of this algorithm is to find the features which have the highest variance, and thus, we can perform feature extraction instead of the manual feature selection.

So, suppose that we have ten features in our dataset, and they are highly correlated. PCA transforms these ten features into two features, for example, depending on your choice, where these two features construct a linear combination of the original ten features. Thus, our new feature space contains features which are not in the dataset itself, but rather a combination of the dataset's features.

Now, our feature space is only 2D instead of 10D. The first dimension, also called the first principal component or the first basis vector, points in the direction of the data with the maximum variance. The second dimension, which is also called the second principal component or the second basis vector, points in the direction of the data with the second maximum variance, and so on.

The following equation is used to formulate the PCA problem.

$$Z_i = \sum_{j=1}^{n} w_{ij} X_j$$

Where the basis vectors are Z, we can calculate Z_1 as follows:

$$Z_1 = w_{11}X_1 + w_{12}X_2 + w_{13}X_3 + \cdots + w_{1n}X_n$$

The mathematics behind the calculation of these principal components is pretty complex and out of the scope of this eBook. However, if you are interested, we can point out the steps needed to do so.

The first step is to subtract the mean of the data, and preferably standardize the data. Then, we calculate the covariance matrix, which is the variance between the different variables structured into a matrix. After that, we calculate the eigenvalues and the eigenvectors of the covariance matrix, which is pure linear algebra. Following that, we construct the transformation matrix w_{ij} with the rows being the eigenvectors that correspond to the k largest eigenvalues, where these eigenvectors represent our new basis vectors.

You do not really need to worry about all of this. Instead, you should only now that PCA is used for dimensionality reduction and can be combined with any unsupervised or supervised machine learning algorithm to speed up the training without sacrificing the accuracy. The other thing you have to worry about is how to implement PCA using Python, which we will tackle in the final section of this chapter.

6.3.2. PCA Pros and Cons

As we have just said, PCA can reduce the training time tremendously while also preserving the model performance. Also, it can be used as a preprocessing step with any machine learning algorithm without any restrictions. Moreover, it can provide us with useful insights into the data itself. For example, we might have two totally dependent features, but we cannot really notice them because the dataset contains dozens of features. Using PCA, we can eliminate one of them from our data.

The only thing that you need to consider while using PCA is that normalization is a must. Other than that, PCA is a very powerful tool in your hand.

6.3.3. PCA in Python

The first step is, as usual, to import the libraries and fix the path.

```
import numpy as np
import pandas as pd
import os
import matplotlib.pyplot as plt
from scipy.stats import pearsonr
from sklearn.decomposition import PCA
from sklearn.preprocessing import StandardScaler
from sklearn.pipeline import make_pipeline
import matplotlib.pyplot as plt
```

```
os.chdir("D:")
os.getcwd()
```

We then import and plot our dataset, which contains only the width and the length of the grains.

```
grains=pd.read_csv('grains.csv',header=None)
```

```
width = grains.loc[:,0]
length = grains.loc[:,1]
plt.scatter(width, length)
plt.axis('equal')
plt.show()
```

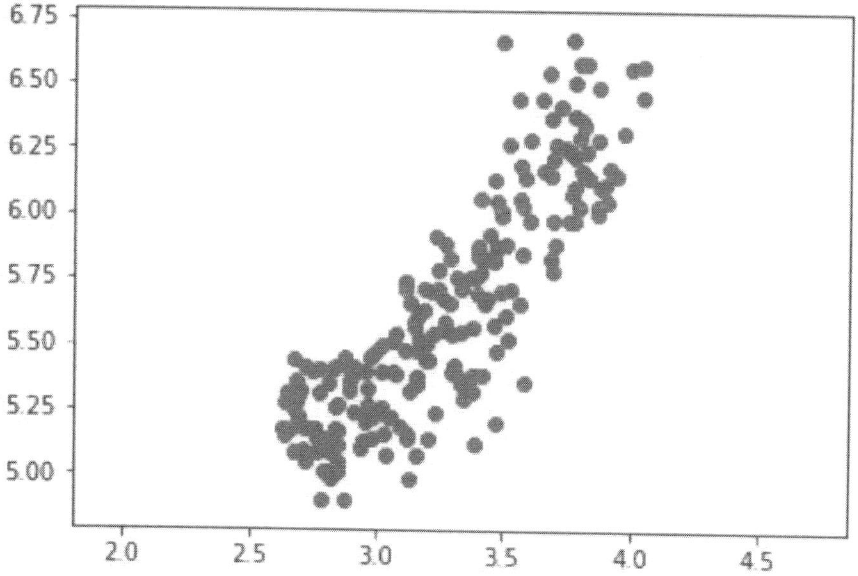

Following that, we calculate the correlation between these two features. By doing so, we find that they are highly correlated.

```
correlation, pvalue = pearsonr(width, length)
print(correlation)
```

```
0.8604149377143467
```

Thus, we create our PCA model and fit it into our dataset.

```
model = PCA()
pca_features = model.fit_transform(grains)
```

We can now plot our transformed features and observe that they are not correlated.

```
xs = pca_features[:,0]
ys = pca_features[:,1]
plt.scatter(xs, ys)
plt.axis('equal')
plt.show()
```

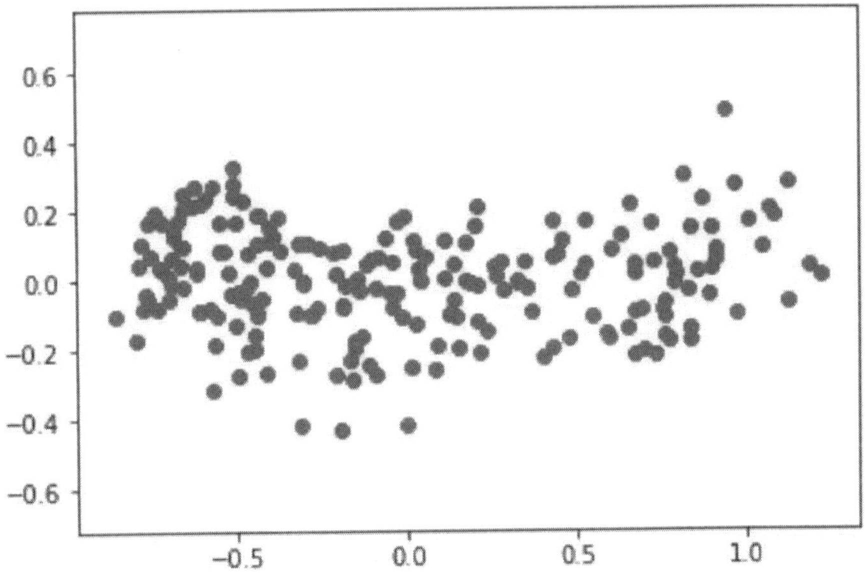

We can make sure of that by calculating the correlation again, but now using the transformed features. We see that they are not correlated at all.

```
correlation, pvalue = pearsonr(xs, ys)
print(correlation)
```

```
1.7440856098723766e-16
```

Then, we can do the same again but with the addition of plotting the basis vectors that we explained earlier on in the original dataset plot.

```
plt.scatter(grains.loc[:,0], grains.loc[:,1])
model = PCA()
model.fit(grains)
mean = model.mean_
first_pc = model.components_[0,:]
second_pc = model.components_[1,:]
plt.arrow(mean[0], mean[1], first_pc[0], first_pc[1], color='red', width=0.01)
plt.arrow(mean[0], mean[1], second_pc[0], second_pc[1], color='green', width=0.01)
plt.axis('equal')
plt.show()
```

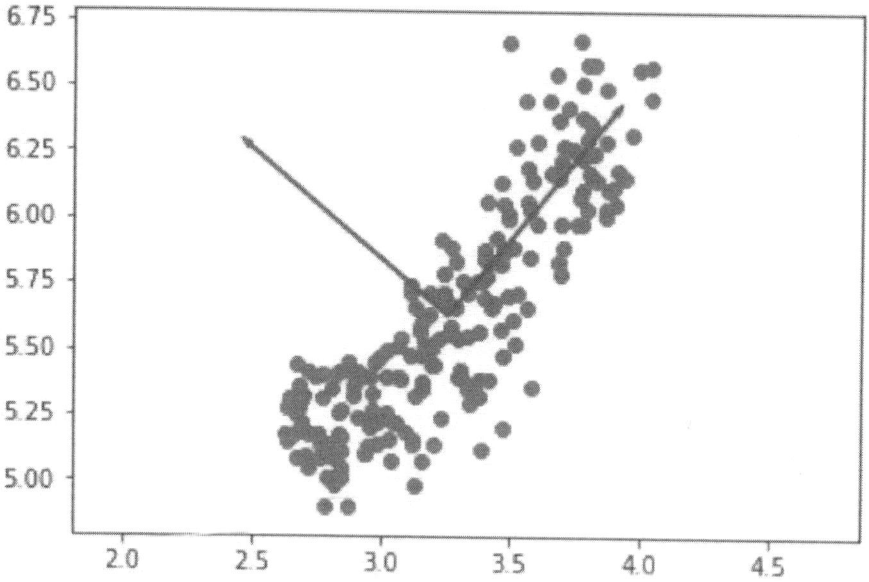

Now, let's do one more exercise using the fish dataset, which contains five features and one output column corresponding to the fish species.

```
df=pd.read_csv('fish.csv',header=None)
samples=df.loc[:,1:]
species=df.loc[:,0]
```

We make a pipeline which performs the normalization and the fitting in one step.

```
scaler = StandardScaler()
pca = PCA()
pipeline = make_pipeline(scaler,pca)
pipeline.fit(samples)
```

Finally, we can plot the variances explained by each feature.

```
features = range(pca.n_components_)
plt.bar(features, pca.explained_variance_)
plt.xlabel('PCA feature')
plt.ylabel('variance')
plt.xticks(features)
plt.show()
```

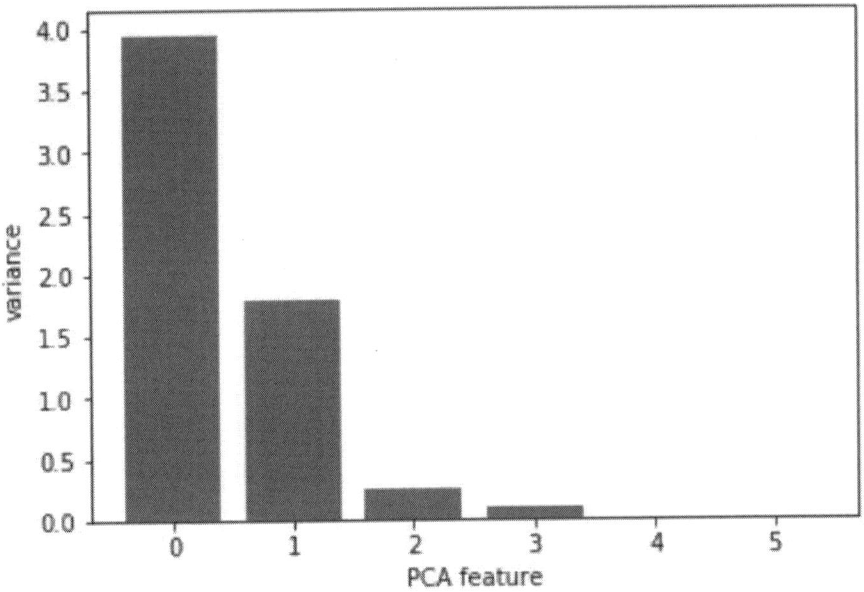

As we can see, we can use only the first four PCA features, and we will not lose any information at all or use only the first two PCA features, and we will lose a little bit of the variance.

7

Neural Networks and Deep Learning

By now, you should have a solid understanding of all supervised and unsupervised learning algorithms. There is only one branch of machine learning, reinforcement learning left, which we will explore in the following chapter.

In this chapter, we will focus on neural networks and go into deep learning from there. Neural Network is considered a supervised machine learning algorithm like linear regression and SVM. However, we are dedicating a whole chapter to it.

So, you might be asking why we did not treat neural network as all the other supervised learning algorithms and cover it in chapter 5. Simply, because neural networks became powerful in the last few years, and there are dozens and even hundreds of use cases for this specific algorithm, and you will have the chance to write code for a few of them by the end of this chapter.

We will start with an introduction to neural networks and machine learning, in which we will discuss the factors that led to the current success of deep learning and neural networks and then define what is meant by deep learning.

After that, we will have a whole section on Artificial Neural Networks -ANN- where we will dive into the details of this brilliant algorithm and see how we can implement it using Python and different frameworks such as Keras.

Finally, we will discuss one of the most successful variations of ANN which is Convolutional Neural Networks -CNN- that is currently deployed and used all over the world in different fields but especially in face detection and recognition. As always, we will dive into the details by working on hands-on projects.

7.1. Neural Networks Introduction

7.1.1. Reasons for Neural Networks Success

It might be obvious to you, when after finishing this chapter, why neural networks outperform any other supervised machine learning algorithm in many scenarios. However, a few years ago, this was not the case, and neural networks were usually suppressed by SVM and other algorithms. So, we'll now discuss the three main reasons that lead to this dramatic change.

The first reason is the availability of the data nowadays, which the neural networks' algorithms depend on heavily. By having this massive amount of data, the capacity of the model can increase safely without worrying that much about overfitting as before. Of course, it is still a burden, but not as before.

The second reason for this massive success is the availability of better hardware, especially the graphics processing unit -GPU- which is used for performing all the training. This was really important for neural networks to succeed because until a few years ago, the training process of neural networks would take days and even months to finish, which made people shift to other faster algorithms. But currently, using the light-speed GPUs, these days and months can be shortened to minutes and even seconds.

Finally, the third reason is the introduction of better and improved algorithms for training and preprocessing the data. We will explore most of these algorithms throughout the chapter, and you will know by then how valuable these modified algorithms are and to which extent they helped in making the neural networks and the deep learning success massively.

7.1.2. What is Deep Learning?

Before we start diving into the details of neural networks, let us take a moment to define what is meant by deep learning. I assume that as you've reached this chapter, and you are interested in being a machine learning expert that you've heard about deep learning before.

Deep learning is considered as a subfield of machine learning, which is based on neural networks, but it uses dozens and hundreds of complex non-linear layers; hence, it is called "deep".

The following figure visualizes both the simple neural network and the deep neural network.

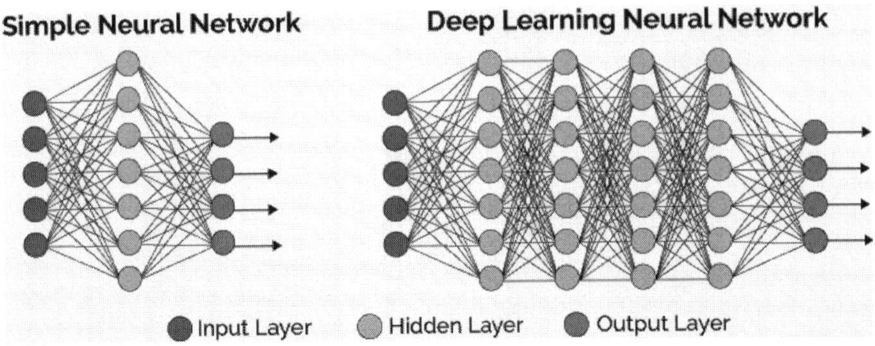

Don't be confused by the connections, the arrows, and the words under the figures. Everything will be clear in the following sections.

However, the takeaway from these figures is that deep neural networks are very complex. In fact, they were developed as a way to mimic the human brain and thus reach the real intelligence.

Although we have even surpassed human performance on some tasks such as image and voice recognition using deep learning, there are still many challenges that face deep learning that are tackled from research worldwide, right now. Also, there's a huge capacity for innovation and design with deep learning, so it is your time to shine after finishing this chapter.

7.2. Artificial Neural Networks

7.2.1. How do Neural Networks Work?

Let's now talk more technically and learn how neural networks actually work.

There are two main steps that are performed in the neural networks' vanilla algorithm, and they are the same for all the variations of ANN like CNN or Recurrent Neural Networks

-RNN-. So, by understanding these two steps, you can confidently say that you understand how all neural networks work, no matter how complex they seem at first glance.

The first step is called forward propagation, and the second one is called backward propagation.

But before we explain what these words mean, let us see why the algorithm was called "neural" networks. Like we mentioned earlier, the people who came up with this algorithm were inspired by how the human brain works and thought about developing an algorithm that mimics the brain-behavior. To do so, they studied the brain structure and designed the algorithm based on that.

In the following figure, we see the structure of the neuron, which is the building block for brain functionality.

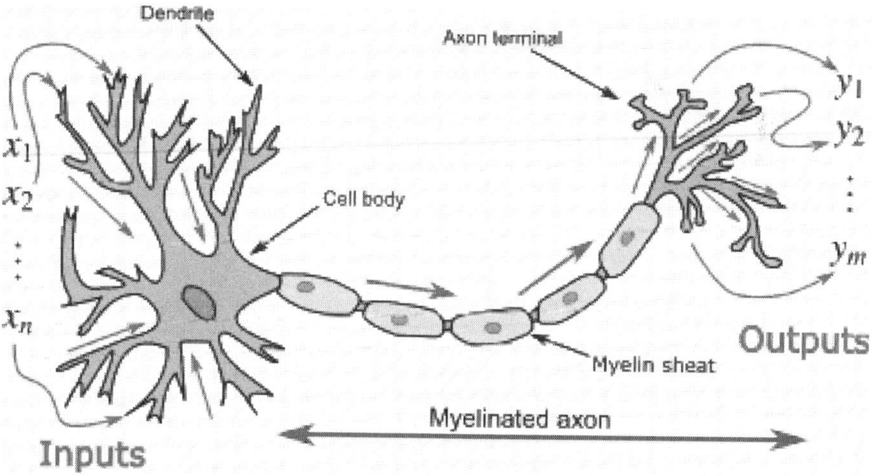

By Egm4313.s12 (Prof. Loc Vu-Quoc) - Own work, CC BY-SA 4.0, https://commons.wikimedia.org/w/index.php?curid=72816083

The input of the neurons is called the Dendrite that is then activated and transformed using the Myelin sheath and then produced as outputs on the Axon terminal.

You can simplify this complex structure to understand what is going on under the hood and then generalize from that. So, to do that, let us revise linear regression, the simplest machine learning algorithm that we tackled. We know by now what is meant by using an activation function such as the sigmoid and the effects of using it. Also, we saw how can take the input, transform it, activate it, and then calculate the prediction using the linear regression equations. This is the simplest forward propagation, which is based on the assumption that we have only one neuron at the input, one neuron in the middle for the activation, and one neuron for calculating the output.

In neural networks, we have "networks" of the linear regression forward propagation. If you think about it this way, it will be much easier for you to understand.

The same with backpropagation, which means calculating the errors based on the predicted outputs compared to the true outputs. Again, you can think about having multiple linear regression gradient descent algorithms running concurrently and parallelly. Concurrently, because you might have more than one neuron stacked together over each other's, so you can do the calculations of different neurons at the same time without any one affecting the others. We call these stacked neurons a layer of neurons or a layer for short. Parallelly, because you might have more than one layer, so the output of layer calculations will affect the output of the previous layer's calculations.

Finally, we call anything between the input layer and the output layer, the hidden layers. By increasing the number of hidden layers, we would have a deep neural network as we will see shortly.

7.2.2. The Activation Functions

If you studied chapter 6 well, then you already know what is meant by an activation function, which is a function used to make our transformation from the input to the output nonlinear.

We talked back then about only one activation function, the sigmoid function, as it was used in logistic regression. The mapping of the sigmoid function is shown in the following figure.

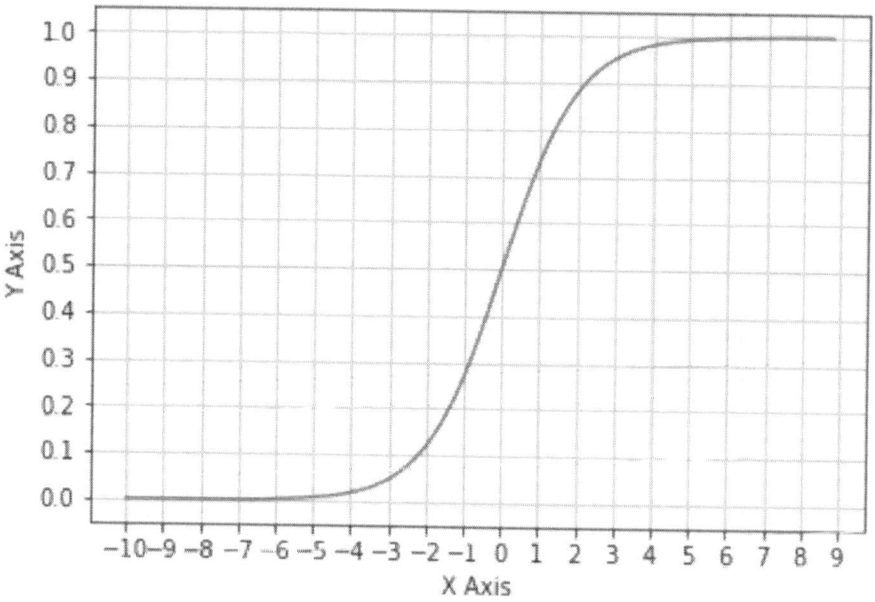

Now, let us introduce other activation functions which are frequently used in neural networks. We have the ReLU activation function which is short for Rectified Linear Unit. Its mapping is shown in the following figure.

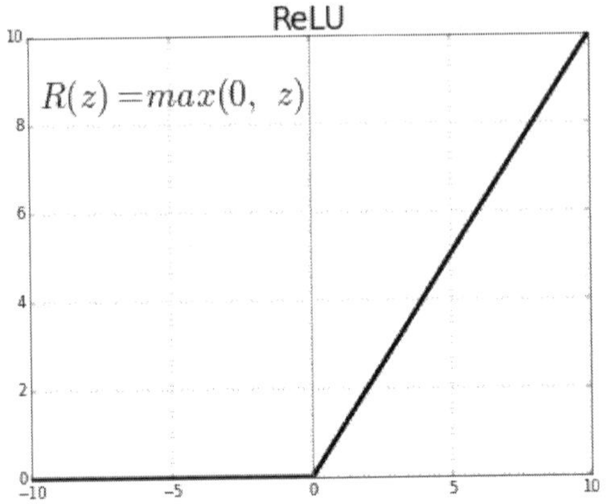

I know that you are now wondering why we might need another activation function if the sigmoid works just fine. The answer is that it does not in many scenarios.

Given that we use gradient descent for backpropagation, we need to calculate the derivative of the output after the activation function. Mathematically, the sigmoid function performs terribly when the input is more than positive one or less than negative one and is nearly zero. We did not suffer from that or notice it while working with logistic regression because we scaled our input to be in the range of -1 and 1 before feeding it to the sigmoid. But now, we cannot do this, because even if we manage to do so for the first layer, then the outputs from it will need scaling again and with the following layers.

In deep learning, this is impractical and time-consuming. Thus, we use the ReLU activation function as it does not suffer from this saturation problem.

However, it has two problems. The first one is that it cannot be interpreted at the final output. The solution is to use ReLU for all the hidden layers and then use a sigmoid function for the final output layer.

The second problem is that the inputs must be all positive, or they will be mapped to 0. There are two solutions for this problem. The first one is to calculate the absolute of the numbers that are fed to the ReLU before each layer. This solution, of course, is not the best one as it requires more preprocessing.

The second solution is to use a modified version of the ReLU which is the leaky ReLU. The graph for this function is shown below.

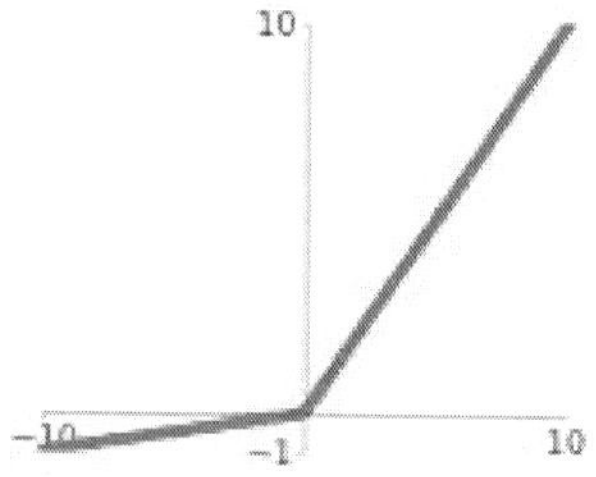

Leaky ReLU

$$f(x) = \max(0.01x, x)$$

We know that the sigmoid function is used for binary classification problems, but if we have a multiple classification problem, then we need another activation function, which is the SoftMax function. This function is simply a normalized average of the sigmoid function.

Finally, we have the tanh activation function, which is also a modified version of the sigmoid function.

In summary, we usually use ReLU or Leaky ReLU for the hidden layers, and a sigmoid/SoftMax/tanh for the output layer depending on whether we have a binary classification problem or not. Of course, there are many other different functions, but they are not used as frequently as the ones that we've discussed. However, you should always experiment with different functions while working on a project because it is an iterative and explorative process.

7.2.3. Numerical Example

Given that we now know how the neural networks work theoretically, it would be fantastic if we could test our understanding by working with a numerical example.

We have our simple neural network below which contains only two inputs which are i1 and i2, one hidden layer consisting of two neurons h1 and h2, and an output layer containing one neuron "out". Also, we divided the neurons of both the hidden layer and the output layer into two parts which are the input to the neuron "i" and the output of the same neuron after activation "o".

So, the first step is to initialize the weights "w1, w2, w3, w4, w5, w6" with random numbers. Let us assume that we did so, and we have the following weights.

w1 = 0.15, w2 = 0.2, w3 = 0.25, w4 = 0.3, w5 = 0.4, and w6 = 0.5

Also, assume that we have the input and the output as follows:

I1 = 0.05, i2 = 0.1, out_o = 0.7

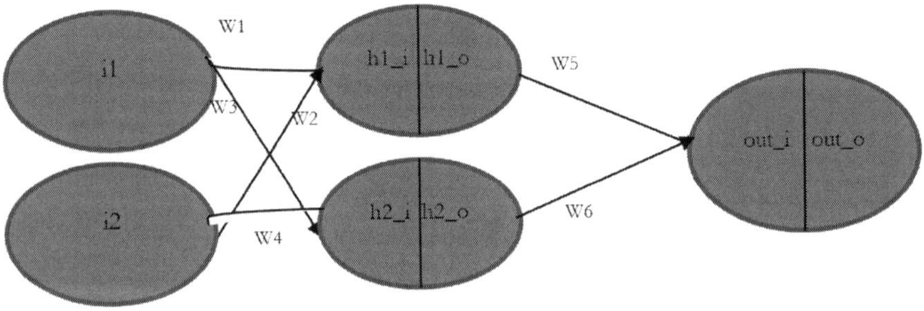

So, let us start the forward propagation calculations.

$$h1_i = i1 * w1 + i2 * w2$$

$$h1_i = 0.05 * 0.15 + 0.1 * 0.2 = 0.0275$$

$$h1_o = sigmoid(h1_i)$$

$$h1_o = sigmoid(0.0275) = 0.5$$

$$h2_i = 0.05 * 0.25 + 0.1 * 0.3 = 0.0425$$

$$h2_o = sigmoid(h2_i)$$

$$h2_o = sigmoid(0.0425) = 0.51$$

$$out_i = 0.5 * 0.4 + 0.51 * 0.5 = 0.455$$

$$out_o = sigmoid(out_i)$$

$$out_o = sigmoid(0.455) = 0.61$$

And that is it for forward propagation!

Now, for backpropagation, we will use the squared error function along with gradient descent for optimization.

$$Error = \sum \frac{1}{2}(target - output)^2$$

$$Error = \frac{1}{2}(0.7 - 0.61)^2 = 0.0081$$

Now, to perform the gradient descent step mathematically, you need to have a background in multivariable calculus and partial derivatives. We are finding the derivative each time with respect to only one variable as we now have more than one, unlike in logistic regression. The key concept that you need to look up is the chain-rule of calculus. By using it, we can write the derivative of the error as following.

$$\frac{\partial E}{\partial w5} = \frac{\partial E}{\partial out_o} * \frac{\partial out_o}{\partial out_i} * \frac{\partial out_i}{\partial w5}$$

So, we are getting the derivative by multiplying the derivatives backward. Now, let us calculate each of the three derivatives.

$$\frac{\partial E}{\partial out_o} = 2 * \frac{1}{2} * (target - out_o)^{2-1} = 0.7 - 0.61 = 0.09$$

Now, for $\frac{\partial out_o}{\partial out_i}$, it is the partial derivative of the sigmoid with respect to the input of the output neuron, which has the following formula:

$$\frac{\partial out_o}{\partial out_i} = out_o(1 - out_o)$$

$$\frac{\partial out_o}{\partial out_i} = 0.61(1 - 0.61) = 0.24$$

$$\frac{\partial out_i}{\partial w5} = h1_o = 0.5$$

$$\frac{\partial E}{\partial w5} = 0.09 * 0.24 * 0.5 = 0.01$$

Finally, we update the weights using the following equation, where $\alpha = 0.001$ which is the learning rate.

$$w5 = w5 - \alpha \frac{\partial E}{\partial w5} = 0.4 - 0.001 * 0.01 = 0.399$$

The same calculations can be done with all the other weights.

And that is! You now know how neural networks work both in concept and in theory. The final thing that you need to know is how to use neural networks in a hands-on project, which is the topic of the following section.

7.2.4. ANN in Python

Now, let's see how to utilize neural networks in a hands-on project. We will do so in two ways. The first one is by using a high-level but widely used framework called Keras, which does not require performing the algorithm's steps explicitly as it takes care of all the calculations.

The second way is by using another powerful but more low-level framework called TensorFlow, which will require us to define the forward propagation algorithm explicitly but takes care of the backward propagation.

So, let us start by importing all the libraries that we will use in this section.

```
from keras import models
from keras import layers
from keras.datasets import mnist
from keras.utils import to_categorical
import tensorflow as tf
from tensorflow.examples.tutorials.mnist import input_data
import warnings
warnings.filterwarnings("ignore")
```

Now, let us load the dataset that we will use for this project, which is a famous dataset consisting of 70,000 images of numbers from 0 to 9. So, our task is a multi-classification one.

```
(train_images, train_labels), (test_images, test_labels) = mnist.load_data()
```

Then, we print the shape of the train and test images to understand the structure of the dataset better.

```
print(train_images.shape)
print(test_images.shape)
```

```
(60000, 28, 28)
(10000, 28, 28)
```

```
train_images = train_images.reshape((60000, 28 * 28))
train_images = train_images.astype('float32') / 255
test_images = test_images.reshape((10000, 28 * 28))
test_images = test_images.astype('float32') / 255
```

After that, we perform basic preprocessing as we reshape the images, so each image is represented by a (28*28) vector and normalized.

```
train_labels = to_categorical(train_labels)
test_labels = to_categorical(test_labels)
```

Then, given that it is a multi-classification problem, we need to convert the labels into categorical labels.

Now, we define our neural network model, by first using the sequential method as our neural network is sequential by nature. Then, we add one hidden layer consisting of 512 neurons and has a ReLU activation function. Finally, we add an output layer consisting of ten neurons corresponding to the ten classes that we have and has a SoftMax activation function, as we discussed earlier.

```
network = models.Sequential()
network.add(layers.Dense(512, activation='relu', input_shape=(28 * 28,)))
network.add(layers.Dense(10, activation='softmax'))
```

Following that, we compile our model as we define the loss to be the categorical cross-entropy that we used in decision trees, the metric to be accuracy, and we use a modified version of the gradient descent called the RMSprop optimizer. You can check the documentation of Keras and experiment with the other different optimizers.

```
network.compile(optimizer='rmsprop',loss='categorical_crossentropy',metrics=['accuracy'])
```

Then, we train our neural network in a single line of code bypassing the input, the labels, the number of iterations which is also called the epochs, and the batch size. We need the batch size as we can not fit the whole dataset in the memory at once as we did with other algorithms because the dataset is much bigger. Thus, we use a modified version of the gradient descent by training on only one batch, getting the output, and then on the following batch until we reach the end of the dataset.

```
network.fit(train_images, train_labels, epochs=5, batch_size=128)
```

```
Epoch 1/5
60000/60000 [==============================] - 6s 105us/step - loss: 0.2566 - acc: 0.9259
Epoch 2/5
60000/60000 [==============================] - 2s 36us/step - loss: 0.1029 - acc: 0.9691
Epoch 3/5
60000/60000 [==============================] - 2s 36us/step - loss: 0.0677 - acc: 0.9798
Epoch 4/5
60000/60000 [==============================] - 2s 36us/step - loss: 0.0493 - acc: 0.9855
Epoch 5/5
60000/60000 [==============================] - 2s 37us/step - loss: 0.0369 - acc: 0.9890
```

After that, we evaluate our neural network performance.

```
test_loss, test_acc = network.evaluate(test_images, test_labels)
```

```
10000/10000 [==============================] - 1s 52us/step
```

```
print('test_acc:', test_acc)
```

```
test_acc: 0.9782
```

We got 97.8% accuracy, which we could not reach using any other algorithm.

Now, let us do the same task but using TensorFlow.

The first step is to load the dataset using the following method.

```
mnist = input_data.read_data_sets("MNIST data/", one_hot=True)
```

Then, we define all the hyperparameters that we will use in the project. The dropout is a trick used extensively in deep neural networks to avoid overfitting. The trick is to drop a random number of neurons or shut them down at each iteration, so the model is forced to learn using all neurons. It then has a higher chance of learning the correct function instead of relying only on a subset of neurons.

```
learning_rate = 1e-4
n_iterations = 1000
batch_size = 128
dropout = 0.5
```

After that, we split our dataset.

```
n_train = mnist.train.num_examples
n_validation = mnist.validation.num_examples
n_test = mnist.test.num_examples
```

We then define the layers' dimensions as we will use three hidden layers instead of one in Keras.

```
n_input = 784  # input layer (28x28 pixels)
n_hidden1 = 512  # 1st hidden layer
n_hidden2 = 256  # 2nd hidden layer
n_hidden3 = 128  # 3rd hidden layer
n_output = 10  # output layer (0-9 digits)
```

To perform any calculations using TensorFlow, all the variables need to be stored in something called a placeholder.

```
X = tf.placeholder("float", [None, n_input])
Y = tf.placeholder("float", [None, n_output])
keep_prob = tf.placeholder(tf.float32)
```

Following that, we create a dictionary of weights and biases as we calculate them ourselves because TensorFlow performs only the back-propagation step automatically.

```
weights = {
    'w1': tf.Variable(tf.truncated_normal([n_input, n_hidden1], stddev=0.1)),
    'w2': tf.Variable(tf.truncated_normal([n_hidden1, n_hidden2], stddev=0.1)),
    'w3': tf.Variable(tf.truncated_normal([n_hidden2, n_hidden3], stddev=0.1)),
    'out': tf.Variable(tf.truncated_normal([n_hidden3, n_output], stddev=0.1)),
}
biases = {
    'b1': tf.Variable(tf.constant(0.1, shape=[n_hidden1])),
    'b2': tf.Variable(tf.constant(0.1, shape=[n_hidden2])),
    'b3': tf.Variable(tf.constant(0.1, shape=[n_hidden3])),
    'out': tf.Variable(tf.constant(0.1, shape=[n_output]))
}
```

Now, we perform the forward propagation ourselves.

```
layer_1 = tf.add(tf.matmul(X, weights['w1']), biases['b1'])
layer_2 = tf.add(tf.matmul(layer_1, weights['w2']), biases['b2'])
layer_3 = tf.add(tf.matmul(layer_2, weights['w3']), biases['b3'])
layer_drop = tf.nn.dropout(layer_3, keep_prob)
output_layer = tf.matmul(layer_3, weights['out']) + biases['out']
```

Also, we define the error function and the accuracy metric.

```
cross_entropy = tf.reduce_mean(
    tf.nn.softmax_cross_entropy_with_logits(
        labels=Y, logits=output_layer
        ))
train_step = tf.train.AdamOptimizer(1e-4).minimize(cross_entropy)
```

```
correct_pred = tf.equal(tf.argmax(output_layer, 1), tf.argmax(Y, 1))
accuracy = tf.reduce_mean(tf.cast(correct_pred, tf.float32))
```

Then, we train the neural network by initializing the TensorFlow session and running it.

```
init = tf.global_variables_initializer()
sess = tf.Session()
sess.run(init)
```

Finally, we train our model and print the accuracy after every 100 iterations.

```
for i in range(n_iterations):
    batch_x, batch_y = mnist.train.next_batch(batch_size)
    sess.run(train_step, feed_dict={
        X: batch_x, Y: batch_y, keep_prob: dropout
        })

    # print loss and accuracy (per minibatch)
    if i % 100 == 0:
        minibatch_loss, minibatch_accuracy = sess.run(
            [cross_entropy, accuracy],
            feed_dict={X: batch_x, Y: batch_y, keep_prob: 1.0}
            )
        print(
            "Iteration",
            str(i),
            "\t| Loss =",
            str(minibatch_loss),
            "\t| Accuracy =",
            str(minibatch_accuracy)
            )
```

```
Iteration 0      | Loss = 3.1347618    | Accuracy = 0.1640625
Iteration 100    | Loss = 0.49795306   | Accuracy = 0.859375
Iteration 200    | Loss = 0.37250668   | Accuracy = 0.8828125
Iteration 300    | Loss = 0.46936858   | Accuracy = 0.8515625
Iteration 400    | Loss = 0.28120446   | Accuracy = 0.921875
Iteration 500    | Loss = 0.35168704   | Accuracy = 0.921875
Iteration 600    | Loss = 0.40933585   | Accuracy = 0.90625
Iteration 700    | Loss = 0.29759502   | Accuracy = 0.921875
Iteration 800    | Loss = 0.4011727    | Accuracy = 0.90625
Iteration 900    | Loss = 0.22333686   | Accuracy = 0.9375
```

As we see, the maximum accuracy that we reached is 93.75% with three hidden layers compared to 98.7% with only one hidden layer that we got earlier.

You are highly advised to experiment and hyper-tune this neural network yourself to obtain even better results.

7.3. Convolution Neural Networks

7.3.1. What is Convolution Neural Networks?

The results that we obtained from using a vanilla neural network in the last section were outstanding compared to the results that we got from other traditional machine learning algorithms.

However, when we noticed that we needed to preprocess the images and convert each one of them into a vector to feed them to the neural network. This would be a problem if we are working with a more complex dataset. That is why we need to modify the neural network algorithm, so it can be used with images out-of-the-box.

That modification results in the convolutional neural network, which was developed by researchers in the field of image processing and computer vision.

Before the rising of deep learning, image processing researchers and developers extracted the features and the patterns from images using a process called the convolution, which we will discuss in the next section. However, there were many limitations that these methods faced, so they needed a more intelligent way to extract the features from the images.

Then, after the promising results that the deep learning algorithms showed, they integrated the convolution operation with the deep neural networks to get the best of both worlds.

7.3.2. What is the Convolution Operation?

Before we discuss what the convolution operation is, we need to understand how images are stored in the memory. The color images that you see on your mobile phone or your computer are stored in an RGB matrix, which consists of three 2D matrices for red, green, and blue versions of the image as shown below.

Now, given that we know scientifically what is meant by an image let's explore the convolution operation.

Suppose that we want to detect the edges in any picture, the first thing that comes to your mind is to multiply the image by some other image that would help us extract the edges from the first images.

That is correct, but the problem is that it is infeasible, because the images consist of millions of pixels, and, we would need a different detector image each time.

So, the other way to do so is to use a small-sized filter that is multiplied by each region in the image to extract the needed features.

That is exactly why the convolution operation was invented to filter the images in a smart and efficient way. The following filter is widely used in the image processing field to detect edges.

1	0	-1
1	0	-1
1	0	-1

Suppose we have an image which is gray-level, so it has only one 2D matrix as follows:

3	0	1	2	7	4
1	5	8	9	3	1
2	7	2	5	1	3
0	1	3	1	7	8
4	2	1	6	2	8
2	4	5	2	3	9

Now, to perform the convolution operation, we multiply the first window of the image by the filter element-wise and sum up the output.

1	0	-1
1	0	-1
1	0	-1

*

3	0	1
1	5	8
2	7	2

The result would be

$$(1 * 3) + (0 * 0) * (1 * -1) + (1 * 1) + (0 * 5) + (8 * -1) + (1 * 2) + (0 * 7) + (2 * -1) = -5$$

Thus, the output image will have a value of -5 at its first entry.

Then, we repeat the same process after sliding the window that we convolve the filter with.

1	0	-1
1	0	-1
1	0	-1

0	1	2
5	8	9
7	2	5

*

The final output image will have the following values:

-5	-4	0	8
-10	-2	2	3
0	-2	-4	-7
-3	-2	-3	-16

By doing so, we have the output image which contains the detected features.

However, the filter that we convolved our input image with contained specific numbers, which was fine for detecting simple edges. But, if we want to extract more complex features like the eyes or the faces in the images, then we need much more complex filters, and we need many and not just one.

Therefore, the idea was to treat the numbers in the filters as weights which are found using a neural network and can be stacked using multiple neurons and multiple layers. By that, we have the convolution neural network.

7.3.3. Padding Layer

Let us now discuss another important layer, the padding layer, which is found in any CNN architecture.

The padding layer is always used before the filter layer, and it does not have any parameters or trainable weights. Basically, it is used to preserve the dimensions of the input image.

In the last example, we saw that the output image dimensions were four and four, while the input image dimensions were six and six. This can be a huge problem if we are doing the convolution operation multiple times, which we do with deep convolutional neural networks. Thus, the use of the padding layer is crucial.

7.3.4. Pooling Layer

Another very powerful layer, which also does not have any parameters, is the pooling layer. The idea behind this layer is to reduce the number of parameters, as the images consist of millions of values while also preserving the information that we got from the filters.

Max pooling and average pooling are two widely used ways to represent the pooling layer.

The first one is shown in the following figure.

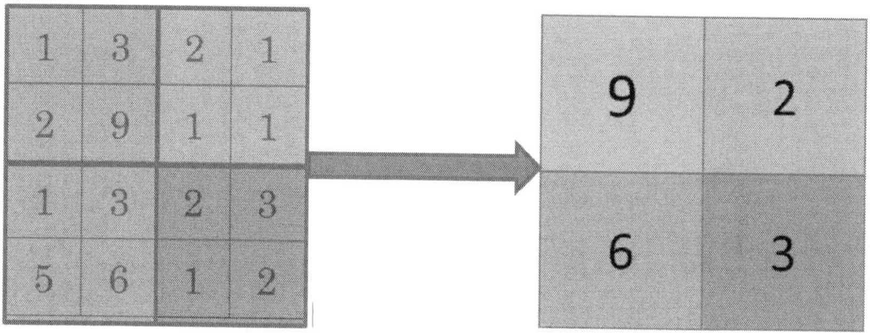

On the other hand, the average pooling is done as follows:

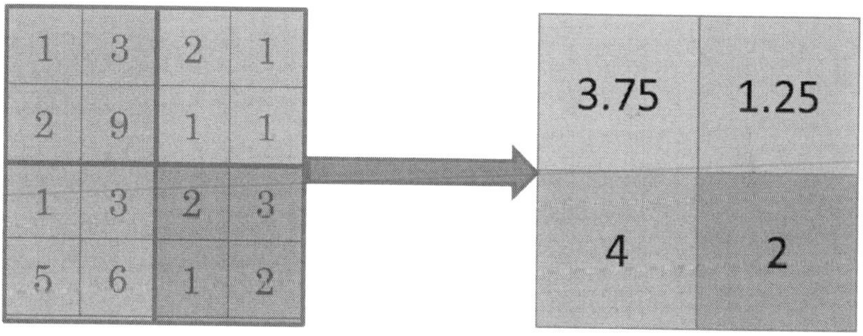

Flattening and Fully Connected Layers

Finally, we should have a fully connected layer at the end of the neural network in order to combine all the different functions that were formulated from the neural network so far. It isn't always necessary or preferred because it may make the model more vulnerable to overfitting. Following that, we have a flattening layer which converts the output into a vector column as we did in the preprocessing step in the neural network project.

7.3.5. CNN Traditional Structure

Although it is highly recommended that you experiment with different architectures, there are some tips and tricks for constructing your CNN. We start the network with a padding layer combined with a convolutional layer which consists of a small number of neurons such as sixteen or thirty-two. These two layers are followed usually by a pooling layer, either maximum pooling or average pooling.

People frequently consider these three layers as one layer, and, this is true for Keras, which we will use in the following section.

However, note that these three layers, which can be considered as a single layer, are repeated many times while the number of neurons increase each time. This is done until the model is not underfitting and before it starts overfitting.

Finally, the CNN would have a fully connected layer and/or a flattening layer.

As we discussed earlier, all the activation functions that use the middle are ReLU, and the final activation function for the outputs is tanh, sigmoid or SoftMax.

7.3.6. CNN in Python

Now, let us see how we can write a Python code for the same image classification task that we did before but using CNN.

We start, as before, by importing the needed libraries, loading the dataset, and preprocessing it.

```
from keras import layers
from keras import models
from keras.datasets import mnist
from keras.utils import to_categorical
```

```
(train_images, train_labels), (test_images, test_labels) = mnist.load_data()
```

```
train_images = train_images.reshape((60000, 28, 28, 1))
train_images = train_images.astype('float32') / 255
test_images = test_images.reshape((10000, 28, 28, 1))
test_images = test_images.astype('float32') / 255
train_labels = to_categorical(train_labels)
test_labels = to_categorical(test_labels)
```

Then, we define our CNN model. Here, we use the Conv2D layer from keras with thirty-two neurons in the first layer and with a filter size of three by three. Also, we notice that the first Conv2D layer has a padding = same while the second one has a padding = valid. The valid padding is equivalent to no padding at all, while the same padding means that the output size of this layer should equal the input size.

So basically, we use padding, convolutional layer with a ReLU activation and max-pooling layer for a few times. If we repeat this too many times, then the model will overfit.

```
model = models.Sequential()
model.add(layers.Conv2D(32, (3, 3), activation='relu',padding ='same', input_shape=(28, 28, 1)))
model.add(layers.MaxPooling2D((2, 2)))
model.add(layers.Conv2D(64, (3, 3), activation='relu', padding = 'valid'))
model.add(layers.MaxPooling2D((2, 2)))
model.add(layers.Conv2D(64, (3, 3), activation='relu'))
```

We can see all the layers names, parameters and shapes using the summary function.

```
model.summary()
```

```
_________________________________________________________________
Layer (type)                 Output Shape              Param #   
=================================================================
conv2d_8 (Conv2D)            (None, 28, 28, 32)        320       
_________________________________________________________________
max_pooling2d_5 (MaxPooling2 (None, 14, 14, 32)        0         
_________________________________________________________________
conv2d_9 (Conv2D)            (None, 12, 12, 64)        18496     
_________________________________________________________________
max_pooling2d_6 (MaxPooling2 (None, 6, 6, 64)          0         
_________________________________________________________________
conv2d_10 (Conv2D)           (None, 4, 4, 64)          36928     
=================================================================
Total params: 55,744
Trainable params: 55,744
Non-trainable params: 0
_________________________________________________________________
```

Finally, we add a flatten layer along with two fully connected layers. The final fully connected layer should have several neurons equal to the number of classes that we want to classify along with a SoftMax activation function.

```
model.add(layers.Flatten())
model.add(layers.Dense(64, activation='relu'))
model.add(layers.Dense(10, activation='softmax'))
```

```
_________________________________________________________________
Layer (type)                 Output Shape              Param #   
=================================================================
conv2d_1 (Conv2D)            (None, 26, 26, 32)        320       
_________________________________________________________________
max_pooling2d_1 (MaxPooling2 (None, 13, 13, 32)        0         
_________________________________________________________________
conv2d_2 (Conv2D)            (None, 11, 11, 64)        18496     
_________________________________________________________________
max_pooling2d_2 (MaxPooling2 (None, 5, 5, 64)          0         
_________________________________________________________________
conv2d_3 (Conv2D)            (None, 3, 3, 64)          36928     
_________________________________________________________________
flatten_1 (Flatten)          (None, 576)               0         
_________________________________________________________________
dense_1 (Dense)              (None, 64)                36928     
_________________________________________________________________
dense_2 (Dense)              (None, 10)                650       
=================================================================
Total params: 93,322
Trainable params: 93,322
Non-trainable params: 0
_________________________________________________________________
```

Then, as before, we compile, fit, and evaluate the model.

```
model.compile(optimizer='rmsprop',loss='categorical_crossentropy',metrics=['accuracy'])
```

```
model.fit(train_images, train_labels, epochs=5, batch_size=64)
```

```
Epoch 1/5
60000/60000 [==============================] - 12s 198us/step - loss: 0.1621 - acc: 0.9492
Epoch 2/5
60000/60000 [==============================] - 6s 93us/step - loss: 0.0451 - acc: 0.9858
Epoch 3/5
60000/60000 [==============================] - 6s 94us/step - loss: 0.0323 - acc: 0.9904
Epoch 4/5
60000/60000 [==============================] - 6s 93us/step - loss: 0.0240 - acc: 0.9927
Epoch 5/5
60000/60000 [==============================] - 5s 91us/step - loss: 0.0191 - acc: 0.9940
```

```
test_loss, test_acc = model.evaluate(test_images, test_labels)
```

```
10000/10000 [==============================] - 1s 69us/step
```

```
print('test_acc:', test_acc)
```

```
test_acc: 0.9925
```

We see that we got 99.25% accuracy which is mind-blowing and surpasses even human accuracy!

8

Reinforcement Learning Techniques

Now, the time has come to explore reinforcement learning, the final branch of machine learning. We will start by introducing the reinforcement learning definition, along with the common terminology that we will use throughout the chapter.

Then, we will explore upper confidence bound and Thompson sampling, two widely-used reinforcement learning algorithms. Of course, we will, as always, explain the algorithms theoretically. Then, we will have a hands-on exercise on them.

8.1. Reinforcement Learning Introduction

8.1.1. Reinforcement Learning Definition

Let's start by defining reinforcement learning. Unlike supervised learning, there are no labels or values that we want to predict or classify. Also, unlike unsupervised learning, our target is not to cluster the data or reduce the dimensionality.

Reinforcement Learning is something completely different. Our goal is to teach the "agent" how to perform certain actions in a given environment in order to maximize his reward.

While this might seem vague right now because of the new terminology, it will be clear after the following section.

8.1.2. Reinforcement Learning Elements

Reinforcement Learning was invented as a subfield in psychology, not in computer science. To understand it in-depth, let us take an example.

We'll imagine that you have a dog that you want to train. When you first get the dog or if it is a newborn, it doesn't know anything. Thus, it explores the environment around it by interacting with it and doing actions. If it obeys you and listens to what you are saying, then you reward it with a small snack. If it does something wrong, then you will punish it by delaying its meal by an hour or so. By doing so, you train your dog by giving it positive or negative rewards as a response to its actions with the environment.

In machine learning, reinforcement learning is the same. We are trying to teach the agent, which was the dog, how to interact with the environment. Every time the agent does an action which affects the environment, and the environment responds to this action with a positive or a negative reward, which changes the state of the agent, and so on. You can visualize this more by the following figure.

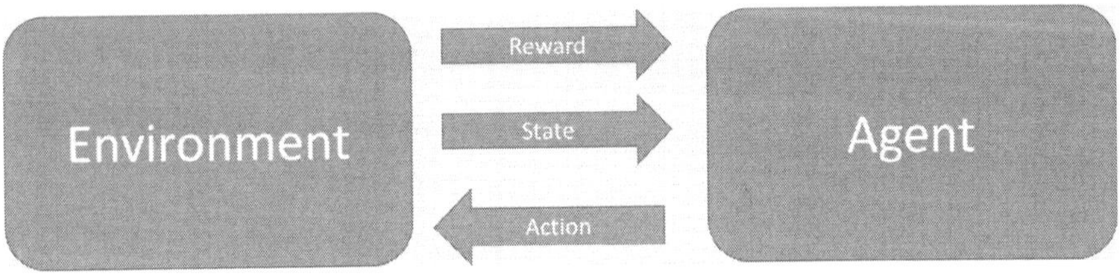

Let us define the reinforcement learning elements once again:

- Agent: Our objective is to make it learn as it performs some action in an environment to get some reward.
- Action: The different interactions that the agent can perform.
- Environment: The virtual scenarios that the agent can tackle.
- Stats: The new position which is a response from the environment.
- Reward: The evaluation from the environment of the action that was taken, either positive or negative.
- Policy: The algorithm or the strategy that the agent uses to select the next action based on the previous reward and the current state.
- Value: The long-term reward

8.1.3. Reinforcement Learning Example

To make sure that we understood everything clearly, let us mention an example of RL used in real-life. Imagine that you want to control a robot's movement so that it can walk without falling or getting stuck. If you treat this as a supervised learning problem, it will be so difficult it cannot be solved practically. So, let us treat it as a reinforcement learning problem.

Here, the agent is the robot's brain, while the environment can be the robot's body, the obstacles around it and the physics constraints. Also, the states would be the joints' angles of the robot, the distance from the next obstacle, the type of the obstacle and so on. Moreover, the actions that the robot's brain can take are the controls and the commands for its joints and limbs. Finally, you can design the reward to be proportional to how much the robot walked without any falling or getting stuck.

This is a very simple, yet practical example of a reinforcement learning use case. In the following three tables, we sum up the differences between supervised learning, unsupervised learning and reinforcement learning.

N	X1	X2	Y
1	155	1	1
2	156	0	0
3	165	0	0
4	948	1	0
5	757	0	1
6	598	1	0
7	901	1	1

N	X1	X2
1	77	54
2	156	77
3	105	100
4	77	14
5	757	55
6	598	78
7	501	91

Step	State	Action	Reward
1	S1	A1	-1
2	S2	A2	0
3	S3	A3	-1
4	S4	A4	0
5	S5	A5	0
6	S6	A6	1
7	S7	A7	0

8.2. Upper Confidence Bound

8.2.1. The Multi-armed Bandit Problem

In this chapter, we will discuss two of the most widely used RL algorithms: the Upper Confidence Bound and the Thompson Sampling. But first, we need to understand the difference between exploration and exploitation, which is a very critical concept.

We will do so by thinking about the multi-armed bandit problem. Imagine that you went to a nightclub in Las Vegas and you see twenty slot machines in a row and every one of them says "Free to play" where the maximum payout is 20$. Given that you know that each slot machine has an average payout which can be different from the other ones, you want to know these averages, so you can maximize your profit.

There are extreme approaches that you might take. The first one is to choose one random machine and play there until the time is over. This is not good because if you're not lucky, the average payout of this machine might not be good, and you will not gain that much money. This is a pure exploitation approach, as you decided to take the safe route.

The other approach is to play on each slot machine for $\frac{1}{20}$ the time. By doing so, you will not gain a very bad profit, but you're also not maximizing it. This is a pure exploration approach.

The trick here is to use a combination of exploration and exploitation, and that is what the following algorithms are addressing.

8.2.2. Upper Confidence Bound Intuition

The first algorithm that we will discuss is the most widely used algorithm to solve the multi-armed bandit problem that we have just explained. It is based on the premise of optimism while facing uncertainty. This means that the more we are not sure about or know about a specific state or "arm", the more it becomes important to explore and tackle.

Suppose that we want to have personalized ads for our website users. In this case, the ads that we display for the users each time they open our website will be the arms d. We will represent each time the user opens the website as round n.

Now, every time the user opens a new website, we display only one ad for him. Thus, we can represent the reward for each ad `i` as follows:

$r_i(n) \in \{0,1\}: r_i(n) = 1 r_i(n) \in \{0,1\}: r_i(n) = 1$ if the user clicked the add and 0 if he did not.

Our objective is to maximize the total reward or the value function as we mentioned earlier.

There are three main steps for the algorithm.

The first one is calculating the sum of rewards R, or the value function, and calculating the number of times the ad `i` was selected N. This should be done in each round, of course.

The second step is to calculate the average reward of ads from the beginning to the current round.

$$\underline{r_i}(n) = \frac{R_i(n)}{N_{i(n)}}$$

Also, we calculate the confidence interval, which is represented by the following equation:

$$[\underline{r_i}(n) - \Delta_i(n), \underline{r_i}(n) + \Delta_i(n)]$$

$$\text{Where } \Delta_i(n) = \sqrt{\frac{3 log\ (n)}{2\ N_i(n)}} \Delta_i(n) = \sqrt{\frac{3 log\ (n)}{2\ N_i(n)}}$$

The third and the final step is to select the ad `i` that has the maximum upper confidence bound $\underline{r_i}(n) + \Delta_i(n)$

By performing these three steps, you can combine both exploration and exploitation to find the best action for each state.

Note that this algorithm is deterministic, which means it gives us results which we can trust without any questioning. But also, it suffers from having to be updated at each round.

8.2.3. Upper Confidence Bound in Python

Now, let us see how we can implement the algorithm using Python and compare it to the pure exploration algorithm.

The first step is to import the needed libraries and fix the path as usual.

```
import numpy as np
import matplotlib.pyplot as plt
import pandas as pd
import os
import random
import math
```

```
os.chdir('D:')
os.getcwd()
```

We then read the dataset that we will use in this project, which is an ads dataset corresponding to the response of thousands of people to ten different ads.

```
dataset = pd.read_csv('ads_dataset.csv')
```

	Ad 1	Ad 2	Ad 3	Ad 4	Ad 5	Ad 6	Ad 7	Ad 8	Ad 9	Ad 10
0	1	0	0	0	1	0	0	0	1	0
1	0	0	0	0	0	0	0	0	1	0
2	0	0	0	0	0	0	0	0	0	0
3	0	1	0	0	0	0	0	1	0	0
4	0	0	0	0	0	0	0	0	0	0

Now, we start with the pure exploration algorithm. We have 10,000 records which are represented by the variable `N`. We implement the algorithm by choosing a random ad each time without any considerations.

```
N = 10000
d = 10
ads_selected = []
total_reward = 0
for n in range(0, N):
    ad = random.randrange(d)
    ads_selected.append(ad)
    reward = dataset.values[n, ad]
    total_reward = total_reward + reward
```

If we plot the histogram, which represents how many times each ad was selected, we notice that nearly all of them were selected equally.

```
plt.hist(ads_selected)
plt.title('Histogram of ads selections')
plt.xlabel('Ads')
plt.ylabel('Number of times each ad was selected')
plt.show()
```

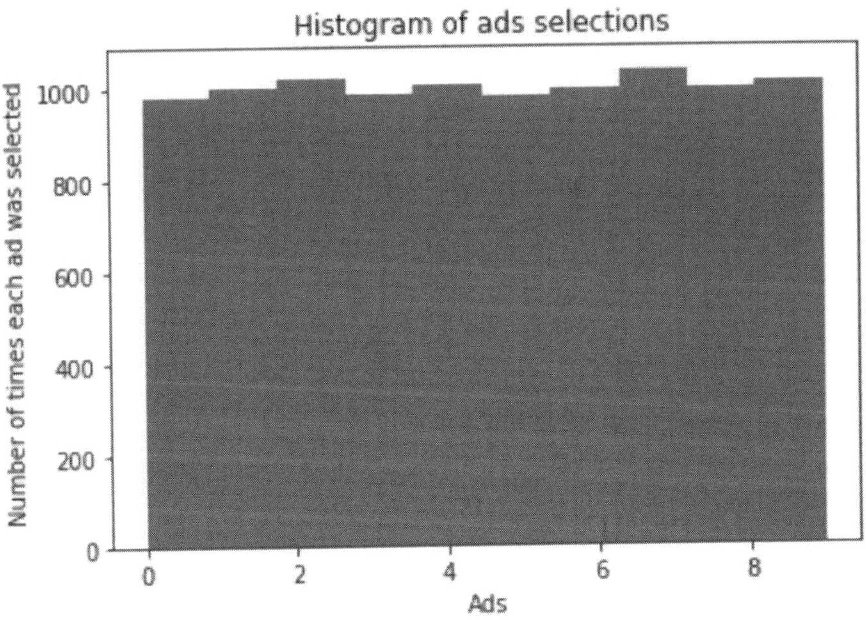

Finally, we record the total reward that we get from this pure exploration policy, which is 1255.

```
print('Total reward using Pure Exploration',total_reward)
```

```
Total reward using Pure Exploration 1255
```

Now, using the same dataset, let us implement the UCB steps and equations which are straightforward as follows.

```
ads_selected = []
numbers_of_selections = [0] * d
sums_of_rewards = [0] * d
total_reward = 0
```

```
for n in range(0, N):
    ad = 0
    max_upper_bound = 0
    for i in range(0, d):
        if (numbers_of_selections[i] > 0):
            average_reward = sums_of_rewards[i] / numbers_of_selections[i]
            delta_i = math.sqrt(3/2 * math.log(n + 1) / numbers_of_selections[i])
            upper_bound = average_reward + delta_i
        else:
            upper_bound = 1e400
        if upper_bound > max_upper_bound:
            max_upper_bound = upper_bound
            ad = i
    ads_selected.append(ad)
    numbers_of_selections[ad] = numbers_of_selections[ad] + 1
    reward = dataset.values[n, ad]
    sums_of_rewards[ad] = sums_of_rewards[ad] + reward
    total_reward = total_reward + reward
```

The total reward is much bigger, and the histogram shows clearly that the fourth ad is the one that gives the highest reward.

```
print('Total reward using UCB:',total_reward)
```

```
Total reward using UCB: 2178
```

```
plt.hist(ads_selected)
plt.title('Histogram of ads selections')
plt.xlabel('Ads')
plt.ylabel('Number of times each ad was selected')
plt.show()
```

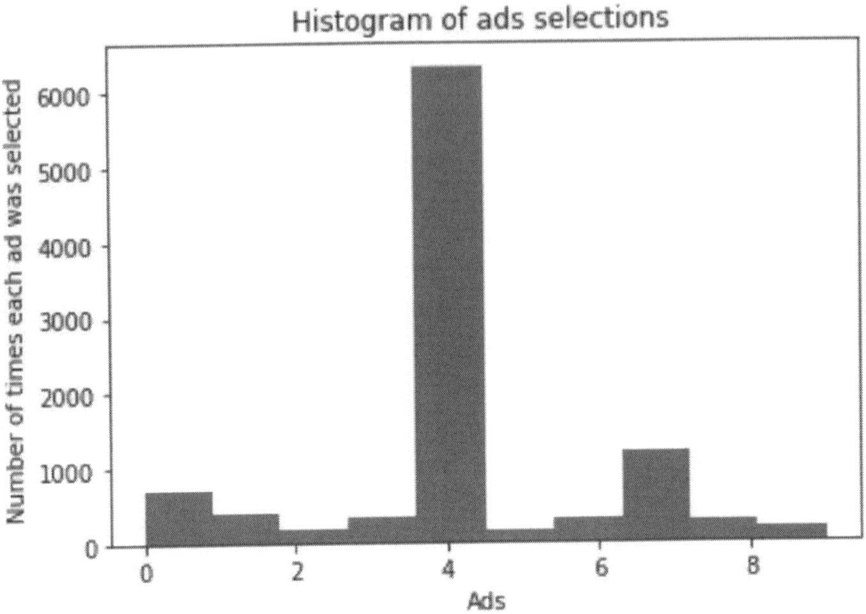

8.3. Thompson Sampling

8.3.1. Thompson Sampling Intuition

Now, let us discuss the second interesting algorithm, which is Thompson sampling. This is one of the oldest heuristic-based algorithms in the field of RL for solving the multi-armed bandit problem. Although it is very old, it was proven recently to be better than the state-of-the-art algorithms.

Like UCB, the algorithm consists of three main steps. The first step is to calculate for each round `n` the number of times the ad `i` got reward 1 up to the current round $N_i^1(n)$ and the other way around $N_i^0(n)$.

The second step is that for each ad, we take a random draw from the following distribution.

$$\theta_i(n) = \beta(N_i^1(n) + 1, N_i^0(n) + 1)$$

You do not really need to understand the previous equation as it needs a very solid mathematical background.

The third step is to select the ad with the highest reward $\theta_i(n)$

These are the three main steps that this algorithm needs to run. However, there is one issue with this algorithm. As it is probabilistic, we cannot trust its results without monitoring. On the other hand, this algorithm can handle any delayed feedback, unlike UCB.

8.3.2. Thompson Sampling in Python

Now, let us see how to do this in Python.

We will import the libraries, fix the path, and load the same dataset.

```
import numpy as np
import matplotlib.pyplot as plt
import pandas as pd
import os
import random
import math
```

```
os.chdir('D:')
os.getcwd()
```

```
dataset = pd.read_csv('ads_dataset.csv')
```

Then, after implementing the Thompson algorithm, we start by defining the number of ads and the number of people. After that, we define a list for both the rewards of 0 and the rewards of 1. Finally, we implement the second step of the algorithm using the `beta variate` module from the random library.

```
N = 10000
d = 10
ads_selected = []
total_reward = 0
numbers_of_rewards_0 = [0] * d
numbers_of_rewards_1 = [0] * d
ad=0
```

```
for n in range(0, N):
    ad = 0
    max_random = 0
    for i in range(0, d):
        random_beta = random.betavariate(numbers_of_rewards_1[i] + 1, numbers_of_rewards_0[i] + 1)
        if random_beta > max_random:
            max_random = random_beta
            ad = i
    ads_selected.append(ad)
    reward = dataset.values[n, ad]
    if reward == 1:
        numbers_of_rewards_1[ad] = numbers_of_rewards_1[ad] + 1
    else:
        numbers_of_rewards_0[ad] = numbers_of_rewards_0[ad] + 1
    total_reward = total_reward + reward
```

As we see below, the algorithm chooses also the fourth ad like UCB did, but with much higher confidence.

```
plt.hist(ads_selected)
plt.title('Histogram of ads selections')
plt.xlabel('Ads')
plt.ylabel('Number of times each ad was selected')
plt.show()
```

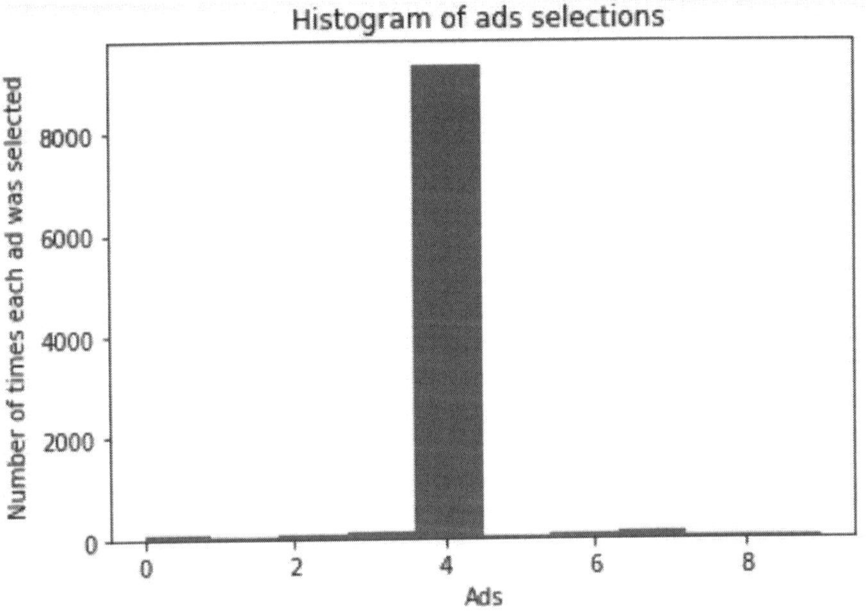

Also, we see that the reward is higher than the UCB.

```
print('Total reward using Thompson Sampling:',total_reward)
```

```
Total reward using Thompson Sampling: 2606
```

Free eBook in Neural Networks and Deep Learning with Python

Hey Data Scientist,

Congrats on completing this book. You now have a baseline understanding of the key concepts of Data Science.

As a way of saying thank you for your purchase, AI Publishing is offering you a free eBooks in data science at this link:

https://www.aispublishing.net/introduction-neural-networks

If you are just starting out into AI and data science, you will find this free eBooks extremely useful.

Until next time, happy analyzing :)

If you want to help us produce more material like this, then please leave an honest review. It really does make a difference.

If you have any feedback, please let us know by sending an email to **contact@aispublishing.net**.

This feedback is highly valued, and we look forward to hearing from you. **It will be very helpful for us to improve the quality of our books.**

From the same Publisher

Printed in Great Britain
by Amazon

32920507R00149